ASPECTS OF SHEFFIELD 2

ASPECTS *of* SHEFFIELD 2

Discovering Local History

Edited by
Melvyn Jones

Series Editor
Brian Elliott

Wharncliffe Publishing Limited

First Published in 1999 by
Wharncliffe Publishing Limited
an imprint of
Pen and Sword Books Limited,
47 Church Street, Barnsley,
South Yorkshire. S70 2AS

For up-to-date information on other titles produced under the Wharncliffe imprint, please telephone or write to:

Wharncliffe Publishing Limited
FREEPOST
47 Church Street
Barnsley
South Yorkshire S70 2BR
Telephone (24 hours): 01226 - 734555

ISBN: 1-871647-58-4

A CIP catalogue record of this book is available from the British Library

Cover illustration: View of the town of Sheffield from the south east, 1844, by Henry Perlee Parker, *courtesy of Sheffield Galleries and Museums Trust.*

Printed in Great Britain by
Redwood Books, Trowbridge, Wiltshire

Contents

Introduction

by Melvyn Jones

The *Aspects* series goes from strength to strength. There are already five volumes in the *Aspects of Barnsley* series, three volumes in the *Aspects of Rotherham* series, and single volumes so far on Leeds and Wakefield. Parallel with this second volume on Sheffield, *Aspects of Doncaster 2* is being published. Volumes on the Yorkshire Coast, Blackburn and Huddersfield, and a second volume on Wakefield are in the late stages of preparation. What all these volumes illustrate is the vitality and wide range of local history research and writing in England.

The present volume continues the *Aspects* tradition of bringing a wide variety of studies in local history to the attention of the general reader. They are all written by local experts with long experience of researching their subjects, with an intimate knowledge of the sources that will give up the secrets of their chosen topic, and illustrated with a bewildering variety of maps, diagrams, photographs and other illustrations, many never before published. The articles should have a strong appeal to long-established Sheffield residents and newcomers alike.

It will come as no surprise to find that half of the contributions in this volume are connected with Sheffield's long industrial history. Ian Medlicott's study of John Curr's long association with the Duke of Norfolk's Sheffield collieries, during which time he introduced rail roads, four wheeled corves, conductors, tipplers, inclined planes and flat ropes, shows how this outstanding engineer made the Duke's collieries the most technologically advanced of their time. Trevor Lodge's authoritative study of Sir Henry Bessemer and the introduction and development of Bessemer steelmaking, shows that far from being innovative, Sheffield's steelmaking establishment took up the new technology with some hesitation.

There are three articles dealing with Sheffield's light trades. Dennis Smith's meticulous research illustrates how Sheffield cutlery was traded in the Baltic region in the late seventeenth century; Peter Machan's history of John Watts & Co. demonstrates the ways in which a long-established firm has adapted to changing circumstances and adopted new lines as markets have changed; and Jackie Richardson's study of early assay masters and assay offices throws interesting light on this important aspect of the silver and silver plate industry.

Finally on an industrial note, many readers will be familiar with the once extensive range of domestic products marketed under the Izal name - from disinfectant to shampoo and toothpaste and toilet paper - but few will realise that they originated from a by-product of coke making at a local iron manufacturing and engineering firm. Joan Jones's illustrated history of Izal makes fascinating reading.

The remaining six articles cover community history, transport, literary biography, the church and the cinema. Andrew Walker's study of religion, politics and leisure in mid-Victorian Attercliffe reveals the way in which the local working-class population of this rapidly growing district shaped their social and cultural lives; Howard Smith's largely visual essay on the evidence of early road development in the Sheffield area shows the diversity and richness of surviving features; Chris Morley's and Melvyn Jones's studies of different aspects of literary activity in Victorian Ecclesfield shed new light on the Gatty family - sometimes referred to as the Brontës of South Yorkshire; the long and varied career of the Rev. James Wilkinson is carefully revealed by Malcolm Mercer; and, last but not least, the history of cinema in Sheffield is expertly chronicled by Clifford Shaw and Christopher Stacey.

I would like formally to thank all the contributors. They have met all my expectations and the result is a volume of studies of infinite variety and interest and, I hope, an encouragement to others with an interest in researching the history of the area and finding an outlet for that research.

The book could not have been produced without the help and support of a number of other key individuals. I would like to thank Charles Hewitt of Wharncliffe Books for his continued support for the *Aspects* series and to Paul Wilkinson and Mike Parsons at Wharncliffe for their sterling efforts. I also wish to acknowledge the help of Hazel Proctor and Jane Scothorne with word processing and Neil Donovan for technical help with disks. The help given to contributors by staff in the Local Studies Library at Sheffield Central Library and at Sheffield Archives is also gratefully acknowledged. Finally, I would like to acknowledge the wise advice of Brian Elliott, the overall series editor.

1. John Spencer's Baltic Trade in Sheffield Wares

by Dennis Smith

THE SPENCER FAMILY ESTABLISHED THEMSELVES at Cannon Hall near Barnsley (Figure 1) during the middle of the seventeenth century. Over a few generations they had become farmers, landowners and industrialists. John Spencer, 1655-1729, continued the family interest in local ironworks, whilst also farming on a considerable scale and managing his estates. Spencer's surviving notebooks contain jottings on household expenses, money loaned with rates of interest, buying and selling sheep and livestock at local fairs and markets and the ploughing, rotation and reaping of crops on his lands. Interspersed with these matters are references to sales of bark to local tanners, taxes paid for Barnby blast furnace and to its suppliers of charcoal, and of ironstone mining at Hugsetts near Silkstone. However these notes conceal the fact that, like his grandfather, Spencer also had merchant interests. These interests are revealed by a few surviving notes and letters scattered through Spencer's papers and accounts.

Spencer and the Baltic trade

Spencer was engaged in the export of linen and Sheffield goods to areas of present-day Estonia during the latter part of the seventeenth century. Spencer's partner or agent abroad was William Watson who shared profits and presumably losses on a fifty-fifty basis. Watson was possibly a distant relative of Spencer's, as a female cousin is known to have married one

Figure 1. Cannon Hall and its park, the home of John Spencer. The Spencers were leading partners in the gentry syndicate that dominated the charcoal iron industry in South Yorkshire and North Derbyshire.

John Watson. Goods were carried overland to Wakefield, thence by boat to Hull (Figure 2) for shipment to the Baltic region.

The chief destination of goods appears to have been the Estonian port of Narva, then, like the greater part of the Baltic, in Swedish occupation (see Figure 3). Possibly goods were distributed overland from Narva into Finland or even Russia, a country that became a threat to Swedish domination as the seventeenth century wore on. Watson's earliest surviving account is an invoice of 6 November 1688 when the sum of money for a parcel of Sheffield goods, 'sold at several times and to sundry persons' was '22 pounds 17 shillings'. Watson was writing to Spencer from Stockholm on 13 January 1689 having had a bad journey of five weeks between Narva and that city.[1] Watson advised Spencer that Joseph Lindall's ship carrying linen was 'lost about 40 English miles from Narva, but all the goods saved, praise be to God'. He lamented that the linen did not come to hand as it could have been disposed of during that winter, together with some Sheffield goods. Some presumably damaged linen together with sales invoices was returned to Spencer. Watson had brought a parcel of Sheffield goods overland to Stockholm. He noted that 'Peter Coats counterfeit tortoiseshell (hafted) knives had changed colour' and remained unsold. 'Winter's spring knives are gone. I have nothing of his goods left but a dozen knives without forks at 10 shillings per dozen.' He continued:

Figure 2. Hull, Sheffield's gateway to the Baltic, *c.*1640, by Wenceslas Hollar. *Hull Maritime Museum*

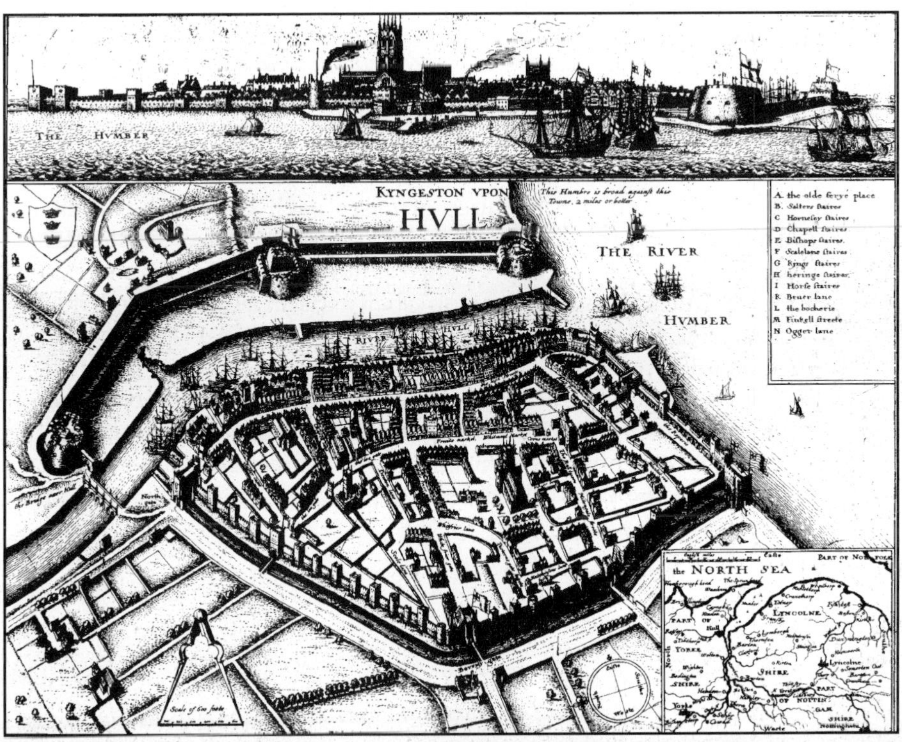

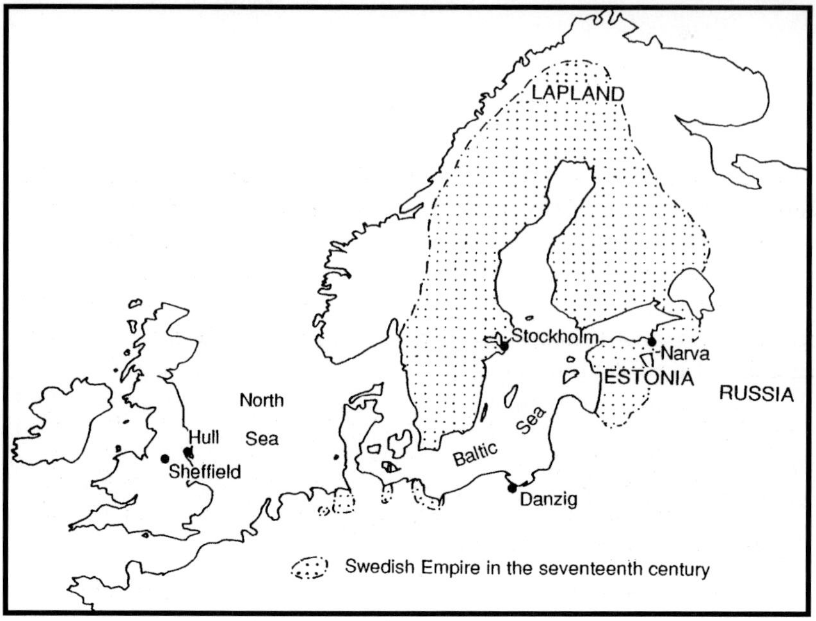

Figure 3. Map of places mentioned in the text.

> *I depart for Narva again the latter part of this month, if we get no harder winter than we have at present I must go north overland for the Narva, if so I shall see some part of Lapland which will be seventeen or eighteen hundred English miles. The way I come hither was seven hundred miles, but in the greatest danger imaginable.*

In addition to the perils of overland travel and of shipping of goods, letters took three months or more to reach Spencer in England.

A memorandum of goods[2] to be sent to Watson, written in John Spencer's own hand exists, dated 4 July 1690. Spencer notes:

> *...our parcel of Sheffield goods is not altogether according to your order, though I bespoke them exactly so, but considering what sort of cutler we have to deal with they are not much amiss. The greatest fault is want of red in Winter's spring knives, which was promised but as you will find unperformed.*

John Winter supplied a number of cases each containing knife, penknife and fork, various hooped and unhooped knives and forks, and some spring knives. Peter Coats was supplying knives, penknives and forks, some with studded tortoiseshell and others with horn hafts. Another cutler, Stephen Fox, supplied knives, forks, razors with silver capped handles, penknives and inkpots. Charles Stewardson supplied a few cases of studded and plain tortoiseshell-handled knives and forks, noted as 'for trial'. Buttons, listed with the maker or supplier's name 'Staniforth' completed the parcel of Sheffield goods.

After noting the cost of carriage to Hull, i.e. three shillings and sixpence and the payment of one shilling and sixpence to the carpenter for a box, Spencer wrote, 'this day these goods go to Hull, so be ready, and when I hear of the arrival of the linen and the shipping of these, shall give you account of the other charges'.

Another memorandum in Spencer's hand dated 20 August 1690 related that he had had notice from Mr Joseph Field of Mr Hans Knache's safe arrival at Hull:

by which I have your letter dated 22nd May, but cannot observe your additional order therein for some low priced knives. I have made up our parcel of Sheffield wares, which has lain some time at Hull with Mr Joseph Field in order to be shipped per return of said Knache, and consigned to yourself at Narva.

Written at a later date on the same document is Spencer's reference to the death of partner William Watson in April 1691:

I gave order to Mr William Beaumont at Narva to enquire into my concern with Mr Watson, and procure me an account, or take the goods undisposed of into his custody and dispose thereof upon my proper account.

William Beaumont was one of the Beaumont family of Bretton, probably the gentleman of that name who resided at Oaks in Darton. He was a man of substance, a considerable owner of properties and lands at Darton, Cawthorne, Staincross, Flockton, Barnsley, Sandal near Wakefield, and elsewhere in Yorkshire. Beaumont himself may have had merchant connections and another seventeenth century member of his family is referred to as 'Dantzick Merchant'. Danzig was the name given to the town of Gdansk in Poland, a river port of the Baltic opened up centuries earlier by German merchants.

On 28 May 1692 Beaumont wrote to Spencer from Narva:

You may well wonder that in all this time I have given you no account of your concerns with the deceased Mr Watson. One main reason whereof hath been that those that are empowered to look after his affairs are no merchants but men of great employment otherwise. Mr Watson having kept his books in English, they are not able to understand them, so that it is a long time before any man can get an account from them.[3]

Beaumont sent sales accounts of the first parcel of knives Watson brought with him, and an invoice for three packs of linen. The last parcel of knives sent via Hans Knache had remained unsold. Spencer was asked for accounts, and for authority to settle affairs with Watson's executors and to take unsold goods into his keeping enquiring also into payment by Watson for his half share in merchandise.

Spencer's suppliers of Sheffield cutlery

Having detailed John Spencer's export dealings, it is of interest to look at the surviving documents, largely wills and inventories left by the Sheffield cutlers who supplied goods to him. It becomes evident that these were small manufacturers as opposed to 'run of the mill' journeyman cutlers. Examples of the types of knives that might have been involved in the Baltic trade are shown in Figure 4.

Peter Coats, rather unusually for the son of a London merchant, was apprenticed to Sheffield cutler Thomas Spooner in 1674. He was buried at Sheffield in November 1702. Stephen Fox was possibly the cutler who died in 1697, leaving goods to his wife Sarah together with lands at Chelmorton in Derbyshire. He may have been the man referred to in Charles Stewardson's list of debts as 'Razorsmith'.

Charles Stewardson, the supplier of knives and forks for trial, was the son of a farmer, and was apprenticed to a cutler at Walkley in 1676 and died in 1694. Stewardson leased a Sheffield house and also a farm at Spittlefields, where there was a small amount of livestock. His Sheffield house comprised six well furnished rooms, including a buttery, kitchen-cum-brewhouse and a chamber - possibly a servant's room over the kitchen. His possessions included books, a clock, a fowling piece and other weapons. He may also have kept a beerhouse, suggested by the listing in his inventory of brewing implements, 20 gallons of ale, debts owed for six gallons of brandy together with six pairs of bowls, and a sign. His two-storeyed workshop contained no less than seven vices, a glazer, six pairs of boring stoops and other small tools all being valued at £4 10s. Wire and a parcel of tortoiseshell were valued at one pound two shillings. Money was owed to people at Rotherham and Birmingham. Other debts were owed for excise, for manure and for school wages (fees) for children.

Mentioned in both lists of packages of Sheffield goods that survive were buttons supplied by Staniforth or Stanyford. Possibly there was a specialised buttonmaker supplying Spencer with these items, though no 'Staniforth' appears to be traceable in the trade at that period. Another possibility is that Spencer traded with the Staniforths of Attercliffe, pinmakers and hardware dealers. Spencer may have supplied wire to the family trade. A Samuel Staniforth, pinner of Attercliffe, died in 1692, and although his home appears to have been small, a portion of it was used as a warehouse and workshop. In the latter part were six stithies, fourteen small hammers, a punching lead, punches and other tools with a large quantity of iron and steel wire for pin manufacture. Shop goods included cloth, tinplate, seeds, medicines, whalebone, writing paper, foodstuffs, books including testaments and hornbooks, and cards of buttons including 'alcony' buttons.

'Winter' is mentioned as the supplier of a variety of designs of knives and forks. The Winter family supplied many workers in the cutlery trades. John Winter senior, who died in 1709, had been a Master Cutler in 1682. He was a person of some consequence living in a well furnished house comprising nine rooms, if buttery, kitchen, chambers and a cellar are counted. His goods included books, pewter and a little silver and delftware. His smithy contained two pairs of bellows, two anvils and stocks, a glazer, four vices and other tools, so that other members of his family and probably apprentices, worked alongside him.

Although John Winter Senior may have supplied goods to Spencer, two notes undated but *c.*1690 are in the very individual handwriting of his son, also John, who lived until the year 1718.[4] One note had accompanied '1 dozen spring knives at eight shillings the dozen - all I have at present ready'. The other note headed 'Sheffield May 22nd', read as follows:

> *Sir according to your order I have sent you 1 dozen ivory knives and forks at 15 shillings the dozen and 1 woman's knife and fork. I give you that three of the forks are Sheffield forks, and are handsome and well wrought on the shanks, the other three are London forks, not so neat, but far harder as you may perceive if you please to cut on the grains* [i.e. prongs] *with a knife, you may have whether you please if you do but write, so I rest sir, your servant, J Winter.*

John Winter Junior bequeathed houses and land to his wife Anne in his will of March 1717, with household goods going to brother Luke. His personal goods valued in 1718 totalled seventy four pounds and sixteen shillings. Smithy tools included only one anvil and a pair of bellows, indicating that he worked alone or only with an apprentice, on a small scale. Other goods of the trade were work tools valued together at £2 7s 6d, and thirty pound in weight of shell for hafting cutlery.

Another list of cutlery intended for an export parcel survives[5], undated but *c.*1690, written in John Spencer's own hand. This list extends the number of cutlers known to

Figure 4. Examples of late seventeenth and early eighteenth century Sheffield knives. *Simon Moore*

have supplied goods and also introduces varieties of cutlery not before noted. Stephen Fox, previously noted, supplied a few dozen painted penknives, including some apparently incorporating an inkhorn, or having this item made to match the knife. Peter Coats, who appears in an earlier list, supplied large tortoiseshell knives at twelve shillings per dozen, a few forks and three dozen counter-knives at six shillings per dozen, the latter presumably intended for use in chopping or paring foodstuffs or similar items in shops. John Winter, another previous supplier, provided spring knives and forks with half slope joints of varied types and sizes, specified as for male or female use. He also supplied knives and forks decorated with silver hoops, these costing fifteen shillings per dozen.

Four new names among the suppliers were William Sherman, Joshua White, Joseph Downes and Thomas Spooner. William Sherman, a cutler who died in Sheffield in 1698 supplied painted knives and forks at prices ranging from three to ten shillings per dozen. These items were presumably a cheaper type of cutlery with painted wooden handles, popular in the area Spencer was trading with. Joshua White, the son of a sheather who died in 1720, was providing two dozen knives. Joseph Downes, a cutler who died in 1712 supplied what appear to be servants' penknives. Included in the list are 'penknives paynted red and black', and these were almost certainly of the 'desk' knife type as opposed to the present day folding penknife.

Thomas Spooner, another new supplier, appears here as supplying large and small studded tortoiseshell knives and forks, together with some plain knives noted as all tortoiseshell with half square joints. Thomas Spooner made his will on 15 February 1691 dying within two weeks of that date. He was the copyhold tenant of an estate at Loadbrook in Bradfield Chapelry. His Sheffield house and its contents were bequeathed to his eldest son Thomas. The four younger children were allocated the sum of one hundred pounds each, and as the sum of four hundred pounds was owed to Spooner at the time of his decease, debt collecting must have been a major preoccupation of his executors. The Sheffield house comprised eight rooms, plus a buttery. Part of the premises are designated 'the warehouse', which contained tortoiseshell to the value of ten pounds. Lest we regard Spooner and his family as mere common workpeople we should note the degree of literacy indicated by the presence in his home of 'books, maps, landscapes, pamphlets' etc., to the value of six pounds. Also the 'pair of virginals', which indicate a degree of musical practice and a level of culture unknown in many contemporary families. Trade tools in the smithy were the usual stithy and stock, cool trough, bellows, glazer and vices. In the smithy chamber were sixteen dozen tortoiseshell knives and forks valued at four pounds sixteen shillings and a parcel of blades valued at nine shillings.

The last word on Spencer's dealings in Sheffield goods for export appears to be a letter from William Beaumont[6] written from Wakefield on 25 May 1694. The postscript of this letter refers to Beaumont's son, George, having shown him a letter from his brother William.

> *Who sayeth something trifleing about your business which he hopes shortly to perfect, but is delayed by the persons concerned who say that some of the Lap Sheffield wares are unsold and that the persons that have them are the kind of masters in town whom he would not willingly force by any lawsuits fearing ill success.*

No further details of Spencer's merchant activities in the Baltic appear to exist, though there are bonds for payments to William Beaumont spread over a further period. For example a bond for the payment of £211 payable to Beaumont was drawn up in 1698 and the money not paid off finally until 1703, but the purpose of these payments is not known. John Spencer's involvement in the local wire mills and in complex partnerships involving Yorkshire ironworks must have occupied much of his time. At the end of the seventeenth century trade in the Baltic must have been disrupted by the political and military upheavals which culminated in the battle of Narva of 1700.

From 1716 Spencer[7] was incapable of managing his industrial interests and later allowed his son William £50 per annum to attend to his business regarding the ironworks. Merchant activity emerged again in the lifetimes of John Spencer's grandsons.[8]

Notes and References

1. Spencer Stanhope Muniments in Sheffield Archives, 60502/55.
2. Spencer Stanhope Muniments, 60502/60.
3. Spencer Stanhope Muniments, 60502/65.
4. Spencer Stanhope Muniments, 60502/98 and 99.
5. Spencer Stanhope Muniments, 60685/1.
6. Spencer Stanhope Muniments, 60630/5 loose paper in pocket of J. Spencer's almanac for year 1694.
7. Spencer Stanhope Muniments, 60494.
8. John Spencer had three grandsons. John Spencer, 1718-75, country gentleman and sportsman, had industrial and mining interest in South Yorkshire and Derbyshire. William Spencer, 1725-59, was apprenticed to Wm Hardman, Liverpool merchant between 1743-52. Benjamin Spencer, 1725-59, twin brother of William, was apprenticed to a London merchant in 1742, became partner with Lucas Steinman, merchant of London, and part-owner of several trading ships including the *Cannon Hall* and the *Benjamin*, and traded with Holland, Germany Spain, Jamaica and France.

Additional source: R. E. Leader (1905) *History of the Company of Cutlers in Hallamshire in the County of York*, Vol. 2, Pawson and Brailsford, Sheffield.

Acknowledgements

Acknowledgements are due to S. W. Fraser Esq and the Director of Leisure Services for permission to quote material from the Spencer-Stanhope Muniments in Sheffield Archives, and to the Borthwick Institute, York, for permission to quote extracts from the following documents in their possession: will of Stephen Fox, Sheffield 1697; inventory of Charles Stewardson, Sheffield 1694; will and inventory of John Winter, Sheffield 1709; will and inventory of John Winter, Sheffield 1718; inventory of Samuel Staniforth, Attercliffe 1692; will and inventory of Thomas Spooner, Sheffield 1692.

2. Early Sheffield Assay Masters and Assay Offices

by Jackie Richardson

In the context of this article an assay office is a place set up by Act of Parliament where articles made of precious metals (in this case silver) are sent to be tested to ensure that the correct standard of metal has been used in their manufacture. The operation of testing the standard is called the assay after the Old French 'assai' *meaning examination. Pieces that pass the examination are hallmarked.*

WHEN SHEFFIELD WAS FINALLY granted permission to establish a local Assay Office, the first problem was that of finding a suitable Assay Master. Or at least, so the local silversmiths expected. However, as they very soon discovered, he had already been selected and his appointment at the inaugural meeting on 5 July 1773 was simply a formality. The choice of a Londoner, Daniel Bradbury, came as a surprise to some. John Parsons, for example, one of the leading local silver plate manufacturers, had fully expected a Sheffield man, William Fullard, to be appointed:

> *The Company here have Elected Mr Bradbury as Assay Master for this Town, a Circumstance when we were in London I had not the most distant thought of, but our Company here thought it indispensably their Duty to comply with the Letter of the Law and to elect a Person skilld in the Art of Assaying...Mr. Bradbury in his Petition set forth the great Mystery in the Art and that it was impossible to acquire it without Long Experiences...Lord Effingham who presided declard himself in favour of Bradbury and the election was carried in his favour Nem Con.*[1]

Parsons would have been even more surprised had he realised that a year earlier Bradbury had been turned down for a post at the London Assay Office because 'he did not seem to have (the) proper character for the office.'[2] Or that Matthew Boulton himself, Sheffield's greatest rival, might well have been involved in Bradbury's appointment. His bill to Birmingham Assay Office for expenses incurred in obtaining the Act of Parliament which set up the Offices records two payments, to 'Daniel Bradbury (Carey Lane, London) the Assayer', one described as 'a present'.

Bradbury took the Assay Master's oath, as required by law, before the Master of the Mint on 21 July 1773, naming James Ross of Wardour Street, Gentleman, and John Lewis of Little Moorfields, Silk Dyer, as his sureties.[3] Then he returned to Sheffield to start his new life. He began work immediately on 5 August 1773, at a salary of £50, making private assays of both silver and gold, although officially the Office was only allowed to hallmark silverwares. The Rough Day Book records his expenditure on the equipment necessary for the job: items included a memorandum book, bricks from Walkley Bank, an anvil, charcoal, scales, crucibles, quills, a hammer, pliers, a penknife, a table and a candle, together with 14/- (70p) Window Tax, and plenty of beer and tobacco pipes for the masons. Apart from the four Wardens appointed by the Guardians, his only assistant was a boy who was paid 1/- (5p) per week.[4]

Daniel evidently settled into provincial life and by 1779 had apprenticed two sons to local cutlers - Richard Walter Whitfield to Samuel Garlick, and William to Benjamin Henfrey. The Office was only open on Mondays and Thursdays for official business, although Bradbury was allowed to open for a third day for private work, as long as all the takings from this were paid to the Office. He later supplemented his income by making silver coin weights for sale - a task also undertaken by the Assay Masters of Chester and Birmingham. Evidently they acted as the unofficial local Weights & Measures Inspectors of the time, as well as checking that the coinage was up to standard by assaying it for local merchants and bankers.

Where Bradbury originally lived when he took up his post is unknown, although his contract allowed him to live at the Office if he wished. The first Assay Office was on Norfolk Street 'wherein Mrs Eleanor Green deceased lately dwelt' and was rented from George Elliott. Henry Tudor and John Winter, both prominent local silversmiths, citizens and newly elected Guardians, were empowered to be responsible for the tenancy agreement - including paying the rent of £7 7s 0d (£7.35) per half year until they could be reimbursed by hallmarking charges. Norfolk Street was a good site for the Assay Office, since most of the prominent silver and plating firms were in the area. Hancock & Rowbotham, Thomas Law, William Marsden & Greaves & Wilson were all actually on Norfolk Street, whilst John Winter was on High Street, Tudor & Leader on Sycamore Street, Richard Morton on Fargate and Fenton, Creswick & Co. on Mulberry Street. (Figure 1).

Evidently this first property was not to the Guardians' liking, because in April 1774 they rented a different house at the lower rent of £5 5s 0d (£5.25) per half-year in a court off Norfolk Street from Joseph Mitchell, Thomas Boulsover's son-in-law, who leased it from the Duke of Norfolk (Figure 2). It was described as:

All that Building or Tenement lately a dwellinghouse with all

Conveniences and appurtenances thereunto belonging as the same were lately occupied by Mr Thomas Bolsover [sic] *situate up a Court in Norfolk Street.*

The tenancy agreement allowed rights of access to the Assay Office and permitted the Guardians to build hearths or furnaces in one of the ground floor rooms 'thereby doing as little damage as may be to the Walls of the said Building.' The house was not to be used as a resi-

Figure 1. Thomas Jefferys' plan o Sheffield, 1772. The first Assay Office was on Norfolk Street, ther the south-eastern edge of the tow

dence without Joseph Mitchell's express consent. The Company took formal possession of the new Office from 24 June, though Mitchell allowed them to make alterations before they moved in. The Cash Book records a payment to Robert Brownell for carrying goods and another of 3/- (15p) to his wife for three days work cleaning the new Assay Office on 21 May1774. From 16 June the Office spent £1 6s 0d (£1.30) on wine, perhaps to celebrate their move, or congratulate themselves on a good first year's work.

There must have been occasions when Bradbury regretted his move up north. Charges for assaying were calculated on the weight of the goods, just as they had been at Goldsmiths' Hall. But Sheffield wares were thinly stamped out with steel dies, using much less silver than their London equivalents. Consequently, the Sheffield Office had twice as many articles to test and mark for the same cost. And unfortunately for Bradbury, local blade and handle manufacturers, whose goods were exempt from hallmarking because they were so light, realised that the hallmark was a useful guarantee of quality. They sent in large quantities of their goods for the Office to assay. By 1776, another assayer had to be appointed to cope with the workload and Bradbury's salary was increased to £80, but by 1780 the Office could only afford to pay him £15 per quarter, the remainder to be paid 'at the same time and in the same proportions as the Wardens shall receive their salaries.'[5] By 1784, the Office was more than £145 in debt, despite a loan of £100 from John Winter. Something had to be done, or the Office would be forced to close.

Fortunately, most silversmiths had by now realised the advantages of having a local Office and subscribed to a second Act of Parliament[6] to change the way charges were calculated. The new method of charging for small wares by count - 6d (2.5p) per dozen - rather than by weight improved the finances of the Office dramatically. By the time Bradbury died in 1789, the Office was solvent. However, he had not made his fortune. Although his salary had only been paid a couple of weeks earlier, his estate was less than £50. As a result of his death, the Office closed for two weeks until his successor

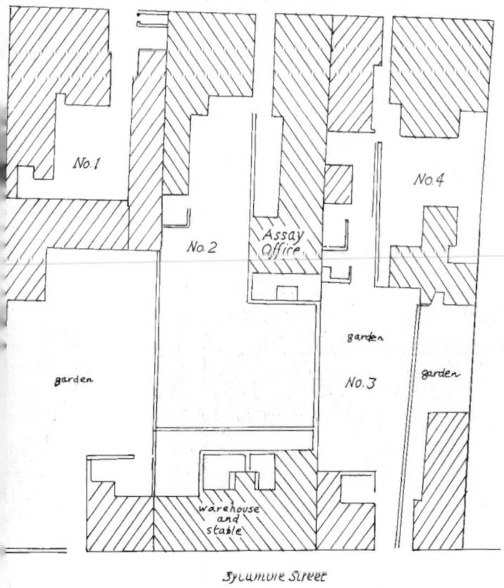

No. 1 Joseph Ibberson; house and several workshops and a garden. Contains 927 square yards.

No. 2 The tenement, warehouse and grounds held of the Earl of Surrey by Joseph Mitchell. Contains 927 square yards.

No. 3 Ann Genn; several houses and two gardens. Contains 585 square yards.

No. 4 Thomas Liddell; house, yard and workshop. Contains 320 square yards.

Figure 2. A re-drawing by T. Rose of a sketch plan by W. Fairbank, 1780, showing the site of the second Sheffield Assay Office, 1774-1795. *Sheffield Assay Office*

could be sworn in.

The post was advertised nationally, attracting replies from at least six Londoners, including Thomas Smith, who seemed to view Sheffield as a useful bolt-hole. In his letter of application, dated 23 July1789, he boasted of his many years' experience in the silver trade, but also hinted at some shadow hanging over him:

...and although I have been unfortunate of late in my plans, yet I hope that no one can accuse me of acting intentionally deshonest, the many have raised unkind & untrue things to the hurt of my Reputation...

Meanwhile, in his application, J. Dechever was less than complimentary about Sheffield:

Having seen your advertisement several times in the Daily Advertiser, take this method of answering it, at all hazard, as you do not mention any, but thought you meant a writing one for it would not be consistant that any one could undertake to go to Sheffield upon an uncertainty;Therefore, if you will be so kind to inform me of the particulars, relative to the Bond and securities as in every other respect answer your demand.

The Guardians finally chose a local man, George Dickinson (Dickenson), to take up the post. He originally worked for John Read's refinery, where he first appears in the wages list in 1779, earning 18/- (90p) per week. Whilst an employee at Read's he is reputed to have brought the book-keeping into shape and to have been John Read's right-hand man. He went on journeys to Birmingham and London on behalf of the firm and spent the summer of 1788 in London in charge of their branch there, shipping the sweeps (jewellers' waste) that he bought there up to Thorne.[7]

Born into a local Quaker family, he married out of the sect. In his Bond he is described as 'Refiner'. John Read himself was one of his sureties; the other was Samuel Marshall, ironmonger - also from Sheffield.

During Dickinson's time as Assay Master, the Office prospered sufficiently for the Guardians to consider erecting their own building. In 1793 they resolved 'that a dwelling house be erected for the Assay Master and an Assay Office' and a committee was set up to find a suitable piece of land and to have plans drawn up. By July 1794 the committee had agreed to purchase a lease for £70 from Edward Sheppard for premises on Fargate. It was resolved:

To treat with a builder for erecting an Office and assayer's House in the course of the present summer upon the site of the said premises on such plan as they shall judge most convenient the estimate whereof not to exceed the sum of £600 to be paid out of the moneys in the hands of the Treasurer (John Turner) and the accumulations of the Office.

A surviving note, not dated, gives the dimensions:

In front to Far Gate - 14 yards
to the Cock Lane - 12 do.
in depth on the Eastside - 15-1 foot
Do. on the Westside abt. 19 yards
Whole content 222 yards.

The builders chosen were John Senior and Edwin Whitehead Drury, working from plans drawn by Joseph Badger & Son, joiners and carpenters. A year later the Committee was authorised to draw another £60, since building costs were higher than expected. An agreement was prepared, allowing Dickinson to live in the house for 5/- (25p) plus all taxes, with a penalty of £100 if he failed to pay them. By 1803, although his salary remained £60, the Office began paying all his taxes. From this time, the Office continued to prosper, evidently well enough to hire a manservant, since a bill survives for £2 3s 11d (£2.20) for fine brown and scarlet cloth, trimmings, linings and buttons, plus a pair of new shoes for one David Senior. By 1810 the building, described as 'Brick built & slated', was insured with the Sheffield Fire Office for £500 (see Figures 3 and 4).

Problems arose in April 1807 when Mr. Dickinson became ill and unable to complete the Office accounts. Read, Watson and Proctor, three of the Guardians, were authorised to settle them. By July, Dickinson was obviously no better and a special meeting was held:

The Infirmities of Mr Dickinson the Assay Master having rendered him incapable of transacting the business of an Assayer, Ordered that Hand Bills be forthwith put out in Sheffield advertising for an Assay Master and included in both the Sheffield newspapers and also in the 'Courier' [London newspaper] *& Aris's 'Birmingham Gazette' for any person to apply to Joseph Read or John Greaves Esq. who are requested to communicate such applications to the Guardians and to call meetings as occasion may require.*

That the account Books be locked up by the Wardens as also the Apartments used as Assay rooms and that the keys thereof be kept by the Wardens who together with Mr. Read, Mr. Watson and any other of the Guardians chusing to attend, are requested to examine and settle the Accounts.

Figure 3. A nineteenth century photograph of the Assay Office, Fargate, 1795-1881. *Sheffield Assay Office*

Despite advertising nationally, the Guardians once again appointed a local man, Samuel Hancock, on 10 August 1807. At a special meeting held nine days later, the principal manufacturers of the town unanimously agreed that the Guardians should 'make such liberal allowance to Mr Dickinson as might be thought necessary from time to time under his present infirmity'. Because the house went with the post, Dickinson had to leave so that Hancock could move in. Sadly, he did

Figure 4. Drawing of Sheffield Assay Office, Fargate, 1795-1881 by Walter Revill after a watercolour by Topham. *Sheffield Assay Office*

not survive for long, dying in November that year, aged 55.

Samuel Hancock was one of eight applicants. He was already a Guardian as well as a Warden, but he resigned from both these positions in order to be considered for the top post. Presumably the Guardians were happier to appoint someone they knew, and someone who could take over the work very quickly; someone who, in fact, was already doing the job, as Warden. Each time the Assay Master was ill or died, the Assay Office had to close, presenting problems and delays for local manufacturers. By appointing Hancock, the Guardians ensured a quick succession. Hancock, too, was from a family of silver-platers, being one of the last of Joseph Hancock's children by his first wife and had originally been apprenticed as a cutler. His brother, Ebenezer Hancock, silversmith, and Joseph Burdekin, merchant, were his two sureties. Unfortunately, though, things did not turn out quite as planned: Hancock himself died suddenly in May 1809. Yet again the Office had to close, this time for a month, until his successor, Matthew Sayles, was appointed and sworn in.

Matthew Sayles, unlike his predecessor, knew nothing about assaying. His Bond reveals him to have been a book-keeper. He appears in the Cutlers' Company list of apprentices and freemen as 'Warehouseman, purchase, knife maker - Freedom 1794'. His two sureties were equally unskilled; William Farnsworth was also a book-keeper, and William George Frith a surgeon.

One of his sons, Francis, who was also apprenticed to a knifemaker, Joseph Hutchinson, in 1807, later appears in Gell's 1825 Directory as 'Watchmaker, goldsmith, lapidary and working jeweller' at 30 Fargate. Another son, Frederick Allan, was apprenticed to George Barker, knife-maker in 1813. However, his skills obviously lay in using knives, rather than making them, for he later appears in directories as a surgeon-dentist, handily situated above a sweet shop, also in Fargate.

By 1818, because of the difficulties of ensuring continuity when the Assay Master died, it was recommended that Sayles should instruct one of his sons in the art of assaying. At a meeting of the Guardians on 6 July 1818, it was reported that his second son, Lewis Charles, had been so instructed. A Committee was appointed to enquire into Lewis's character and qualifications. Presumably they were satisfied by what they found, since he was appointed Assistant to his father, to act only when instructed by the Guardians, and he was ordered to be duly sworn in at the Mint, with the Office paying the expenses for his time and trouble in going to London. His sureties were John Law, cutler, and Leonard Cowley, liquor merchant. In July 1827 Lewis was paid three guineas for taking on the Acting Warden's duties during his illness, but it was not until 1833 when his father died that the question of the legality of his appointment arose. The Office was not closed after Matthew's death, but partly as a result of circulars received from manufacturers by the Guardians, they called a special meeting to consider the situation. Lewis produced various documents to prove that he had been legally appointed. The Guardians submitted a case to C. A. Milner Esq, Barrister-at-Law, for Counsel's Opinion. He duly reported that:

> *Upon the whole, he was inclined to think that the election of Mr Lewis Charles Sayles must be considerd as having been complete and that he now holds by law the office of an assayer.*

The impression that the Guardians were not overjoyed at this decision is strengthened by the Minutes of 3 December 1833, in which it was reported that:

> *Lewis Charles Sayles had proposed certain charges against the Law Clerk for improper conduct in his office and the same having been enquired into by the Guardians present at this meeting these charges appear to be frivolous and vexatious and the Guardians are of the opinion the Law Clerk has not exceeded the duties of his office.*

Relations appear to have improved by 1834 when the Guardians agreed to reimburse more than £120 which Sayles had spent on improvements and repairs to the Office, and they also increased his salary (at his request).

During most of his time in office, Lewis, like his brother Frederick, was also a dentist. Since the Office was still only open on Mondays and Thursdays, it must have been quite easy for him to combine the two occupations. Life in Fargate was not without its difficulties. In July 1839, Sayles complained to the Guardians about problems with his neighbour, Mr Christian Kramer, who was killing pigs next door and upsetting the delicate assay balances. Presumably the noise deterred potential dental patients, too. Proceedings were threatened, but by the following Annual Meeting, Sayles reported that the problem had ceased. In 1844, Sayles complained again, this time because Kramer was using some kind of machinery, possibly steam-powered, to chop meat 'that when used it causes a vibratory motion which renders the premises unfit for use as an Assay Office and less fit as a residence by himself and family.' He called another special meeting in November 1844 to persuade the Guardians to take further action, but although mention was made of the Law Clerk taking the opinion of Counsel, no more was heard on the subject.

At the Annual Meeting in 1854, the Guardians accepted Lewis's resignation from the post of Assay Master. The original legislation which established the Assay Office did not allow the Assay Master to retire, but the Guardians were either unaware of this, or chose to ignore it. The meeting was adjourned until 22 August for the election of a new Assay Master and also to look at Sayles's claim for expenses incurred in improvements he had made. Advertisements were placed in all three Sheffield newspapers for an Assay Master or Masters, and John Watson was duly elected, at an annual salary of £130 and the use of the house.

Meanwhile on 28 August Mr Sayles submitted his valuation of £340 for improvements made to the buildings at his own expense. The committee inspected these, and although agreeing that he had indeed made improvements in accordance, felt that:

> *The Guardians were not legally liable, especially since he had enjoyed these improvements for upwards of 20 years. Still, they found the house and buildings considerably improved and conceded that he had an equitable claim for compensation and therefore determined that the sum of £175 should be allowed on condition that the fixtures, including chimney pieces & grates, should be left as they now stand.*

Sayles continued to ask for further compensation, but his demands were ignored.

In his application for the post of Assay Master, John Watson stated that he had been a Guardian for nineteen years, succeeding his father. He was brought up in the family firm of Watson, Pass & Co. as a manufacturer of silver and plated wares and had a thorough knowledge of the trade. By 1854 he was head of the firm of John Watson & Sons, Leopold Street, Stock and Sharebrokers, which his father had founded in 1845, when Watson, Pass & Co. like many silverplating firms in Sheffield had got into difficulties after the invention of electroplate. Watson was not only a Stock and Sharebroker - he was also an agent for Chubb's locks and safes, and for the Scottish Widows Fund and the Life & Fidelity Guarantee Assurance Society. It was fortunate for him that the Office was still open only two days per week!

On his appointment, the Guardians evidently decided to show who was in charge. They stipulated that the Assay Master was to be entirely responsible for the care of the Assay Office, and that if he did not choose to live there, he must employ a caretaker and not sub-let the house. The front large room was to be kept for Guardians' Meetings. The name of the Assay Office, in silver, was to be fixed in some conspicuous part of the front of the building, and a brass plate with the Assay Master's name on it affixed to the front door:

Mr Watson being sent for expressed his desire to meet the wishes of the Guardians and the requirements of the trade as to the days and hours of business.

He took his oath in September 1854, his two sureties being John Jobson Smith of Roscoe Place, Sheffield and Thomas Porter of Pitsmoor - 'both highly respectable and wealthy gentlemen' according to the Law Clerk, Henry Watson.[8]

His time in office was not without its problems. There were intermittent complaints from manufacturers about slovenly marking. Nothing more was heard of Kramer, the pig-slaughterer, but in March 1856 the Guardians ordered Mr Watson to:

take steps to secure the abatement of nuisance of melting tallow in premises occupied by Mr Crowther and also the obstruction caused by a weighing machine in the passage at the back of the Office.

This last resulted in the purchase of new balances and alterations to create space to put them in. In 1856 gas lighting was installed, and in 1861 apparatus for wet assaying, whilst 1866/67 saw the introduction of a gas furnace invented by his son Arnold[9] (Figure 5). John Watson was something of a moderniser.

By the Annual Meeting in 1868 it was resolved that William Henry Watson should be elected assayer to assist his father, not only to avoid problems when John Watson died, but also because of the increased workload. William Henry was duly sworn in on 31 July 1868, with his father and his uncle, Jarvis Radley of Beighton, farmer and gentleman, as sureties.

On 2 October 1878 the Guardians met:

to express their regrets on the death of the late Master Mr John Watson which took place on 9th August last & to record their appreciation of the efficient and highly satisfactory manner in which he invariably discharged the duties of his office for a period of close upon 24 years. Resolved that Mr William Henry Watson, son of the late Master and who was himself elected as assayer to assist his father at the Annual Meeting in 1868,

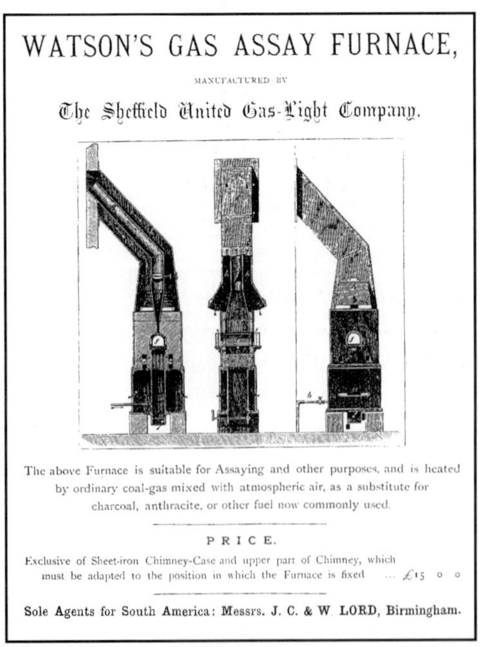

Figure 5. Watson's gas furnace.
Sheffield Assay Office

be the Assay Master at a salary of £200 pa, commencing from the date of his father's death. That Mr Arnold T. Watson, brother of the Master be elected as an Assayer without salary to assist him.

Although initially only William was sworn in as Assay Master, both he and Arnold shared the work between them. William, in a reply to the Law Clerk on 24 July 1879, about who should sign any cheques, stated that 'I do not know that there is any difference between his position and mine as I believe we are both Assay Masters'.[10] (Apart from the salary, that is.)

Evidently not all local manufacturers were happy at the change of Master. In a letter to James Dixon & Sons dated 10 December 1878, concerning goods which failed because they included base metal, Arnold was at pains to refute any suggestion that the work was not done as well as in his father's time:

I return portion of wire so that your Mr Cunningham may satisfy himself on the point:- I think that this should prove to him that the unfair implication which he made this morning to the effect that there was now in his opinion either less ability to make reliable assays, or less care used in making them than in the lifetime of the late Mr John Watson, was quite unmerited. I feel sure that he was only expressing his own idea when he said that we appeared to be always 'on the look-out to catch you'.

Towards the end of the nineteenth century, Sheffield city centre was undergoing major reconstruction. The Fargate site, at its junction with Pinstone Street, was needed for the new Town Hall. Mr. Flockton, the Corporation Surveyor, suggested a site on Firth Street (now Leopold Street), opposite Firth College and the Central Board School. Flockton and Gibbs, the chosen architects, put forward two proposals - one for an office of the same size and one for a much larger building. Mr. Fowler, the Surveyor employed by the Office, described the existing Fargate building as 'strong, substantial and in fairly good repair, although old' and felt that the Guardians would be well compensated for the compulsory purchase. Fortunately, many contemporary letters give an insight into what went on behind the scenes:

The street improvements for which our offices are required I understand will be carried out by the Town Trustees and as several of them are Guardians of this office I don't anticipate any difficulty in our arrangement. [11]

As you may possibly be aware the town of Sheffield is at the present time undergoing improvements in the hands of the Corporation & amongst the property to be pulled down this Office is fortunately included. As we are about drawing out plans for new buildings we think we can probably obtain some useful hint by an inspection of your Hall. [12]

Memories of Lewis Sayles's difficulties with Kramer the butcher obviously lingered in the memory: the Guardians were not going to be caught out again:

Assay Office & Corporation
When speaking with you upon the subject of the site which is offered to the Guardians of the Assay Office in exchange for the one at present occupied, we omitted to name that the adjoining premises should not be let for any purpose where machinery was brought into play - say even as a steam sausage chopping machine or anything of this kind, as it would create a vibration which would quite upset the accuracy of the work of the delicate balances by which the assay office operations are carried out. [13]

There are hints that the Guardians and Assay Master did not always agree:

We have looked over the plans and elevation of the proposed New Offices and as far as we can see with very slight alteration they would do very well, but we think they will have to be submitted to the Guardians for approval at the next Quarterly Meeting which will be on the 6th Oct before it will be advisable for you to get out Quantities of Estimates, as what will suit us, possibly might not suit them, and so your trouble might be thrown away. [14]

Apparently the Guardians were persuaded and the larger building was chosen. The final account shows that the Office actually made a profit of £52 on the change of site. Somewhat belatedly, in February 1881, the design of the building had to be altered when Parkin & Bacon, the occupants of neighbouring premises in Orchard Street, complained that the frontage of the new buildings would be four feet higher than the old ones and would interfere with their right to light. Rather than go to litigation at this late stage, the plans were modified slightly and the upper storey set back a few feet.

The rooms were papered by Chadwick & Co in sage green, the marking-hall was colour-washed and the waiting-room whitewashed, to cover all the pencil-markings left on the walls by the contractors. The floors were woodblock. The Watsons also looked after their home comforts:

Will you please get from Longden & Co a small cooking stove consisting of oven & range. We think there will be need for a boiler attached, but we want a thoroughly good stove capable of roasting a joint in front of the fire and baking a dish in the oven. [15]

Not only a stove was asked for but also a meat-safe, to be fitted outside the building.

Watson also had the lion (reputed to be by Mosley, one of Chantrey's pupils) removed from the Fargate Office and put it in the passage in the new Office. Later, he asked for dark ground glass to be put in the ground floor windows instead of the plate glass which had been fitted originally. The move finally took place during August 1881, after a slight dispute with the Rating Officer.[16] The Sheffield Red Book for 1882 describing the new Office, states:

The new buildings are erected in Leopold Street, immediately opposite the School Board Office, and consist of furnace, weighing, making [sic] *rooms, and workmen's waiting-room with an entrance from Orchard Street, and suitable offices with an entrance from Leopold Street. The front is in Huddersfield stone, in the style of English Renaissance* (Figure 6).

Everything must have been rather a mess, since there is an apology at this time to the Royal Mint for not having paid their bill, which had got lost, and to Roberts & Belk for failing to answer a letter which had been inadvertently placed under some other papers. Complaints about the new building continued to preoccupy the Watsons for some time, culminating in a catalogue of problems:

about the WCs:

The water closets do not work at all satisfactorily & at times cause such a nuisance in the offices as to be perfectly unbearable. The fact is the

Figure 6. Drawing of the Assay Office, Leopold Street, by Walter Revill.
Sheffield Assay Office

pan is so shallow that it does not contain enough water to cover the excrement, hence a great smell & this is driven into the passages and front offices by the strong down draft through the ventilator: I think you will have to change the pans for 'Underhays' or something similiar.

about ventilation:

The office ventilation will also have to be completed as originally intended; we have named this to Mr Bradford. [17]

about dirt getting in through the skylight:

The skylight of my office also admits smuts to sprinkle my desk & papers all over with them: this is caused I think by the want of proper puttying at the lower ends of the glass, so that smuts from the roof blow through.

about a need for glass panels in the door to the WC:

There should be corrugated glass panels to the door of the lavatory & WC as it is so dark if the doors are kept closed: there should also be springs to keep the door closed. The urinal also as already named is very unsatisfactory.

about the heating of rooms:

The Chairman of our Board of Guardians has today been looking over the premises & strongly objects to the mode of heating the waiting-room viz by Perkin's apparatus, and insists on having the cupboard which now fills the fireplace removed to some other part of the room & an open fireplace substituted for the hot water pipes. - We must say that they are a complete failure & quite useless... [18]

about the front door bell:

P.S. The front door bell is still out of order : cannot be made to ring unless pulled to the very extreme. [19]

and after various complaints about ventilation, the smoking chimneys:

All the chimneys on the Orchard Street side of the building smoke badly & something will have to be done to them either in the way of raising or fixing revolving chimney pots. [20]

Despite the complaints, others found the new surroundings only too congenial - Arnold Watson had to write to Candlish & Baxter, who had a tobacco factory on Orchard Place, asking them to stop their workpeople using the Assay Office waiting-room, and he frequently

Figure 7. Arnold T. Watson, Assay Master and President of the Sheffield Literary & Philosophical Society. *Sheffield City Libraries, Local Studies Library*

complained to manufacturers about the behaviour of their messenger boys, who disrupted the work and played football in the street outside.

The offices on the second floor were occupied by the Watson family stockbroking firm. The Assay Office paid all the rates and taxes for this business, and in return, the firm supplied much-needed clerical assistance. Despite the move to larger premises, the Office was still only open on Mondays and Thursdays, although the local silver trade was growing rapidly. From 1884 the Office opened for a third day, but the Watsons were not allowed to pay more staff to cope with the increased workload.

After William died in 1890, Arnold continued with the help of his nephew, Bernard. Arnold's interests lay elsewhere, particularly in marine zoology, and in the Sheffield Literary & Philosophical Society, of which he was twice President (Figure 7). By 1898 he had had enough, and resigned so that a younger person could take over and the Office could expand. Bernard succeeded him, reigning with a rod of iron for 43 years, through two world wars and immense changes. After 125 years, Sheffield finally had a full-time Assay Master.

Notes and References

1. Letter to Matthew Boulton, 14 July 1773, Birmingham City Archives. I am grateful to Gordon Crosskey for pointing this out.
2. Evidence of Samuel Smith to the Select Committee on Assay Offices, 30 March 1773. Birmingham City Archives.
3. The Act of Parliament which set up the Sheffield & Birmingham Assay Offices - 13 Geo.III C.52 - laid down the oath which the Assay Master had to swear, and also demanded that he provided two sureties and the sum of £500 to be paid to the Master of the Mint in case of any fraud or neglect on his part.
4. The Act appointed 30 'Guardians of the Standard of Wrought Plate within the Town of Sheffield' to oversee and control the running of the Office. Of these local men, ten were local gentry, ten merchants / bankers and nine silversmiths, with the number made up by one refiner.
5. Assay Office Minutes 3 July 1780.
6. 24 Geo.III C.20, 1784. This Act also allowed platers to register their marks with the Assay Office.
7. Much of the information on Dickinson is from *Two hundred precious metal years* by Ronald E. Wilson, London, 1960.
8. Despite his surname, Henry Watson (later Sir Henry) was not related to John Watson. The Watsons who were the Assay Office Law Clerks were descended from Thomas Watson, an innkeeper. The Assay Master's family was descended from one of the early silversmiths, William Watson.
9. In July 1868 Arnold Watson was presented with £21 for *the expense he has been at & the time he has devoted to the completing of the new furnace for assaying as heated by gas, which is found (after being in constant use for the past 15 months) to be a considerable improvement in the working as also a saving in cash as compared to the charcoal furnace heretofore used.* Guardians' Minutes 6 July1868.
10. William Henry was 39 when appointed; Arnold Thomas was 32.
11. Letter from John Watson to W. Westwood, Birmingham Assay Master, 20 July 1877.
12. Letter from Arnold Watson to W. Westwood, 7 July 1880.
13. Letter from William Watson to J. Flockton Esq., 23 June 1880.
14. Letter from Arnold Watson to Flockton & Gibbs, 10 September 1880.
15. Letter from John Watson & Sons to Flockton & Gibbs, 6 May 1881.
16. William Watson complained that, although the new site was marginally larger, the land on Fargate was more valuable, and although there were three more rooms in the new Office, two of them were smaller than those in Fargate, and anyway the Office had been compulsorily purchased so the Council could not expect them to pay more than the £66 they paid for the Fargate premises.
17. Complaints about the plumbing continued intermittently until 1922, when new drainage and toilets were finally installed.
18. Letter from Arnold Watson to Flockton & Gibbs 16 December, 1881.
19. Letter from William Watson to Flockton & Gibbs, 10 October 1881.
20. Letter from Arnold Watson to Flockton & Gibbs, 11 October 1881.

3. REV. JAMES WILKINSON AND THE CHURCH IN SHEFFIELD, 1754-1805

by Malcolm Mercer

As a great public character, commanding respect by a dignity in person and manners rarely to be met with, the Rev. James Wilkinson was deservedly looked up to and consulted upon every occurring occasion, whether for the relief of the poor, the defence of his country, the protection of every useful institution, the encouragement of merit in any situation, or of any plan calculated in any way to improve or benefit society in general, but more particularly the town and neighbourhood of Sheffield. Robert Ernest (1824)[1]

SHEFFIELD'S MOST INFLUENTIAL FIGURE in the second half of the eighteenth century was the Vicar, the Rev. James Wilkinson, parson, squire and magistrate (Figure 1). A countryman by birth, field sports were in his blood. He revelled in the chase and 'hunted with avidity'. He acquired the manly sport of boxing and enjoyed convivial company. He conducted his affairs with 'unaffected piety' and when appointed magistrate he dispensed justice with 'inflexible integrity'.

The fourth of seven sons, young James was earmarked for the Church from an early age. Well educated, he was schooled in the classics at Beverley and graduated at Clare College, Cambridge, where he prepared for ordination. He became a Bachelor of Arts in 1752 and MA in 1755. His father, Andrew Wilkinson of Boroughbridge, described as 'principal storekeeper of the ordnance' succeeded his father in law, Judge William Jessop of Broomhall, Sheffield, as MP for Aldborough and Boroughbridge, both of whom supported the Whig party in government. Andrew Wilkinson inherited the rights of patronage to the benefice of Sheffield through his marriage to Barbara Jessop, Judge William's eldest daughter.

Although James was still at university and not yet ordained deacon when John Dossie, the unlamented vicar of Sheffield, died on Christmas Eve 1753, he was offered the living by his father. Ordained deacon in York on the 9 June 1754, he was inducted vicar of Sheffield on the 25 September shortly after his twenty-third birthday.

Figure 1. Bust of the Rev. James Wilkinson by Sir Francis Chantrey in Sheffield Cathedral.
Drawing by Charles Ashmore

Figure 2. Broom Hall in 1819. This sixteenth century house was inherited by Vicar Wilkinson in 1754. *Sheffield City Libraries, Local Studies Library*

His ordination to the priesthood took place twelve months later.[2]

Having inherited the Broom Hall estate from his Jessop ancestors, Vicar Wilkinson chose to live in this rural retreat away from the hammering, grime and soot of the industrial township (Figure 2). He added an east wing to his home in 1760 from where he occasionally administered justice.

Church and Parish

At this point in time, Anglican places of worship were the Parish (Trinity) Church, the 'new' church of St Paul's (1740) and the chapel of the Shrewsbury Hospital. The chapels in Ecclesall and Attercliffe served the people in the outlying townships. Since the Reformation, parochial responsibility was vested in the vicar together with three assistant ministers. Appointed by the Church Burgesses, these assistant clergy officiated conjointly with the vicar in reading prayers, preaching, administering the sacrements, visiting the sick and burying the dead, but they were free from any legal control or direction by the incumbent - an anomaly that had worked well in the past but was to mar the early years of Wilkinson's ministry.

Entrusted with the 'cure of souls' at his induction, the young vicar saw his parochial duty as a responsibility to be shared with his assistants as part of a caring team - each one taking a week by turns in regular rotation - 'all striving together in the work and labour of love'. This conviction immediately provoked a dispute between himself and John Dickenson, curate of Ecclesall. Dickenson, a pluralist, also held the living of Parson Drove in the Fenlands, three days' ride away. Because he was not prepared to live in the parish or perform any pastoral duty outside the chapelry, the churchwardens of Sheffield and Ecclesall reported his negligence to the Archbishop of York. He had been absent for over six months, refused to visit the sick outside the chapelry and was serving without a licence. In 1756 Dickenson resigned the curacy but retained his position as assistant minister which generated a legal dispute until 1763.[3]

When the Rev. John Downes - appointed assistant minister in 1766 - was denied the curacy of Ecclesall, he also objected to the vicar's direction. Wilkinson maintained that all he asked of Downes was that he should attend the parish church every Sunday and preach but twice a month. Downes argued that he should perform such duties as he thought fit without let or hindrance. This wrangle was not resolved for another seven years.

Vicar Wilkinson maintained the preaching rota operated by John Dossie.[4] He preached in the parish church on the first, fourth and fifth Sundays of each month, in Attercliffe on the second and Ecclesall on the third. The curate licensed to the parish church was normally present every Sunday morning and preached in the afternoon. When the vicar preached in the outlying chapels the curates who ministered there were expected to officiate in the parish church.

The gloomy parish church of Sheffield (Figure 3), so graphically described by Samuel Roberts, was a maze of high boxed pews and galleries ill lit by candlelight - not unlike Whitby parish church today.[5] The manorial pew inherited by the Dukes of Norfolk straddled the chancel arch. This chaotic clutter of seating was the outcome of pew holders erecting their own pews as to size, height and shape for their own exclusive use. Only a hundred seats were nominated 'free' so few of the poorer folk could find room to sit or stand and were effectively precluded from most services. The charity school children were admitted in the galleries and four knock-nobblers (peace keepers) were employed to keep order. I suspect that an 'orderly sober atmosphere' was rarely achieved.

Leather fire buckets decorated the chancel and the distant altar was obscured by the expensive rood loft and eclipsed by the sepulchral remains of the noble Talbots. In his recollections of the church of his

Figure 3. Sheffield parish church from an engraving by T. Harris, 1793. Note the newly-built St James' church at the head of St James' Row and the presence of the military in the foreground. *Sheffield City Libraries, Local Studies Library*

childhood, Samuel Roberts born in 1763, recalled the symbolic link between church and state - the Royal Arms that filled the apex of the chancel arch 'painted most gloriously and magnificently large'. The ubiquitous tablets revealing the Ten Commandments, Lord's Prayer and Creed repainted at the instigation of Nathan Drake in 1703 had no lasting effect on young Samuel's memory. The real focus of attention was the three decker pulpit (Figure 4). Expounding 'the word' clearly took precedence over the administration of the sacrament in eighteenth century Sheffield.

Holy Communion was in fact celebrated monthly in the parish church, plus the major festivals of Christmas, Easter - which included Palm Sunday and Good Friday - and Whitsun. This compared favourably with many parishes in the Diocese of York where four celebrations per year was the norm. In 1743, John Dossie recorded 500 Easter communicants in the parish. Ten years after his induction Wilkinson was able to record that 850 had celebrated Easter communion though this total may have been boosted by Wesleyan attendance. Monthly celebrations attracted 150 and Michaelmas was added to the list of

Figure 4. The three tier pulpit in Sheffield parish church. The pulpit was installed in front of the choir and organ pipes when the church was reordered in 1805.
Sheffield City Libraries, Local Studies Library

festival celebrations.[6]

However, the administration of the sacraments in the Church of England declined significantly in the latter part of the eighteenth century.[7] John Lloyd, vicar of Rotherham, recorded 130 communicants on Good Friday and 180 on Easter Day in 1764 compared with 500 twenty years earlier. Holy Communion was celebrated there on the first Sunday of the month 'or at least six times within the year'. In Ecclesfield the sacrament was administered on major festivals, the first Sunday in August, and the Sunday preceding Michaelmas 'providing the parish clerk gave sufficient notice and it was not inadvertently forgotten'. Easter communicants in Ecclesfield numbered 284.[8]

Towards the end of the century the progressive decline in attendance at Holy Communion in Sheffield was so serious that the assistant minister, Rev. George Smith, not only preached a sermon *On the Prevalent and Encreasing Neglect of the Holy Communion* - he published it, together with statistical evidence.[9] He began by saying:

> *In our own church we can readily determine the relative proportion of those who remain behind to receive the holy sacrament which is certainly very small indeed, and with grief I add appears to be rapidly declining.*

He also chastised the inhabitants of Ecclesall and Attercliffe for their non-attendance at the quarterly celebrations in the parish church.

> *It is the general custom to shut up the Chapels on the mornings of the great festivals of the Church in the hope and expectation that the congregations of those colonial chapels will come.*

Holy Communion was celebrated in the outlying chapels on the Sunday following the great festivals only for the convenience of those unable to attend the previous assembly in the parish church. Smith pointed out that the combined Easter communicants were down from around 340 in 1780 to barely 200 at the end of the century.

It is clear that many more folk were attending church than received the sacrament and the decline in communicant numbers is not the only yardstick for measuring church growth or decay. Wilkinson arranged for evening prayers to be said daily in the parish church and in 1778 introduced a Sunday evening service that attracted congregations of well over 2000. He enabled a more commodious chapel to be built at Ecclesall in 1787 (Figure 5) and initiated the erection of St James' Church on the vicarage croft adjacent to the parish church in 1789. This proprietary chapel was dedicated to St James in honour of the vicar expressly for the emerging middle class who could afford £50

Figure 5. Ecclesall church. Vicar Wilkinson ensured that the Enclosure Commissioners allotted a portion of the common lands at Ecclesall for a new church built in 1787 to replace the old chapel of 1622. Note the adjacent stocks - frequently occupied by Sabbath Day tipplers. *Sheffield City Libraries, Local Studies Library*

each for the purchase of a pew in perpetuity plus an annual rent of one shilling in the pound.[10] This is perhaps inconclusive evidence of spiritual growth but Wilkinson certainly strengthened the church during his tenure of office.

Baptisms were permitted in the chapels at Attercliffe, Ecclesall, St Paul's and St James' and a few were conducted in the Nonconformist and Catholic chapels. The parish church was the only church licensed for weddings - a legal requirement reinforced by Lord Hardwick's Marriage Act of 1753 and a continued affront to the religious feelings of Protestant Dissenters and Roman Catholics alike. Burials became an increasing problem for the parish church. Anyone who brought a body for burial after 4 p.m. was fined 20 shillings. The charnel house where the bodies were laid was north of the chancel (now St Katherine's chapel). It was replaced by a vestry in 1777 when the Church Burgesses erected a meeting room for themselves.

Music in worship was frowned upon by the seventeenth century Puritans who silenced the organ and allowed it to fall into disrepair. After the Stuart Restoration church services were accompanied by a small band of fiddles, hautboys and bum basses plus a choir of loosely woven voices. It was recorded in 1770 that:

> *before the west window high above the gallery was a kind of immense large box hung in chains into which by the aid of a ladder musicians and singers, male and female contrived to scramble.*[11]

Congregational participation hinged on Tate and Brady psalms and paraphrases together with a local collection of psalm tunes published by Joseph Turner in 1715. In 1761 the Methodists introduced their hymn book and gradually hymns and anthems were incorporated into Anglican worship. By the turn of the century St Paul's, St James' and the Parish Church had their own individual collections of hymns and psalms.

With the growth of parish schools where the Church Catechism was usually taught, the clergy were released from the grind of daily teaching but they were required to catechise children and servants in preparation for confirmation. When Archbishop Drummond asked the vicar to report on the diligence of parents in sending them to church, Wilkinson reported that he conducted his examination every Sunday between Easter and Whitsun from one o'clock till evening service which in 1764 was 3 p.m., although 'the people have been generally remiss in sending the children and servants except when notice has been given for an intended Confirmation.'[12] 1777 was an exceptional year when 'Dr. William Markham, Archbishop of York, confirmed about 5500'.[13] Many eighteenth century clergy including Thomas Bright, vicar of Ecclesfield, regarded afternoon catechising more beneficial than preaching as 'thereby the younger sort are taught in a plain manner the Principles of Religion and early imbibe the Doctrines and Truths of Christianity'.

As and when Vicar Wilkinson introduced additional services he ensured that the assistant ministers, sexton and parish clerk were remunerated accordingly. The benefice income in 1764 was only £120 per annum depending on the payment of small tythes, Easter dues and fees for marriages, burials, churchings, etc., there being but little glebe.

Scale of Fees in 1801[14]

Marriage by Banns	2s	
Marriage by Licence	5s	
Burial		3d
Burial in the church	6s	8d
Burial in the chancel	10s	
Mortuaries received by the vicar:		
For every householder inhabitant in the parish dying worth £40 and upwards	10s	
£30	6s	8d
£30 marks	3s	4d

Easter offering
For every person 16 years of age or upwards in the parish 2d
For every garden 1d. Suista 1/2d

As Vicar Wilkinson outlived his brothers who all remained single except one who died without issue, he inherited much of the family wealth which enabled him to purchase the Duke of Norfolk's two-thirds share of the tythe and so improve the stipend of successive vicars of Sheffield.

The stipends of the assistant ministers were barely adequate but assured. Since the creation of the Church Burgesses Trust in 1554 the curates no longer relied on seasonal fairs and congregational giving but received a regular income. In 1764 the curate of Attercliffe was 'passing rich' on £40 a year. The curate of Ecclesall received £44 10s and the parish church assistant was paid £50 annually. Their income accrued from pew lettings in their respective chapels and £20 per year from Queen Anne's Bounty. By the end of the century the Ecclesall curate's stipend had risen to £100 whilst the minister at St James' Church received £120 per annum entirely from pew rents.[15]

Nonconformist ministers also relied on the letting of pews. The Rev. Joseph Evans, the minister at Upper Chapel (1758-98), received £70 per annum occasionally boosted to £80. The pastor at Nether Chapel, Rev. John Pye (1748-73), was in receipt of £100 per annum. At the other end of the scale Rev. Samuel Smith at Stannington rarely received more than £12 plus his house. The itinerant Methodist ministers had a continual struggle to survive.[16]

By 1790 it was apparent that 't'owd parish church' was in urgent need of renovation and enlargement, and the Church Burgesses were granted a licence to commence work.[17] Piecemeal restoration uncovered 'ruinous decay in the walls, arches, pews, roofs' and other parts of the fabric were 'moulderous, rotten and decayed'. The Archdeacon's Visitation in 1800 accelerated the scale of restitution. The church was reduced to a shell and the refurbishment of the nave was financed by the Church Burgesses and pew holders. The transformation of the parish church, equipped with a more formal seating arrangement and a new organ was completed in October 1805. Because the church was re-pewed at the expense of the pew holders the meagre provision for the poor survived. Vicar Wilkinson never saw the modernisation however. He had died in chronic pain at Boroughbridge nine months earlier.

Although the poorer classes were still excluded from most church services the demands on the clergy for the rites of passage intensified as the population expanded. In 1754 there were 722 baptisms, 185 marriages and 608 burials. In 1804 there were 1807 baptisms, 445 marriages and 1193 burials.[18] John Dossie recorded a population of 'above 2000 families' in 1743. Twenty years later Wilkinson estimated the population had risen to '2833 families living in the township, 570 families in Ecclesall and 536 families in the chapelry of Attercliffe - 3939 families in the parish' which was somewhat of an underestimate:

> *The populousness of this town and the parish and the manner of living amongst the common people, several familys frequently inhabiting the same house have made it impracticable for me to ascertain precisely the number of families.*[19]

It is clear from the bills of mortality for the period that the population was rapidly increasing and had risen to 45,755 by the first national census in 1801 - three times the total of 14,531 recorded in 1736. This population explosion created the chronic overcrowding underlined by Wilkinson and confirmed by James Wheat in 1774 in his *Observations on the Present State of the Poor in Sheffield.*

> *Their houses, if such they can be called, are miserable cabins, small, low close dark and dirty where impolluted air seldom enters - here a father, a mother and their children often reside in one room and often sleep in one bed, or if they happen to be possessed of two, they are generally of such wretched quality as to be fit only to generate filth, vermin and disease.*[20]

Nonconformity

'The most important fact in the religious history of Sheffield was the early and continuing strength of the Dissenting Tradition' wrote Bishop David Lunn in 1987.[21] With Nonconformity emerging in the town from the beginning of the seventeenth century[22] alternative religious traditions took root after 1662 and the gap between the Established Church and the Dissenting congregations widened in the wake of the Act of Toleration in 1689. In 1764 Wilkinson confirmed that:

> *the number of dissenters is very large but cant be well determined. Many persons go to their meetings who declare that they have no reason for not going to church but the want of room. The sect of Methodists is at present the most numerous here, the Independents next then Presbyterians and Quakers the fewest.*
>
> *All the meeting houses are licensed of which there is one of every sort in the town. The largest is now that of the Methodists whose teachers*

are many and those often changed are said to be under the Direction of Mr. Wesley. They have very frequent meetings generally once in every day and often twice. Their congregation is a great concourse of people consisting of some from every other sect and many who profess to be members of the established Church of England.

Towards the end of the eighteenth century the Upper Chapel congregation, denominated Presbyterian, gradually veered towards liberal Unitarianism. The Independents, having formed Nether Chapel in 1715 settled for more orthodox Calvinism and were set to expand rapidly. The Rev. John Pye, minister of Nether Chapel from 1748 to his death in 1773, so invigorated the church that by 1759 'there was not so much as a seat to let in the whole meeting'. On his death disagreement and schism led to secession after secession. Over the next sixteen years five Independent Chapels were erected within the urban township, i.e., Coal Pit Lane (1774), Lee Croft (1780), Garden Street (1780), Queen Street (1784) and Howard Street (1790).[23]

The prosperous if austere Society of Friends (Quakers), numbering 172 in 1736, rebuilt their meeting house in Hartshead in 1764 to accommodate their steadily growing congregation. A return to the Archbishop of York in 1767 recorded 319 Roman Catholics in the town.[24]

Meanwhile, Wesleyan Methodism was gathering its own momentum. Their evangelical enthusiasm threatened the religious *status quo* in the 1740s when mobs were allowed to destroy their meeting rooms unhindered. In 1745 the churchwardens and a constable dragged John Wesley from a private meeting only to discover that his subversive activity was confined to conducting prayer and he was released. Eventually the Wesleyan Society brought an action against the magistrates for negligence at York Assizes. They were ordered to rebuild their meeting house. On his visit in 1757 John Wesley observed, 'How quiet is this country now since the chief persecutors are no more to be seen'.[25] This is clearly a reference to the hostility of the late John Dossie and the advent of Vicar Wilkinson.

In his Visitation returns for 1743, John Dossie had totally ignored the presence of the Wesleyans in the parish and Vicar Steer of Ecclesfield did not expect the Methodists 'to have any long continuance', but the vicar of Tinsley was very concerned.

I do heartily wish yt a stop might be put to ye growth of Methodism among us to such a height of immodesty have they proceeded yt as is currently reported they have washed women naked in a tub full of water under pretence of cleansing em from yr sins.[26]

Imbued with the desire for conversion the Methodists were set to overtake all other forms of Nonconformity in the town. In 1764 John Bright, vicar of Ecclesfield, remarked:

> *Enthusiastic or Methodist I cannot ascertain the number. I believe there are not so many as I found upon my first coming hither tho they swarm at present in the next neighbouring parish to me towards the south namely Sheffield.*

In 1756 Charles Wesley had tried in vain to prevent the Wesleyans from breaking their ties with the Established Church in Sheffield and it is clear from John Wesley's *Journal* that his annual visits excited the townsfolk and strengthened the 'society'. In August 1761, he preached outside Mulberry Street meeting room to three times as many people as it would have contained. By 1771 the number of classes had increased from five to thirteen with a recorded membership of 652. Eight years later Wesley preached in Paradise Square 'to the largest congregation I ever saw on a weekday.' In 1780 he preached at the opening of the new Wesleyan Chapel in Norfolk Street. The Sunday morning following, Vicar Wilkinson allowed him to preach in the parish church. Anticipating a long service and a large congregation, the 78 year old Wesley offered to assist at Holy Communion but the vicar declined his assistance which provoked a curt reply.

> *Sir,*
> *There is no harm done. If you dont want me. I dont want you.*
> *I am your fellow servant,*
> *John Wesley.*[27]

In his Journal for the 2 August 1780, Wesley wrote:

> *At eight I preached at Sheffield. There was after such a number of communicants as was never seen at the old church before. I preached again at five, but many were constrained to go away.*[28]

The Methodist Church continued to grow apace and by 1796 the recorded membership numbered over 3000. Garden Street Chapel was purchased from the Independents and retained until the handsome Carver Street Chapel was opened in 1805. Meanwhile, the Methodist congregation that seceded with the maverick Mr Bryant in 1764 built their own chapel in Scotland Street. On the death of Bryant, Alexander Kilham was invited to be their pastor. He seceded from the Methodist Connexion in 1797 and Scotland Street Chapel gave birth to the democratically inclined Methodist New Connexion, frequently nicknamed Tom Paine Methodists.

In this age of schism the evidence suggests that different strands of dissent were developing and evangelical Nonconformity was expanding. The Established Church was stronger but no appreciable effort was made to match the needs of the rapidly increasing population. The estranged poor were not the only sector outside the Church's sphere of influence. Habits of indifference to organised religion stretched back several generations to the seventeenth century toleration legislation which effectively permitted the inhabitants the right to absent themselves from religious practice altogether.

A Christian Moderate

Characteristic of the Whig Anglican clergy of his day, Wilkinson celebrated the centenary of the Glorious Revolution in 1788 and preached at the commemoration service. The gentlemen and principal inhabitants, all loyal to the House of Hanover, arrived at the parish church wearing their orange cockades. The clergy wore their 'sacerdotal habiliments'. Wilkinson's tolerant attitude and mutual respect for Dissenters prompted Edward Goodwin, Curate of Attercliffe, to describe him as a 'Christian Moderate' in a town 'where no spirit of party prevails'. His theological outlook veered towards the rational and reasonable - an eighteenth century Latitudinarian or broad churchman and somewhat of a liberal. It is significant that when the clergy of the Archdeaconry of York met in 1790 to oppose the repeal of the Test and Corporation Acts which so penalised Dissenters, the assistant clergy of Sheffield were amongst their number but Vicar Wilkinson was not one of them.[29]

Wilkinson's spirit of toleration clearly extended to civil and religious liberty and he actively supported parliamentary reform. Motivated by the totally unrepresentative nature of parliament, political corruption and abuse of public office, he allied himself with many prominent Dissenters. The movement for political reform led to the formation of the Yorkshire Association inspired by the Rev. Christopher Wyvill. In company with Samuel Shore, the Unitarian banker of Meersbrook and Norton Hall, they attended a preliminary meeting in York in December 1779, and regular committee meetings over the next few years.[30] In June 1781 Wilkinson delivered a political sermon in the presence of the Archbishop of York when he held a Confirmation in Sheffield.[31] Wyvill kept Wilkinson informed of William Pitt's attitude to reform well into the 1790s.

Mr Justice Wilkinson

His election to the magistrate's bench in 1763 conferred on Wilkinson the accolade of a country gentleman and confirmed him as an agent of social control. As Justice of the Peace for the North and West Ridings of Yorkshire he frequently presided over the petty sessions in Rotherham, Doncaster and Pontefract and on occasion attended the Quarter Sessions at Knaresborough and York. His responsibility involved the supervision of the churchwardens, the overseers of the poor, the surveyors of highways and a handful of constables all elected by the inhabitants. The gaols and houses of correction, and the licensing of ale houses were also under his control. In conjunction with the more fiery Colonel Athorpe of Dinnington Hall he dispensed justice in the lower room of the Cutlers' Hall - a very strong sanction against disruptive behaviour. However, this dual role of *rex atque sacerdos* - king and priest - was to provoke resentment among the poorer classes towards the end of the century.

Sheffield was not regarded as an unruly town though St Paul's Church was vandalised whilst standing empty in the 1730s and mobs were free to destroy Methodist worship centres until the ring leaders were caught and prosecuted in the 1740s.[32] The rising cost of flour provoked a riot in 1756 and the inflationary rise in the price of coal in 1774 caused another. On the latter occasion the constables and their assistants were forced to barricade themselves in the parish church until sufficient help could be mustered to retrieve the situation.

The suppression of moral delinquency and the restoration of good behaviour guided Wilkinson's judgement when discharging justice. The church gate stocks were regularly employed for Sabbath breaking. Boys caught bathing or adults found tippling during service times were invariably incarcerated there. 'As breaking the Sabbath engenders as much as anything the seeds of vice among the vulgar we cannot too much applaud the vigilence of this careful magistrate' commented the editor of the *Sheffield Register* in January 1788. Disorderly servants and apprentices were committed to Wakefield House of Correction for between a fortnight and two months' imprisonment as were vagrants, deserters, milkmen selling short measure and offenders found guilty of breaking and entering or stealing workshop and domestic items such as sheets, pillow cases or kettles. Because young abandoned children became a charge on the parish, Justice Wilkinson had no compunction in sending single mothers, or both parents if discovered, to Wakefield. Serious offenders were normally sent to York Assizes.[33]

Corporal punishment in the form of a public whipping was

commonplace. Offenders were dragged in a cart from Truelove's Gutter (Castle Street) to the church gates and flogged by the beadle. In August 1763, Wilkinson sentenced a man to be whipped through the markets for stealing the iron axle trees from a grinding wheel. A Manor collier stole an axe from a Darnall collier's cabin in January 1789. He was whipped on Worksop Road and imprisoned for a month. In June 1787, three men were found guilty of 'plucking up several hundred ash plants'. They were sentenced to three months' imprisonment and publicly whipped once a month through the town of Wakefield. When first appointed magistrate, Wilkinson occasionally ordered vagrant women causing a nuisance to be whipped but it became rare. Corporal punishment for women was abolished in 1820. Prisoners sent to Wakefield were invariably marched there in chain gang fashion. In November 1802, it was estimated that about 300 actions were heard in the Sheffield Courts every three weeks but the number of prisoners was only fourteen.[34]

Summary justice was in everyone's interest but it was a combination of injustices that ignited the attack on the vicar's home in July 1791. Joseph Gales the editor of the *Sheffield Register* was 'at a loss to account for it' but it is apparent that the townsfolk were incensed by the threatened enclosures advertised in the *Sheffield Register* and the notices pinned on the parish church door. Bolstered by a gang from Birmingham, the mob first attacked the debtor's gaol in King Street, demolished the gaoler's house and liberated the prisoners. The throng then set out to vent their fury on the property of the vicar at Broomhall, and the Duke of Norfolk's agent, Vincent Eyre, and the home of James Wheat the attorney, the major beneficiaries of the act. Common lands at Ecclesall were enclosed between 1779 and 1788 and Hallam Moors, Rivelin Valley, Crookesmoor and the village greens at Heeley, Newfield and Owlerton became private property. The expanding town was deprived of its open spaces without an acre being allotted for public purposes.

All the vicar's windows were smashed, his library set on fire and four hayricks were completely consumed - satirized in the doggerel:

They burnt his books
and scared his rooks
and set his stacks on fire.

The rioters were dispersed by a troop of Light Horse and the next morning two troops of Heavy Dragoons summoned from York arrived. Additional constables were sworn in before 'tranquility' was restored.

Thirteen prisoners were examined by Justice Athorpe at the *Tontine*

Inn and eight were released without charge. Five youths - all under nineteen - were remanded in custody and marched off to York in irons escorted by a party of cavalry. Four of the youths were set free but the Judge came down heavily on the fifth. John Bennett, a half-witted youth - accused of taking a lighted candle to set fire to the haystacks and to ignite the house - was condemned to be hanged. Setting fire to the home of a magistrate was an offence against public justice and could not be condoned.[35]

At the Cutlers' Feast in September 1791, the Company paid tribute 'to our most worthy vicar and magistrate'. Joseph Gales reported that:

> *the gentlemen who might justly be considered the representatives of the town were almost frantic in their expressions of approbation of his conduct when his health was drunk by accompanying it with three times three.*
>
> *The Mistress Cutler not only drank his health but acknowledged also the eminent services rendered their town and neighbourhood for a series of years by so respectable a magistrate.*
>
> *Such an unequivocal proof of the affection of a large and populous town is a remuneration for services worthy of the acceptance of the Good and the Great.*[36]

The immediate effect of the riot was the billetting of troops in the town. In May 1792, a dispute arose between the garrison officers and a crowd assembled outside the *Tontine Inn*. In the ensuing affray a number of injuries were sustained before peace was restored. Magistrates Wilkinson and Athorpe were both called out. They promised 'redress through the courts rather than revenge'. In admiration, Gales reported that 'Too great praise cannot be given to the magistrates'.[37]

These popular disturbances arose against a background of political unrest spawned by the success of the French Revolution, stimulated by sentiments expressed in Thomas Paine's widely read *Rights of Man* and fostered by Joseph Gales in the *Sheffield Register*. These revolutionary opinions were so popular that junketing and civic feasts were held to celebrate the success of the French armies in November 1792, and even the bells of the parish church rang out. However, the vicar was badly shaken by the mobs and distanced himself from the political agenda drawn up by the newly formed Sheffield Society for Constitutional Information, which he described as almost entirely composed 'of the inferior sort of manufacturers and workers'.[38]

The Sheffield Society for Constitutional Information was founded in December 1791, by a group of five or six 'mechanicks' but by the end of 1792 had over 2000 members. They were intent on the more radical reform of parliament than the vicar or his Nonconformist colleagues could approve. The rapid growth of this radical body was seen as a danger to the stability of the neighbourhood bordering on the seditious. During 1792 Colonel de Lancy was dispatched by the Home Office to assess the security of some of the larger towns. Sheffield was singled out as the storm centre of British radicalism. He proposed that a barracks be built to house the military presence in the town. He also inferred that Vicar Wilkinson kept a low profile and 'avoided the many profligate people' but the columns of the *Sheffield Register* recorded his judgements in the Sheffield Courts and the Rotherham and Doncaster Sessions week by week throughout 1792 and 1793.[39] In August 1795, Wilkinson informed the Home Office that he 'detected a great change in the minds and behaviour of the people'.[40]

In part this was due to the adverse effects of the war with France being felt by the Sheffield trades. With inflation soaring, tempers flared again and more volatile situations erupted. On the 4 August 1795, a troop of local volunteers on 'stand by' fired into the crowd and two men were killed. The bitterness and hostility aroused by this incident was encapsulated into verse by Joseph Mather the radical file-smith and ballad monger:

Corruption tells me homicide
Is wilful murder justified,
A striking precedent was tried
In August 'ninety-five'.
When arm'd assassins dress'd in blue
Most wantonly their townsmen slew,
And magistrates and juries too
At murder did connive.[41]

Repressive action may have successfully driven the ultra radicalism underground but it was a couple of years before Wilkinson could confidently inform the Home Office:

> *I am persuaded that the number of disaffected at this place are diminished, or else their hopes and spirits are so much checked and abated, as to prevent them showing themselves with so much confidence in their cause, and audacious reliance on the strength and number of their party as heretofore.*[42]

In the Public Service

In the absence of the Lord of the Manor and the town not yet a corpo rate borough, James Wilkinson was subordinate to no-one. The basic structure of local government in eighteenth century Sheffield was the parochial system and the inhabitants expected that the vicar's secular responsibilities should at least be equal to his priestly function. His stewardship of the Court Leet was distinct from his magistrate's role. A medieval device for keeping public order, the 'leet' had become much more relaxed since the demise of manorial control. Its jurisdiction, however, still entailed an annual perambulation of the streets - and an excuse for a meal at the Lord's expense - in order to discover and remove all public nuisances and filth and general supervision of the constables, the scavengers who cleaned the streets and the searchers for weights and measures, leather, butter and eggs, oatmeal, corn, flesh and fish.[43] He dutifully fulfilled this pivotal role throughout his incumbency and the monuments to his life's work speak of 'his unwearied zeal in the service of the public'.

For years he chaired one public meeting after another. He adjusted the poor rates with equanimity though they rose from £400 in 1750 to £10,000 at the end of the century owing to inflation and industrial recession.[44] He convened political forums and guided the town's charitable trusts. He mobilised public opinion to petition parliament in favour of the total abolition of the slave trade and liberally endorsed the foundation of the General Infirmary for the sick and lame poor (Figure 6). In his only published sermon on the opening of the Infirmary on the 4 October 1797, he said:

> *and if the advantages of an Infirmary be anywhere evident, no place, probably, can be found more eligible or distinguished with superior degree of local propriety for such an establishment, than amidst the great number of inhabitants in this populous town and its vicinity, many of whom in their daily employments are peculiarly exposed to the hazard of contracting dangerous diseases and of suffering from calamitous accidents.*[45]

Wilkinson sanctioned the use of St Pauls' Church as a theatre and concert hall for the performance of oratorios and other sacred music

Figure 6. Sheffield General Infirmary from an engraving by J. Rawsthorne, 1804. It was erected by public subscription and opened in 1797. *Sheffield City Libraries, Local Studies Library*

from 1768 onwards. Temporary seating above the communion table was permitted for performance of *The Messiah* in aid of the Girls' Charity School and the General Infirmary. These events were a real fillip to the cultural life of Sheffield. When *The Messiah* was presented the orchestra was comprised of 44 local instrumentalists and the amateur choir totalled 118.

On a social level Wilkinson was a member of 'The Monthly Club' instituted by the gentlemen of the town in 1783 and which met at the *Angel*. Two years later he subscribed to the erection of the *Tontine* in the Haymarket (Figure 7). This celebrated hostelry became the mecca for the élite and more prosperous manufacturers for major social, political and business functions.[46]

Education was still considered a religious activity and one of the vicar's earliest tasks was to revitalise the finances of the Boys' Charity School which were in a 'scandalous' condition. He introduced an annual charity sermon for the school and served as treasurer for forty years. In 1784 he affirmed the creation of non-sectarian Sunday Schools - a movement spearheaded locally by the inestimable curate of Attercliffe (1774-1817), the Rev. Edward Goodwin, who opened a Sunday school in Attercliffe in February 1785, addressed a pamphlet *To Parents, Masters and Poor Children* on the merits of the schools in 1786 and defended the movement nationally in the columns of the *Gentleman's Magazine* in 1797. Not until Kilham introduced the voluntary teacher at Scotland Street chapel that same year were the denominations galvanised into widespread activity.[47]

It is significant that the vicar applied for a schoolmaster's licence for the endowed day school at Crookes in 1798 and the township school at Attercliffe in 1799 at a time when the licensing of schoolmasters was regarded as an 'empty formality'. Having been denied the opportunity to elect a schoolmaster for the endowed school at Sharrow Moor I suspect he wished to ensure the incumbent's right to nominate the master.[48]

Maintaining law and order was his magisterial responsibility so it is

Figure 7. The *Tontine Inn,* the focus of social, commercial and political life in Sheffield. It developed as the premier coaching inn until the advent of the railways. It was replaced by the Norfolk Market Hall in 1851. *Sheffield City Libraries. Local Studies Library*

not surprising that the vicar had his critics - not the least was the radical ballad writer Joseph Mather who lampooned him as 'the old serpent, that black diabolical fiend'. Mather clearly harboured resentment having spent time himself in the debtor's prison. He also voiced the accumulated discontent that surfaced over the Enclosure awards of Ecclesall and Hallam and as we have seen, the vicar's connivance at the repressive measures used to contain the violence and revolutionary undercurrents that surged through the town between 1790 and 1802. Any suggestion that the role of Justice and Priest should continue was effectively terminated on Wilkinson's death. As Dr Gatty observed, the duties of magistracy ceased to be compatible with those of Christian ministry.[49]

Duty was the key to his character and his contribution to almost every aspect of Sheffield life was far reaching as he sought to preserve what society considered valuable and leavened the advance of secularism by Christian charity. He preached the Gospel week by week and laboured 'to implant the revealed religion', yet the only ecclesiastical preferment he accepted was a sinecure prebend in the Collegiate Church of Ripon.

In the latter years of this distinguished and 'venerable stately old man' the paralytic shake of his head grew progressively worse and he acquired the nickname of 'Old Niddlety Nod'. Accustomed to driving about in a large family carriage and pair he spent more time in Boroughbridge, his birthplace and final resting place. Hunter recalls him in the parish church vestry receiving his Easter dues 'the last Easter of his life - or last but one'. One of his final public actions was to present his curate, the Rev. George Smith, to the curacy at Ecclesall in January 1805 and on 18 January he died. His interment at Boroughbridge on 3 February was marked uniquely by a day of public mourning in Sheffield where he was hailed as the 'Father of the Town'. When James Montgomery composed his obituary notice in the Sheffield Iris he summed up the endless tributes of the community:

> *His whole life was devoted to the public good. Such was the influence of his superior character - his unfeigned though unostentatious piety - his quick penetration and solid judgement - his mild, modest and conciliating yet dignified manners - his inflexible integrity - his respectable family and fortune - and lastly his venerable age and estimable services - that few persons have had the enviable opportunity of being so eminently useful to society.*[50]

Notes and References

1. R. Ernest (1824), *The Origin of the Sheffield General Infirmary*, p.ii.
2. J. & J. A. Venn (1927), *Alumini Cantabrigiensis*, Vol. 4, Part 1 to 1751, p.411. J. Hunter (1869), *Hallamshire: The History and Topography of the Parish of Sheffield in the County of York*, ed. A. Gatty, pp.271-2. *The Book of Common Prayer* (1662) determined that 'none shall be admitted Deacon, except he be Twenty-three years of age'.
3. Rev. C. V. Collier (1929), 'Letters and other Papers relating to Church Affairs in Sheffield in the Eighteenth Century' *Transactions of the Hunter Archaeological Society (THAS)*, Vol. 3, pp.295-327.
4. Collier, 'Church Affairs'.
5. S. Roberts (1849), *Autobiography*, pp.13-14. For a groundfloor and gallery plan of the parish church see T. W. Hall (1932) *The Fairbanks of Sheffield 1688-1848*, pp.100-103.
6. York, Borthwick Institute of Historical Research, Archbishop Drummond's Visitation Returns (ADV) 1764, Vol. III, Fo.19.
7. A. D. Gilbert (1976), *Religion and Society in Industrial England*, p.27.
8. York, Borthwick Institute, ADV 1764, Vol. III, Fo.19.
9. Rev. G. Smith (1799), *On the Prevalent and Encreasing Neglect of the Holy Communion* L.P. 59, No.16, Sheffield City Libraries.
10. Hunter, *Hallamshire*, p.249-276. St James' Church, (1788), *Conditions of Subscriptions for raising a sufficient fund for building a new Church or Chapel of Ease.* Sheffield City Libraries.
11. A. C. E. Jarvis (1938), *The Cathedral Church of St Peter and St Paul*, pp.58-9.
12. York, Borthwick Institute, ADV 1764, Vol. III, Fo.19.
13. Jarvis, *Cathedral Church*, p.60.
14. Newspaper Cuttings relating to Sheffield, Vol. 25 P.139, Sheffield City Libraries. A *suista* is the medieval Latin name for a pigsty.
15. Collier, 'Church Affairs' *Transactions of Hunter Archaeological Society (THAS)*, Vol. 3, p.305. Hunter, *Hallamshire*, p.349.
16. R. E. Leader (1901), *Sheffield in the Eighteenth Century*, p.7.
17. Plan and Licence of proposed enlargement of Church of Holy Trinity, Sheffield (1790) M. D. S(20) 6m. Sheffield City Libraries. Hunter, *Hallamshire*, p.249. A. Gatty, *Town and old Parish Church of Sheffield.* L. P. 157 No.16, Sheffield City Libraries. Local Notes and Queries, Vol. 5. p.34, Sheffield City Libraries.
18. Bills of Mortality. PR. 138 G1. Sheffield Archives.

	Baptisms	Marriages	Burials
1751	697	170	471
1761	811	239	527
1771	906	241	920
1781	1198	335	1047
1791	1607	453	1147
1801	1482	465	1177

19. York, Borthwick Institute, ADV 1764, Vol. III, Fo.19.
20. D. Hey (1991), *The Fiery Blades of Hallamshire*, p.91.
21. D. Lunn (1987) *Chapters Towards a History of the Cathedral and Parish Church of St Peter and St Paul, Sheffield.* Preface unpaginated.
22. M. Mercer (1997), 'Reformation to Restoration: Emerging Nonconformity in Sheffield 1540-1660' in M. Jones (ed.) *Aspects of Sheffield 1*, pp.25-38.
23. Rev. E. R. Wickham (1957), *Church and People in an Industrial City*, pp.46-49 and Appendix V.
24. Wickham, *Church and People*, p.45. Sheffield Local Register 1767.
25. J. Wesley (1938), *Journal* ed.N. Curnock. 28 June, 1745, and 28 July, 1757.
26. *Yorkshire Archaeological Society* (1929) 'Archbishop Herring's Visitation 1743', Vol. LXXV, p.56-58.
27. Wesley, *Journal*, 29 June, 1761; 15 July 1779; 28 June 1780. M. P. 209 S, Sheffield City Libraries.
28. Wesley, *Journal*, 2 August, 1780.
29. *Sheffield Register*, 27 October, 1788, 28 February, 1790. *Gentleman's Magazine*, (1764) Vol. 34, p.159.
30. G. P. Jones (1937), 'The Political Reform Movement in Sheffield', *THAS*, Vol. 4, p.57.
31. Hunter, *Hallamshire*, p.262.
32. Hey, *Fiery Blades*, pp.243, 297-8.
33. *Sheffield Register*, 7 July, 1787; 8 September, 1787; 19 January, 1788; 26 January, 1788.
34. This section is based on court proceedings reported in *Sheffield Public Advertiser* 1763-1790 and *Sheffield Register* 1787-1793
35. *Sheffield Register* 29 July, 5 August and 19 August, 1791. See also W. H. G. Armytage (1951) 'The Editorial Experience of Joseph Gales 1786-1794', *North Carolina Historical Review*, XXVIII, p.337. J. Stevenson (1991) 'Sheffield and the French Revolution', D. Williams ed. 1789, *The Long and the Short of it.*
36. *Sheffield Register* 9 September, 1791.
37. *Sheffield Register* 11 May, 1792.
38. G. P Jones (1937), 'Political Reform Movement in Sheffield', *THAS*, Vol. 4. pp.57-68. J. Taylor, (1943), 'The Sheffield Constitutional Society' *THAS*, Vol. 5, p.133. A. W. L. Seaman (1957), 'Reform Politics at Sheffield 1791-1797' *THAS*, Vol. 7, pp.215-228. J. Wigley (1979), James Montgomery and the Sheffield Iris 1792-1825: 'A study in the Weakness of Provincial Radicalism', *THAS*, Vol. 10, p.173.
39. See *Sheffield Register*, Court Reports, 13 February, 1792 - 17 October, 1793.
40. F. K. Donelly and J. L. Baxter (1976), 'Sheffield and the English Revolutionary Tradition 1791-1820' in S. Pollard and C. Holmes, eds., *Essays in the Economic and Social History of South Yorkshire*, p.95.
41. Donelly and Baxter, 'Sheffield and the English Revolutionary Tradition', pp.94-5.
42. Donelly and Baxter, 'Sheffield and the English Revolutionary Tradition', p.96.
43. *Sheffield Register*, 5 April, 1793. See also 'The Court Leet of the Manor of Sheffield' *THAS*, (1916), Vol. 1, pp.193-207. D. Hey, *Fiery Blades*, pp.58-60.
44. Leader, *Sheffield in the Eighteenth Century*, p.4.
45. Rev. J. Wilkinson (1797), *A Sermon preached at St Paul's Church in Sheffield upon the occasion of the Opening of the General Infirmary.*
46. Leader, *Sheffield in the Eighteenth Century*, p.118. *Sheffield Local Register*, 29 September, 1785.
47. For the development of Sunday Schools in Sheffield see M. Mercer (1996), *Schooling the Poorer Child*, pp.51-61.
48. York, Bothwick Institute. S. M. Nominations, 15 September, 1798, S.M. Nom. 1799.
49. J. Wilson, ed. (1862), *The Songs of Joseph Mather*, pp.44-45.
50. *Sheffield Iris*, 18 January, 1805.

4. Visual Reminders of Sheffield's Turnpike Roads

by Howard Smith

NB This article is designed to be read in conjunction with chapter 5 (pp 70-83): 'Sheffield's Turnpike Roads' in Volume 1 of *Aspects of Sheffield* (1997).

ALTHOUGH THE CITY'S LAST TURNPIKE, or toll, road closed well over a century ago there is a wealth of visual evidence to remind us of the fourteen highways that played such an important role in the growth of industrial Sheffield. The main reminder is the present network of main roads (with the exception of the Parkway) which are simply turnpike roads suitably modified for motor vehicles and vastly increased traffic. Often wider, sometimes straightened, with Tarmacadam surfaces and better drained, nonetheless many of today's roads are little altered, especially on the rural routes. It is a tribute to those surveyors, particularly those of the earlier years of the nineteenth century, who laid out roads designed for horse-drawn traffic averaging no more than 10 mph which can now be driven along at speeds up to six times greater. Good examples of little-modified roads include the A57 Snake Road from the west of Crosspool all the way to Glossop (with the exception of the stretch between Ladybower and Ashopton), the A625/A6187 from Dore Moor to Chapel-en-le-Frith, the B6054 between Bradway and Longshaw on down to Calver as the A625, and the A621 from Owler Bar to Baslow.

Some stretches of the earlier turnpike roads, later by-passed or abandoned when more advanced roads on better routes were built in the nineteenth century, reveal much of this design and construction. They were only capable of enabling even passenger traffic to progress at no more than 5 mph (8 kph), and 40 or so miles (64 km) in a day was the most that could be expected on a journey. Examples that can be examined are the two mile long (3.2 km) Houndkirk Road (see page 54), another stretch of the original 1758 Sheffield-Buxton turnpike across Fairfield Common, NE of Buxton, and the last 0.5 mile (0.8 km) climb to the summit of the Sir William Hill Road up from Grindleford.

In pre-turnpike days most inns were situated in towns, but with the rapid growth of long-distance passenger and freight traffic, many new establishments were built to cater for this passing trade, or small wayside hostelries were enlarged and modernised. Many examples survive from this period, and two representative samples are shown on page 55.

Whenever there was a tollgate there had to be an adjacent cottage for the keeper as the roads were open day and night. The early buildings were usually very simple structures, often in isolated positions, but with the passage of time much better cottages, or even two-storey houses were provided for the custodians. The proof of this improved quality is demonstrated by the number which survive to this day as private dwellings well over a hundred years after being sold off when the roads were disturnpiked (see pp. 56-57). Some had to be demolished as their bays projected into the highway, thus obstructing the increased flow of traffic in the twentieth century. The former Langsett Road toll house (page 57) survived by sacrificing its gatehouse (roadside bay).

By law, each turnpike cottage had to display a table of tolls laid down by Parliament, usually fixed for a period of twenty-one years. Only a handful of tollboards have survived, but a splendid local example is now displayed in the Kelham Island Museum (see p. 57). The purpose-built rectangular recesses in which the boards were fastened can be seen on many of the surviving cottages. The actual tollgates were usually made of wood and quite heavy, so they were mounted on large stone stoops, some of which have survived by being recycled elsewhere. Examples can be seen on page 58.

Parliament, which established each Trust, stipulated that distances along every road had to be recorded every Statute Mile (as had been defined by an Act of 1593). This was usually done on a roadside milestone, a surprising number of which survive, and several local examples are shown on pages 58 and 59. Most modern travellers are unaware of their existence, even though most are 'listed' grade II, as they are often overgrown by vegetation as the highway authorities no longer have to maintain them as they no longer have an official function. In Victorian times cast-iron mileposts, often well-designed and attractive if painted properly, either replaced missing or broken milestones, or were used on the new lengths of road which replaced earlier unsatisfactory routes (See page 60). The Statute Mile of 1,760 yards, was gradually spread round the country, in our locality replacing the longer customary local mile which measured about ten furlongs, approximately 1.25 miles (2.0 km).

As almost all the early turnpike roads leading out from Sheffield were simply upgraded ancient packhorse tracks, many existing bridges had to be widened and strengthened to cope with wheeled vehicles and much heavier loads. One such example is the bridge at Unstone Green which carried the original road between Sheffield, Dronfield and Chesterfield over the River Drone. Many new bridges were also needed. When the Greenhill Moor and Hathersage Trust constructed their Longshaw to Calver branch, which had to cross the Derwent, they erected a purpose-built 'New Bridge' in 1781. Both bridges are shown on page 61. Simpler bridges can be inspected on Houndkirk Road - the best to see being Thieves Bridge (mr 283825). However, even the carriage-bridges built by the trusts have often had to be widened and strengthened to cope with the demands of twentieth century traffic. Two examples are Saltersitch Bridge at Owler Bar, and Cutthroat Bridge between Moscar and Ladybower. Other visual reminders of the turnpike days are shown on pages 61 and 62.

All the following photographs, with the exception of the Attercliffe and Worksop tollboard on page 57, were taken by the author. All map references are prefixed SK.

FORMER TURNPIKE ROADS

GRAVES PARK: ROAD 1: mr 352824
This former 1756 turnpike road can be discerned running between the double row of trees. This was last used by coaches in 1806 following the opening of a new road through Woodseats (Chesterfield Road) and Meadowhead (road 1b) to by-pass the original route.

HOUNDKIRK ROAD: ROAD 4: mr 274810
Part of the two mile length, dating from about 1758, between Ringinglow and Fox House, abandoned when a by-pass new road was opened between Banner Cross and Fox House via Dore Moor in 1818.

CALLOW BANK: (CUPOLA ROAD): ROAD 3: mr 250820
An ancient packhorse track climbed this 1:5 (20%) incline on its way from Dale Bottom (Hathersage) to Sheffield via Burbage and Ringinglow. It was turnpiked in 1758 but proved so dangerous it had to be by-passed within less than a decade, via Overstones Farm.

INNS

THE PEACOCK, OWLER BAR: ROADS 11, 12 (now A621, B6054) mr 293780
Originally the *Devonshsire Arms* when built to serve the new turnpike from Sheffield to Baslow, it became the *Peacock* when purchased by the Duke of Rutland. It functioned as a coaching inn and port of call for passing freight and passenger vehicles, and always attracted the tourist trade from late Victorian times to the present. Recently it has been extensively modernised and refurbished under new management.

SNAKE PASS INN: ROAD 14 (now A57) mr 112905
Built as Lady Clough House, it soon became a coaching inn being situated roughly halfway between Glossop and Ashopton when the last of Sheffield's turnpike roads was opened in 1821. Its name is derived from the family crest of the Cavendishes (Dukes of Devonshire), owners of the inn in its early years. The road takes its name from the inn, not the other way round as is often assumed: it is coincidence that it is such a sinuous - or serpentine - route.

ROUND HOUSE, RINGINGLOW: ROADS 3, 4 mr 291837
Although this octagonal building is the best-known tollhouse in the Sheffield area it had only a short life in that capacity - from 1795 - *c.* 1825. The design enabled the custodian to look out for traffic on the three roads it controlled by two gates.

PITSMOOR: ROADS 2 and 2a mr 356894
Erected in 1837 on the site of the 1758 original at the junction of Pitsmoor Road (B6070) and Burngreave Road (A6135), controlling two gates. It closed in 1876.

GRINDLEFORD BRIDGE: ROAD 4 (now B6521) mr 245778
Originally a seventeenth century cottage, it was converted into a toll cottage in 1758 by the addition of a two-storey bay to allow the custodian to watch for approaching traffic. It functioned until 1884 before reverting to a private dwelling. Renovated in 1930, it was doubled in size and modernised in the 1950s.

LANGSETT ROAD: ROAD 13 (now B6079) mr 333896
The drawing shows the tollhouse in Victorian times before its gatehouse was removed when it became an obstruction to traffic as the road became busier. It functioned as a tollhouse between 1840-1857.

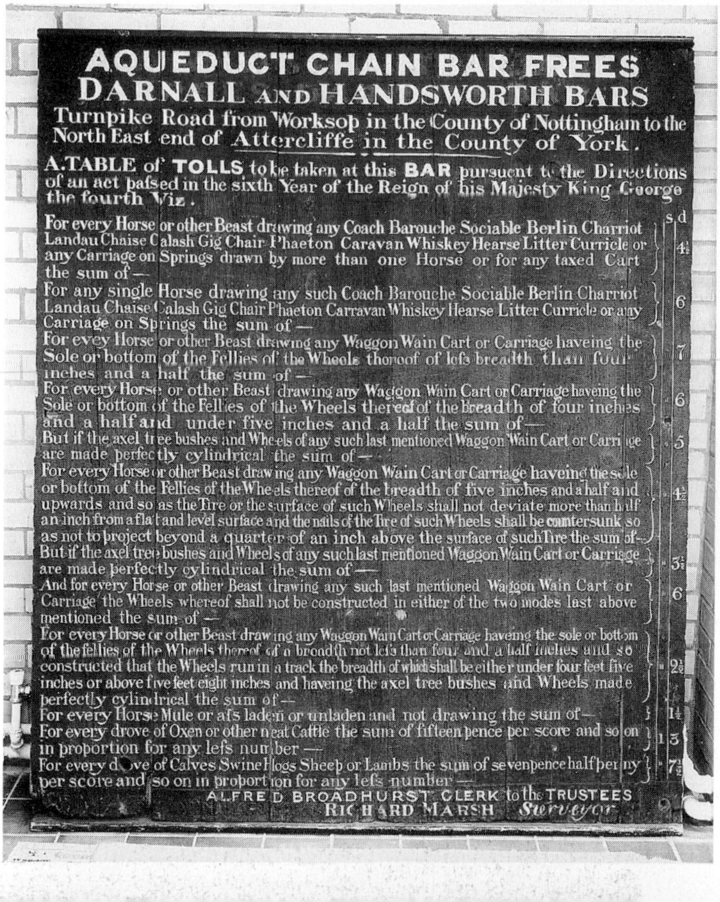

TOLLBOARD
This restored splendid tollboard is a rare survivor from turnpike days. It was removed from the tollhouse at Handsworth (ROAD 8) now B6200, and is currently on display at Kelham Island Museum, Sheffield.

FORMER TOLLGATE STOOPS

(above) **HUNTERS BAR:** ROAD 3b (now A625) mr 332857
Mr Hunter was a farmer here, and his tollgate stood here from 1817 to 1884. It was the last in Sheffield to be removed - to much rejoicing, as the public had tired of paying tolls, and the bars had hindered the inevitable expansion of a rapidly growing Victorian Sheffield. The stoops supported the entrance gate to Endcliffe Park for many years before re-erection in their original site in January 1957.

(right) **MOORWOOD LANE:** off ROAD 12 (now A621) mr 298785
Removed here (together with its five sisters) from one of the two tollgates at Owler Bar.

MILESTONES

(right) **LONGSHAW ESTATE:** ROAD 4 mr 263800
Original milestone Sheffield-Buxton turnpike road 1758 (distance would be 8 miles).

(below) **BIG MOOR:** ROAD 11d (now A621) mr 281743
(date 1818)
SHEFFIELD 10 MILES BAKEWELL 6 MILES

(above) **CROSSPOOL:** ROAD 14 (now A57) mr 311872 (date 1821)
At side of Tavern Service Station, Manchester Road - on reverse SHEFF 2

(right) **OVERSTONES FARM, STANAGE**:
ROAD 3a mr 248829 (date *c.* 1765)
8 = number of miles to Sheffield

(below) **THE CROFTS, HATHERSAGE:** ROAD 3 (now A6187) mr 231815 (date 1758)
10 miles to Sheffield. Moved a short distance from original site.

MOORWOOD, HOLLOW MEADOWS: ROAD 14 (now A57) mr 263874

ONESACRE, OUGHTIBRIDGE: ROAD 13 (now A6102) mr 301942

MILEPOSTS

ASTON: ROAD 8 (off B6067 Worksop Rd, former A57) mr 476853

TINSLEY: ROAD 7 (now A6178) mr 404914
NB: metal plate fixed on side of former milestone

BRIDGES

UNSTONE GREEN BRIDGE:
ROAD 1 (now Whittington Lane) mr 376766
This little-known bridge over the River Drone displays two date stones - 1717 and 1758. The first date refers to its construction as a narrow packhorse bridge on this ancient north-south route, the second to its widening to carriage width when the road was turnpiked between Sheffield and Chesterfield.

NEW BRIDGE: ROAD 11b (now A625) mr 243753
New Bridge (as compared with the old one at Froggatt village, some 1/4 mile (400 metres) upstream on the River Derwent) was purpose-built for the Longshaw-Calver road by the Greenhill Moor and Hathersage Turnpike Trust in 1781. A datestone confirming this is on the centre parapet facing upstream - a little odd, as it cannot be seen from the road.

MISCELLANEOUS

RE-ERECTED TOLLGATE STOOPS (bottom) **and INFORMATION PLAQUE** (right)
BAMFORD: ROAD 3
(now A6187/A6013) mr 207824
These three massive stoops once stood outside the toll cottage at Mytham Bridge (River Derwent) which controlled two gates between 1758 and 1884. After closure, the redundant stoops were used to edge flower-beds before being rescued and re-erected on a safe site in 1985 about 150 yards (135 metres) from their original setting, with a modern wooden gate added for effect. Another two of the original six can be found in Bradwell.

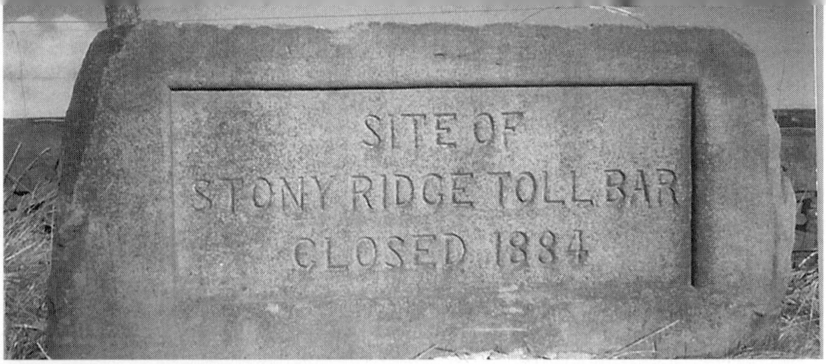

MEMORIAL STONE: ROAD 4c (now A625) mr 277806
The bar functioned between 1818 and 1884. Its accompanying toll cottage survived as a dwelling house until 1915, and was demolished in 1919.

(above) **MEMORIAL STONE:** ROAD 11d (now A621) mr 267733
Stands opposite the site of Cupola toll-bar cottage on Baslow Hill. Now badly weathered, and partly covered by tarmac, the stone (originally the pedestrians' wicket-gate stoop by the side of the tollgate) carries this inscription:
THIS ANCIENT/TURNPIKE/ERECTED IN THE REIGN OF/KING GEORGE II/WAS RE-ERECTED AT/THE CORONATION OF/KING GEORGE V/JUNE 22 1911/BY GM WRENCH MVO

ROAD SIGN: ROAD 13 (now A6102) mr 332905
When an old, free, road was turnpiked, travellers tried to evade tolls by using existing lanes or short-cuts. Parliament gave Trustees permission to erect side bars, often iron chains across the feeder road to 'catch' potential non-payers - hence this road name.

ROAD SIGN: ROAD 6 (now A631) mr 462912
A reminder of the Brecks tollgate which stood near the junction of turnpike roads from Sheffield and Rotherham which met here on their way to Bawtry via Maltby and Tickhill.

MILE PLATE: ROAD 3b mr 346864
Located where the Chapel-en-le-Frith turnpike started, on the side of a building lying between Old Ecclesall Road and Cemetery Road.

5. John Curr, 1756-1823, Mining Engineer and Viewer

by Ian R. Medlicott

DURING THE LATTER half of the eighteenth century the coal mining industry experienced a considerable increase in the demand for coal, due in part to the widespread adoption of coke in the smelting process, the introduction of Cort's reverberatory furnace, and the parallel development in canal transport which facilitated the cheap bulk movement of coal. It was the expertise of colliery engineers such as John Curr, that enabled the continued growth of the coal mining industry during the eighteenth and nineteenth centuries. John Curr was born in 1756, the son of John Curr, coal viewer of Bushblades. The exact location of his birth is uncertain, but he is reputed to have been born at Kyo, near Lanchester, and brought up at Pontop Pike, or born and brought up at Greenside, in Ryton parish, in County Durham.[1] The Currs almost certainly came into contact with the Buddle family, the foremost mining consultants of the time, who

Figure 1. Collieries on the Sheffield estate, 1750-1830.

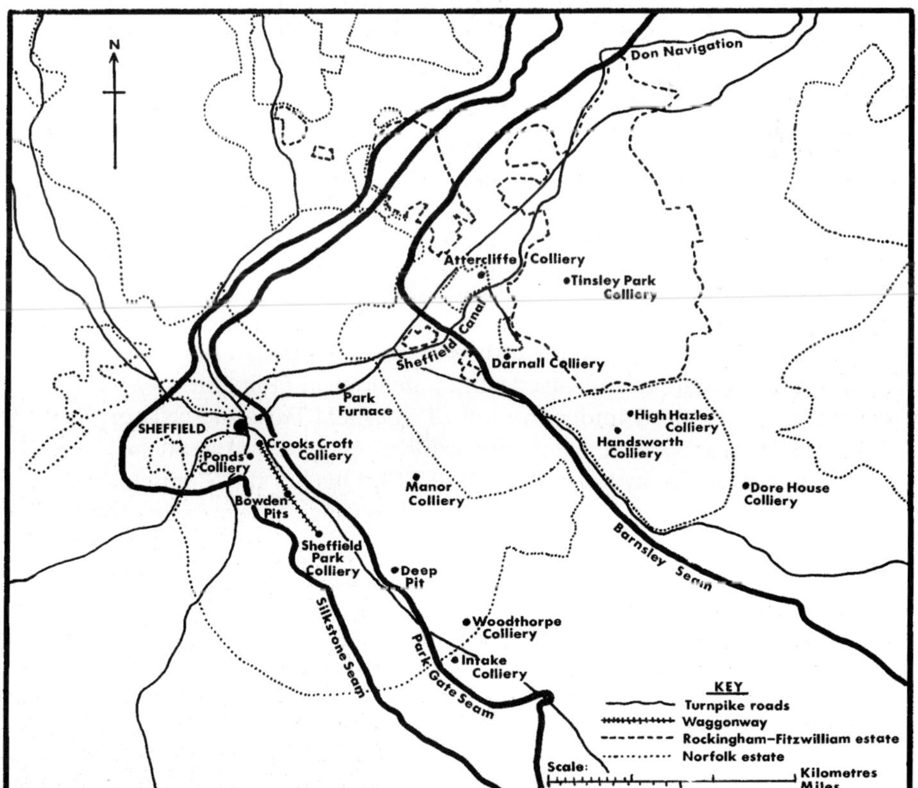

viewed, managed, and owned collieries, especially in the Northumberland and Durham coalfield.

John Curr and the development of the Sheffield collieries

There is some doubt about the precise date when Curr became employed on the Sheffield estate (Figure 1). The first reference to Curr in the estate accounts was on 20 December 1777, in an entry, 'Received of Mr John Curr the Remainder and in full for the overvend both of the Wood & Manor Pits due Xmas 1775 & 1776 - 134. 1. 6', and on 3 December 1778, an account referred to the nature of his employment, 'By John Curr for viewing and examining several collieries 7. 4. 0.'. Curr's employment on the Sheffield estate probably commenced in 1777, after the death of the ninth Duke of Norfolk on 20 September 1777, as the trustees who took over the management of the estate would have required a viewer to assess, value, and report on the condition of the collieries under their charge. [2]

The Wood pits (Sheffield Park Colliery) and the Manor Colliery were under lease to Townsend and Furniss in 1777, with the larger of the two being the Wood pits that worked the Silkstone seam used by the Sheffield cutlers and householders, while the Manor Colliery exploited the Parkgate seam which supplied local farmers and maltsters. A new lease had been discussed in 1774, and shortly before Christmas a waggonway of oak and beech rails was completed that ran from the Wood pits to the Sheffield coal stage at a cost of £3,280, to be paid for by the lessees. A report on the collieries by Curr in 1779 showed that they soon experienced financial difficulties, and even in 1774:

> *The Colliery at this period of time was wrought at a moderate expence by reason of the shallowness of the pits, the quantity of hard in consequence produced, and the short distance to the Town and not withstanding the Rent being something advanced to his Grace, left a little profit to the undertakers but not sufficient encouragement after sinking such a sum.* [3]

The lessees continued reluctantly with the colliery in 1779 in spite of being faced with an increased rental, geological faults, deeper workings as they moved under the hill of Sheffield Park and 'No profits arising from small coal', while the proportion of hard to small coal had declined from 3:5 in 1774 to 1:3 by 1779. This left the Sheffield Park Colliery £60 in debt by Christmas 1778, with an expected loss of not less than £250 for 1779. However, on Lady Day (25 March) 1781, Townsend and Furniss surrendered their lease, from which time the mines came under direct estate management. Curr was put in charge of the collieries and in the *Directory of Sheffield* of 1787, was referred to as the 'Superintendent of the Coal Works of his Grace the Duke of Norfolk'.

In Curr's book, *The Coal Viewer and Engine Builder's Practical Companion*, published in 1797, he wrote:

> *The making and use of rail-roads and corves were the first of my inventions, and were introduced at the Sheffield Colliery about twenty-one years ago; they are doubtless a great acquisition in rendering the article of conveyance much easier and less expensive, and it is not the least convincing proof of their being so, that they have been generally imitated, and made use of in most collieries for the last three years, especially in the southern parts of the kingdom.* [4]

Tramroads or plateways became the common names for cast-iron angled rails, but Curr referred to them as 'rail roads' (Figure 2) with the rails as 'plates' or 'rail plates'. The 'common plate' was six feet long, three inches broad on the 'trod', and half an inch thick. The 'margin' was two inches above the plate and tapered from a half to

Figure 2. 'CAST IRON RAIL ROADS'. *John Curr, The Coal Viewer and Engine Builder's Practical Companion, Sheffield, 1797, Plate 2*

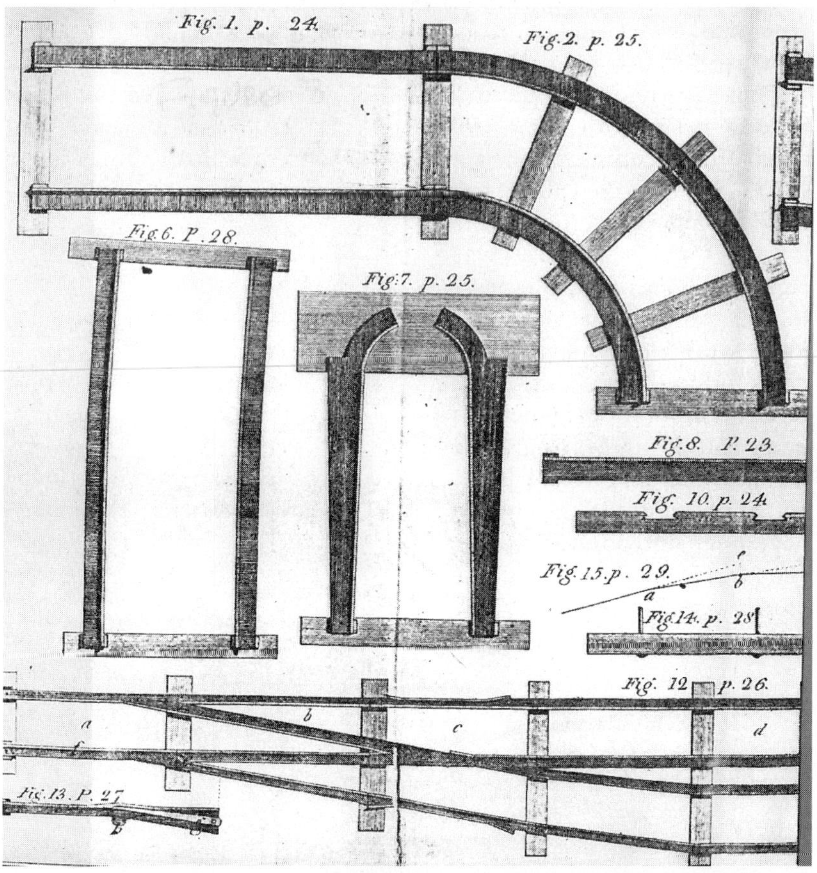

three-eighths of an inch. The plate weighed 47 to 50 lbs. For heavy loads the plates could be strengthened by reducing the length to four or four and a half feet and raising the margins to two and a half inches in the middle, and the thickness by one eighth of an inch. Other plates were made, for example, to go around bends, or to allow corves to pass. The sleepers were three feet four inches long for the wide corf, and three feet two and a half inches for the 'straiter' one, made of oak, four and a half or five inches wide by two and a half inches thick, with the plate sunk one inch deep into the sleeper. The width of the road was recommended to be 22½ inches for the narrow corf and 24 inches for the wide corf.

Curr replaced the hazel kibbles and corves carried on horse-drawn sledge trams by four-wheeled corves of solid board and iron frames (Figure 3). The novelty of Curr's system was that the whole corf could be wound up the shaft without the necessity of unloading at the pit bottom. He developed two sizes of corf, one for 'long way' working, where the roads along the bank face (coal face), were narrow and the coals small, that weighed about three hundredweight (cwt) and held approximately five and a half to six cwt of coal. The outside dimensions were 40 inches in length, 30 inches wide, and 21½ inches high, and cost an estimated £2 16s 6d each to produce. The corf for 'short work', where the coal was extracted in large pieces and the seam not very thick, was 42 inches in length, 31½ inches wide, and 19 inches high, weighed two and three-quarter cwt and cost £2 13s 6d[5].

There is some uncertainty about the precise date when rail roads were first used. In Curr's book of 1797 he wrote that rail roads and corves had been introduced about 21 years previously, but a letter written by Curr in 1801 referred to his invention, 'rail roads', introduced some two to three years before the Duke was concerned with the collieries.

This would leave the years 1776 and 1778 as possible dates for their introduction. As no contemporary evidence has been found suggesting Curr was in Sheffield prior to 1777, and as it is doubtful they would have been introduced during the first few months of his employment in 1777, the following year appears the

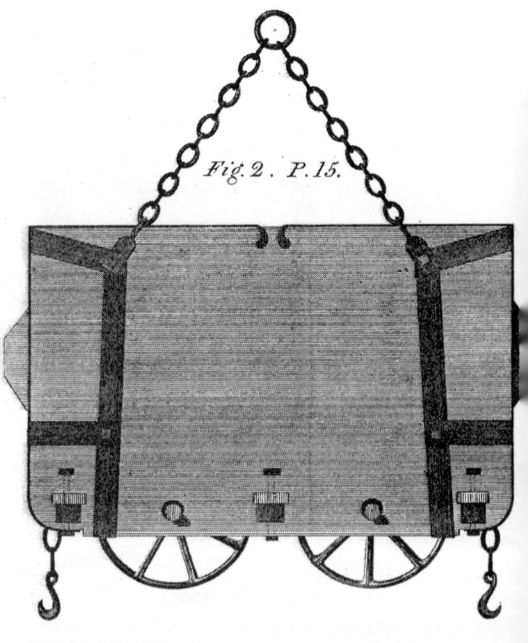

Figure 3. 'THE CORF'. *John Curr, The Coal Viewer and Engine Builder's Practical Companion, Sheffield, 1797, Plate 1*

more likely. However, their use was restricted to one pit in the Sheffield Park Colliery, according to a report by John Buddle I, (1743-1806), in 1787. In fact, wooden waggonways continued to be installed during this period, for example, an estate account for December 1785, referred to laying 596 yards of beech rail at twopence per yard.

On 7 April 1787, John Buddle I gave an independent technical report on the Sheffield Park and Attercliffe collieries that included an assessment of Curr's schemes. In the report he compared Curr's 'rail roads' with the usual method of 'hurrying', which he thought would save £312 10s 0d on the average annual sale of 14,000 waggons of coal from the Sheffield Park Colliery. There followed the large-scale introduction of rail roads and four-wheeled corves into the Sheffield collieries. The Attercliffe Colliery, that was in the process of being sunk to the Barnsley seam, underwent a major expenditure on cast-iron plates. The first recorded entry was on 18 October 1787, and by 28 August 1789, Binks, Booth and Hartop of the Park Iron Works, Sheffield, had supplied rails weighing 92 tons-1 cwt-3 qr-4 lbs costing £1,084 19s 9d. The Sheffield Park Colliery also underwent a period of investment with an initial entry on 16-23 February 1788, 'To Messrs Walker & Co. for Rails 63. 11. 7'. In 1797 each corf contained nineteen pecks Newcastle measure, or about five and a half cwts, and a horse could haul 150 tons 'for a moderate days work', a distance of 220 yards, taking in general, twelve corves at a time, but where the ground fell half an inch in a yard, double the number could be carried. By 1796 rail roads were also being used on the surface. [6]

An increase in the depth of shafts and speed of winding the rectangular shaped corves raised the possibility of a collision between the ascending and descending corves and buffeting against the shaft side. To overcome these problems Curr devised a system of raising the corves two abreast with the aid of conductors or guide rods. Although this had not been introduced in 1787 when John Buddle I wrote his report, his assessment of the system was: 'I have not the least Doubt of Mr Curr's being able to carry out into Execution, with the wished for Effect', and this and all the designs for drawing coal were 'Founded on true mechanical Principals'. The guide rods consisted of two pairs of deal rails measuring four by three inches fixed in the shaft into which a crossbar, that suspended the corves, ran with the aid of rollers in a channel formed by the conductors or guide rods. The guide rods divided in the shaft to allow the corves to pass each other and on reaching the surface they were unloaded automatically with the aid of a tippler (Figures 4 and 5). The weight of coal that could be raised at any one time was increased considerably. A report on the Sheffield

Figure 4. Landing and emptying the corf. *Bland Collection 9/8. Patent No.1660 A.D.1788*

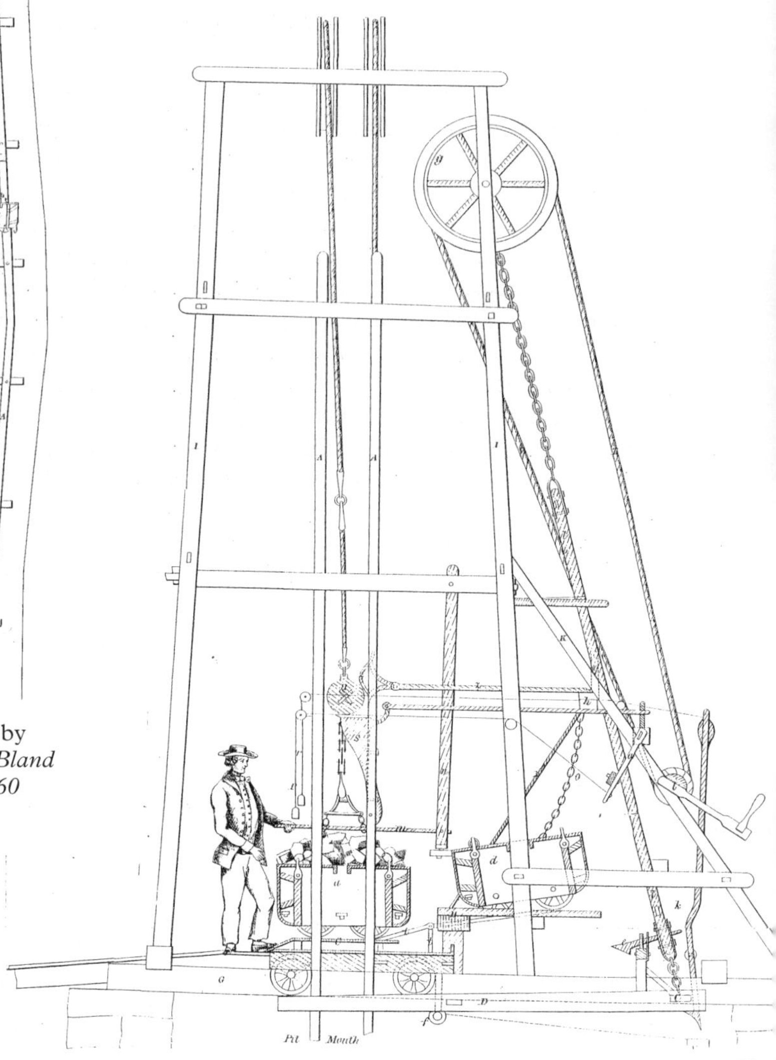

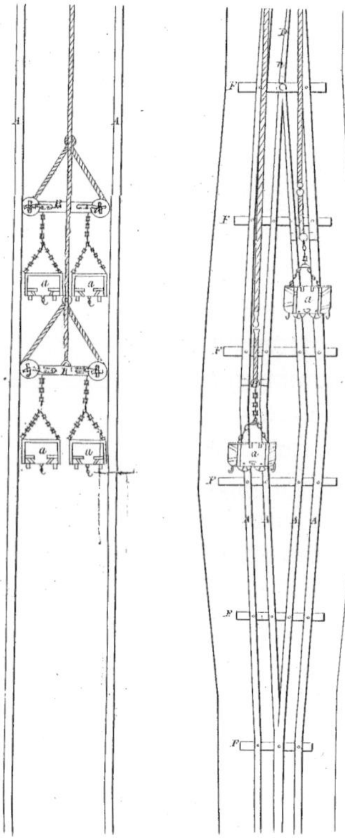

Figure 5. Raising the corf by conductors or guide rods. *Bland Collection 9/8. Patent No.1660 A.D.1788*

FIGURE.19

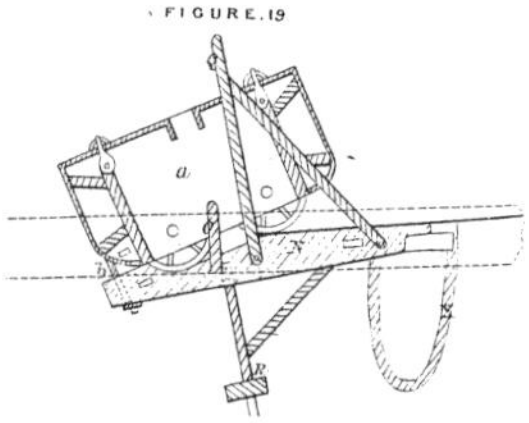

Park Colliery by John Buddle I in 1773, suggested unloading the ten peck (2.89 cwt) kibbles at the shaft bottom into larger sixteen peck (4.63 cwt) corves for winding to the surface, but with Curr's improvements 38 pecks Newcastle measure or about eleven to twelve cwts of coal in two corves could be wound at a time, not including the weight of the corves.[7] On a visit to the Sheffield Park Colliery in 1796, Hatchett wrote:

> *These corves have at the bottom four small Iron Wheels by which they run in the Cast Iron rail roads above and underground... By an ingenious machine worked by water and invented by Mr Curr two of these*

corves are drawn up and two let down at the same time, by the same machinery a Platform slides over the mouth of the shaft and the two full corves are pushed foreward by two empty ones which are next to go down, and the full corves are then rolled by men to the edge of a Platform where by a discharging machine also invented by Mr Curr they are emptied into carts etc. Each corf is guided by friction rollers during the descent and ascent in the shaft, and as these meet about the middle of the shaft this divides there... The loaded corves are brought from the places which are worked for coal (and which are from the bottom of this shaft from 1 mile & 1/4 to 1 & 1/2 mile distant)... along iron roads by a horse guided by a boy, and at every 250 yards, this boy and horse are met by another boy and horse either taking back the empty corves or bringing loaded ones. These boys make an exchange of corves so that each Boy and Horse goes and returns 250 yards in a stated place like a limited stage... by Mr Curr's invention of iron rail roads by the rollers or wheels of the corves and by the passages being nearly perfectly level, one horse is able to draw without difficulty from 12 to 14 loaded corves at one time, whereas before the Iron rail roads were used only two corves could be drawn at once. By this means 200 Tons of coal have been raised at this colliery in one day by the aid of 9 horses, and the machine above ground above mentioned. [8]

The introduction of rail roads, four-wheeled corves, conductors, and tipplers allowed greater quantities of coal to be moved more quickly using fewer hurriers and horses, while the increased quantity of coal hauled up the shaft enabled more colliers or getters to be employed per pit. As coal was able to be worked at a greater distance from the shaft bottom it reduced the frequency of sinking new shafts and erecting winding engines. The use of conductors also extended the working life of the corf by preventing collisions in the shaft.

The increased depth of the shafts and the speed and weight of the coal wound, required advances in rope technology:

The double Rope which I introduced at the Collieries 10 Years ago, produced a great annual saving as the Ropes of the same weight drew more than double the weight of Coals drawn by the single rope... [9]

Curr made further improvements with the introduction of the flat rope that entailed stitching together several round ropes on his 'Flat Rope Lacing Machine'. The rope lapped on itself, which enabled the weight of the rope and the empty corves to assist in counterbalancing the loaded corves as they ascended the shaft, and allowed an initial faster downward movement of the corf which slowed as the rope unwound as it neared the pit bottom. William Bourn, Gainsborough, initially made the flat ropes, but Curr later set up 'The Sheffield Patent Ropery' for their manufacture. In 1801, he claimed:

> [The] *Invention of the Flat Rope (3 years ago) has drawn in one instance 5 times as much as the com.n Round Rope, in another instance 3½ times, and in others 3 and 4 times as much, but the Ropes now in use, being more perfectly manufactured will do 6 or 7 times as much work as the Common Ropes, and thereby save 3 or 4 hundred pounds, per annum in the Duke's Collieries.* [10]

In 1797 Curr commented that it was 'extraordinary, that the drawing by machine had not made greater progress in the southern parts of this Kingdom'. By 'machine' he meant methods other than by a gin or windlass worked by hand. In Sheffield, he used the Newcomen-type pumping engine for colliery drainage and winding the coal. During the summer months the 'Fire Engine' raised the water to the top of a water wheel connected to a winding drum, while in the winter months a nearby stream was used to turn the wheel, as the pumps were required to be used full time to drain the mine. Such engines were at work in the Sheffield Park and Attercliffe collieries.

In 1792 Curr asked Vincent Eyre, steward to the Duke of Norfolk, for permission to establish a foundry:

> *About the year 1792 Fire Engines for drawing Coals were introduced and got fairly under way in the neighbourhood of Coalbrookdale, when I took an opportunity of informing Mr Eyre, that as these Articles were certain to be of great use in our Collieries; to take away the necessity of employing so many horses...* [11]

A foundry was built in Sheffield Park to manufacture engines, rails, and cylinders ranging from fourteen to 32 inches in size. In 1796, Hatchett wrote that at the Attercliffe Colliery, 'a small steam engine as at Coal Brook Dale works Mr Curr's machine for drawing up the corves which here are only two instead of four as at Sheffield Park'.

Curr made improvements and modifications to the Newcomen-type pumping engine, and 'obtained a considerable addition of power, without any increase in fuel'. He found that a better vacuum could be achieved when the injection-cistern was placed about 36 feet above the top of the cylinder. The additional height of the cistern produced a more rapid initial condensation and a better vacuum. He preferred the use of valves which he found more reliable and easier to repair than the 'common regulator and injection cock'. John Farey described an engine built by Curr at the Attercliffe Colliery in 1790, and which he saw at work in 1809. The surface of the water in the injection-cistern was 46 feet above the jet leading into the cylinder. The two boilers were located outside the engine house rather than under the cylinder. Each boiler was enclosed within a bottle-shaped brick construction some 48 feet in height, which not only increased the draught but encouraged the flames to heat a greater surface area (Figure 6). The furnaces consumed ten cwt of sleck or small coal per hour. It had a cylinder of 61 inches in diameter, a piston making a nine feet stroke, although eight and a half feet was usual, at twelve strokes per minute working five pumps.[12]

Curr was also a pioneer in the adoption of self-acting inclined planes, on the surface and underground. One application of this system was to carry coal to the pit stack with the aid of a jinny. A distance of 300 yards was found to be the most practical, with the jinny capable of being revolved in any direction:

> *The ground on which the coals are stacked has a descent of about 3 inches in the yard from the 'jinney', and the momentum of the full*

Figure 6. 'Newcomen's Atmospheric STEAM ENGINE for draining Mines Constructed by Mr. Curr, 1790'. *J. Farey, A Treatise on the Steam Engine, Historical, Practical, and Descriptive, 1827, Volume 1, reprinted 1971, p. 208, Plate V111*

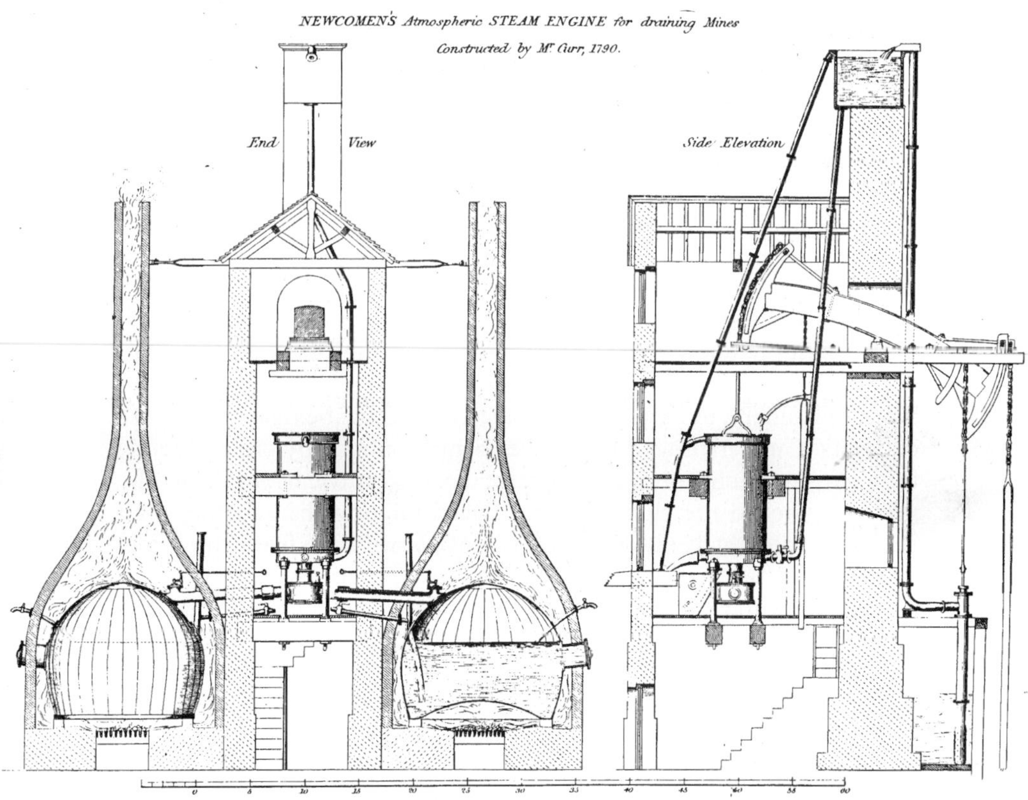

corves going down the inclined plane, with the assistance of the communicating ropes, takes the empty corves back to the 'jinney'. [13]

Curr also devised a machine for the automatic operation of ventilation doors, which enabled corves to pass without the need to employ a trap boy. How practical the trap doors were, and to what extent they were introduced, is open to question, but it does reflect his ingenuity and continual drive to reduce costs.

The original corf design was improved upon. In a letter written to John Buddle II (1773-1843) on 17 February 1800, Curr stated that a 'great improvement in the corf wheel had been accomplished', which entailed lengthening the axis by four and a half inches and leaving two and three-quarter inches of the inner part hollow, with three-eighths of an inch not touching the 'axeltree'. When the hollow was filled with grease the corves could run for 30 or 40 miles without the need for greasing, whereas previously they had to be oiled every three miles with one greasing equal in cost to one oiling. The wheels were placed outside the corf so they could be taken off more conveniently to grease, while lengthening the 'axis' gave 'better direction' and enabled the wheel to work for longer before it became too large. On 23 March 1800, John Buddle II ordered one dozen 'improved corf wheels', with the comment that grease was an important item of expenditure. Curr introduced a light brass bush into the corf wheel through which the axle ran, and instead of the corf wheel being discarded when it had worn out, only a new bush was required, as well as making 'the corf easier in its draught, and consume less grease than iron workg. to Iron'. According to Curr, by 1801, the considerable improvement upon his first corf design saved on horses, grease, and labour, at least £200 per annum in the collieries. [14]

When, in 1787, a new winning of the Sheffield Park Colliery was under consideration at one of two sites, Crooks Croft or the Ponds, as an alternative to sinking deep shafts into the hill of Sheffield Park, Curr devised a system of conveying the coal by 'navigation' through the workings to allow coal to be hauled up a shallower shaft. Although the method was similar to that employed at the Duke of Bridgewater's Worsley Colliery, in Lancashire, instead of the coal being carried loose on boats, Curr envisaged the corves being winched by crane directly into barges, each containing twelve corves, and carried from the 'barrow gate' to the shaft bottom. On evaluating the scheme, John Buddle I thought it the best method of conveyance from the mine, where the depth was upwards of 150 yards, and it would solve the problem of water seeping into the shafts and save on the expense of a waggonway. However, a lack of documentary evidence makes it uncertain whether this method of haulage was adopted in the Ponds Colliery opened in 1789, the Crooks Croft Colliery opened in 1804/5, or the Attercliffe Colliery opened in 1789, where John Buddle I agreed it could also be used to advantage.

As superintendent of the collieries Curr received a total income of £190 per annum, which consisted of £100 for the Sheffield Park and Manor collieries, £70 for the Attercliffe Colliery, and £20 for the Hesley Colliery, with a further £25 when called upon to view and measure the coal and ironstone mines under lease. These sums remained fixed throughout his period of employment, in spite of the considerable rise in inflation during the last twenty years of the eighteenth century:

> *having for all my trouble and Inventions, and including the Risque of Moneys deposited in my hands no more than £190 per annum; and when I have deducted an assistant Clerks salary, whom I was obliged to Keep: the Keep of only 1/2 my Riding Horse, House Tax, Coals, Candles for Office, and a sufficient Agents House to live in, all of which are in general found by the proprietors of collieries; I have not pocketed towards the maintenance of myself and family more than £80 or £90 per annum.*[15]

Curr was placed under financial pressure from Norfolk who deducted a fixed annual rental from each colliery amounting to: £1,000 at Sheffield Park Colliery, £75 at Manor Colliery, and £500 at Attercliffe Colliery, with anything above this designated as 'profits and interest on monies expended'. After the deduction of the fixed rent, the Sheffield and Manor collieries returned a 'profit' of £673 15s 2d in 1781/2 rising to £2,973 15s 8d in 1791/2. However, by 1800 the Sheffield collieries were working at a financial loss, which prompted Norfolk to dismiss Curr in October 1801, after more than twenty years' service.

Several factors contributed towards the dramatic decline in the profitability of the collieries. The adoption of Curr's schemes in the Attercliffe Colliery encouraged the opening of the Ponds pit which adversely affected the former as the increase in output of 'hard coal', that was preferable for the 'Cutlers Hearths', led to the rise in the output of 'small coal', in direct competition to the Attercliffe Colliery. The flow of water into the Attercliffe Colliery from the River Don, and later from two neighbouring mines increased production costs, necessitated the installation of at least four powerful pumping engines and the loss of some of the deep coal. The demand for coal declined after 1792, following the acute economic depression in Sheffield, a situation exacerbated by competition from the Darnall, Dore House, and Intake collieries, which prevented a rise in coal prices to compensate for the increase in the costs of production. In relation to the Dore House Colliery:

> *The loss to themselves in Interests and money sunk has been about £8,000, but the loss sustained (in being deprived of their consumption, and keeping down the price of Coals) has been 3 times as much to the Duke's Collieries.*

The collieries in general experienced:

> *The high prices of hay and Corn, Workmens wages on acct. of the high price of Provisions, Punch Wood and leading, Deal Timber, Powder, Ropes, Candles, Iron, Cast Iron, & oyl & have for 2 years past been distressing* [16]

Curr was surprised at his dismissal, 'unconscious as I was of any cause for so unexpected a dismissal', and concerned for his professional reputation. In reply to his letter of 'expostulation', Norfolk stated:

> *...the want of success in concerns so important to myself & the trade of Sheffield, has appeared to me a sufficient reason for placing the management of them in other hands, to try whether different measures may not produce better consequences.* [17]

Norfolk went on to state that the situation of the collieries may have been due to his judgement, but not his integrity. However, coal sales and profits were already improving by 1801; the Darnall Colliery had been purchased in 1798, the price of coal was increased in 1799, and the Norfolk coal monopoly further reinforced by the purchase of the Dore House Colliery in 1801. Many of the problems that faced the collieries in the late 1790s were probably beyond Curr's control, and he may have been correct in stating, '... bad as the Collieries have lately proved, they would have been worse if I had not made the improvements I have stated'.

The national significance of John Curr as a mining engineer

The importance of Curr as a mining engineer would not have been so great without the widespread influence of his expertise and adoption of his improvements and innovations. In 1801, he stated that by his invention relating to conductors and tipplers, 'I have received something handsome for the Patent Rights from sundry Proprietors of Collieries', and that his rail roads had been adopted in Yorkshire,

Lancashire, Shropshire, Derbyshire, Staffordshire, Warwickshire, Wales, near London, and in the neighbourhood of Newcastle upon Tyne. Although tramroads were widely adopted for overland transport, it was left to engineers, such as William Jessop and Benjamin Outram, to more fully exploit their use, with rails produced at their Butterley Ironworks, in Derbyshire. They built tramroads throughout the country, including the Merthyr Tramroad, 1793, the Peak Forest Tramway, 1794, and the Surrey Iron Railway, 1801, the first public railway that ran between Croydon and Wandsworth, London.

By 1793 Curr's reputation had spread as far as the Coalbrookdale Company in Shropshire who sought his advice on improving the communication between their ironworks and the Shropshire Canal at the Brierly Hill terminus near Coalbrookdale. Shafts had been sunk from the canal to tunnels 120 feet below to gain access to the Coalbrookdale works. Curr suggested the installation of platforms or cages in the shafts with rails that could hold two trucks side by side, and when the containers arrived from the canal they could be lifted by crane onto the trucks and pushed into the cage for descent to the tunnels below. According to a sketchbook of William Reynolds, engineer, the scheme appears to have been adopted.[18] Curr gave advice to George Overton, prior to the construction of the Merthyr Tramroad, Glamorgan, in 1793, and around 1801 he was employed to reorganise and set on a sound financial basis the Castlecomer collieries, in County Kilkenny, Ireland: '... to endeavour to re-arrange matters after a proper form; but it does not appear that much was affected, the master colliers having so great a hold of the property'.[19] John Buddle II was sufficiently satisfied with Curr's competence that on 12 February 1804, due to other business commitments, he asked Curr to give detailed information on 'Wykin Colliery', near Coventry, in which he had an opportunity of taking a share, and on 27 February1804, he again wrote of a possibility to purchase shares of a colliery in South Wales, which may have been the one Curr 'had in hands last year', and would appreciate a report on the mine.[20]

Determined attempts were made to break into the Northumberland and Durham coalfield, aided by a close professional relationship with John Buddle II, who assessed Curr's schemes, and provided orders from collieries in which he had an interest, managed, or viewed. In July 1800, Curr advised John Buddle II on holding corves on a descending road where a 'jenny' could not be introduced, and in September 1802, Buddle sought information on whether Curr had seen or erected winding engines for drawing waggons along the horizontal or up ascents one in two. Curr was a pioneer in the use of stationary steam engines, and around 1805 he used one for the first time to haul coal between Birtley near Gateshead and Black Fell.[21]

It was in the development and exploitation of flat ropes that Curr applied many of his innovatory skills after 1798, with patents for twisting and laying the ropes, for their use on a ship's windlass, capstan and drum, on horse-gins, steam winding engines and for catching whales. John Buddle II had introduced flat ropes into the Wallsend Colliery by February 1800, but technical problems initially prevented their efficient application. In reply to a letter from John Buddle II, Curr was concerned that the '... New flatt Rope is inclin'd to contract so bad a habit in its infancy as you state of turning upon the Pulley Wheel...' He thought the problem may have been caused by the greater depth of the collieries in comparison to those in Sheffield. Difficulties continued, and it was not until 13 August 1800, that Curr was able to write that a solution had been found to prevent the rope 'distending and turning over', which involved taking special care to twist each rope that made up the flat rope with an equal number of turns. He was sufficiently confident of the sale of flat ropes that on 30 August 1800, he wrote to John Buddle II stating that he believed there was a need for a machine for 'lacing' at Newcastle, with the quayside a good place to locate, as he also proposed to have a warehouse for 'rail roads' that his agent would look after. By 1804, flat ropes had been adopted in many collieries in Northumberland and Durham.[22]

After the expiry of his patent in 1812, Curr would have come under pressure from other flat rope manufacturers, and according to Dunn, writing in 1844:

> *He also invented the flat-rope, which he manufactured himself; but the difficulty of stretching all the four strands alike, with the then machinery, was so great that his patent yielded him little or no advantage; especially as the numerous improvements of the round rope were brought into powerful competition.* [23]

Curr stopped rope making in 1818, sold some of his machines to R. & W. Furley & Co, Gainsborough, and provided them with his connections, in return for a percentage on all flat ropes sold. Colliery proprietors continued to use hemp and later wire flat ropes in the nineteenth century.

At least from 1800, John Buddle II purchased substantial quantities of rails from Curr, with the plates four feet and eight inches long due to the heavier loads carried, and in December 1800, he stated his intention to install conductors at the Wallsend Colliery. By May 1803, Curr's son, John Curr II, was working in the Sheffield Park Foundry, and in correspondence with John Buddle II concerning orders for engines, pipes, rails, flat ropes, and technical matters.

In September 1800, Curr suggested a new idea for the 'improvement in the Waggon for Conveying Coals on a Rail Road upon the Top of the Ground', which could be adopted for use in John Buddle II's new 'winning'. A similar scheme had been introduced at Sheffield some two months earlier which he claimed would save half the initial erection cost of a staithe. The novelty of the idea lay in the carriage, that held one and a quarter tons of coal, being adapted to discharge its load on either side, by tilting sideways, to a breadth of four feet on either side of the rail road. Once a bank of coal had been built up in the staithe the 'Rail Road' only required to be moved laterally.

Curr was also a pioneer in steam powered boats, although little evidence appears to have survived. In 1814 he had interests in the Norwich Iron Foundry that constructed paddle boat steam engines. John Buddle II was interested in the purchase of the 'Tyne Steam Packet', and turned to Curr for technical advice. There followed several exchanges of letters on the relative merits of steam driven boats. Curr's engine had two cylinders of thirteen inches diameter, equal to one of about eighteen inches diameter, with paddles eight feet in diameter that took 25 turns per minute, travelling at six and three-quarter miles per hour and 'cut water' at three and three-quarter miles per hour. The boat weighed 33 tons, the engine 17 tons, making 55 tons in total.[24]

A lack of documentary evidence prevents the emergence of a clear picture of Curr's professional activities after 1815. However, ill-health persuaded him to settle in Paris during the early months of 1820. The family house, *Belle View*, in Sheffield Park, was advertised for sale by auction on 20 March 1820, at the *Tontine Inn*, Sheffield. The premises were extensive and reflect a person of some wealth and social position within the community. They included the house, hothouses, greenhouse, stables, coach house, outhouses, part of the pleasure grounds and gardens, with two small tenements for labourers at the back leased from the Duke of Norfolk, along with a further 20 acres and three roods of land adjoining the house. Curr returned from Paris after a stay of upwards of eighteen months, and after staying with friends settled in the western suburbs of Sheffield. He continued to live in Sheffield until his death at the age of 67 on 27 January 1823, and was buried at St. Marie's Roman Catholic Church, Norfolk Row, Sheffield.

Conclusion

John Curr deserves recognition as one of the prominent mining engineers of his time. The introduction of rail roads, four-wheeled corves, conductors, tipplers, inclined planes, and flat ropes placed the Sheffield collieries among the most technologically advanced in the country. His improvements and innovations were widely adopted and made a major contribution to the expansion of the coal mining industry. John Curr was a mining engineer of considerable expertise, ingenuity, and practical knowledge.

Notes and References

Abbreviations: ACM: Arundel Castle Manuscripts, in Sheffield Archives; DRO: Durham Record Office; NEIMME: The North of England Institute of Mining and Mechanical Engineers.

1. J. Curr, *The Coal Viewer and Engine Builder's Practical Companion*, Sheffield, 1797. Second Edition, 1970, Preface by C. E. Lee.
2. Under the 1767 settlement of Edward, 9th Duke of Norfolk, Charles Howard of Greystoke inherited the dukedom, whilst his son the Earl of Surrey (1746-1815), received the profits of the Sheffield estate which remained under trustees until 1786, when he inherited the dukedom and the estate.
3. ACM, S217. The price of hard coal was 3s 4d and small coal 2s 2d per load in 1773. The small coal was used for domestic consumption and later as fuel in the Newcomen engine.
4. Curr, pp. 5-6.
5. Curr, pp. 15, 20-21. For overland tramways stone blocks were commonly used as sleepers, which allowed the horse to move unheeded between the rails. The corf wheel had no flange and could be used on surfaces other than rails.
6. ACM, S223.
7. ACM, S215.
8. A. Raistrick, (Ed.), *The Hatchett Diary. A Tour Through The Counties Of England And Scotland In 1796 Visiting Mines And Manufactories,* Truro, 1967, pp. 70-76.
9. ACM, S214.
10. ACM, S214.
11. ACM, S214.
12. Figure V11. J. Farey, *A Treatise on the Steam Engine, Historical, Practical, and Descriptive,* 1827, Volume 1, reprinted, 1971, pp. 208-210, Plate V111.
13. Curr, p. 30.
14. DRO, NCB/JB/346, ACM S214. Buddle was using light basket corves in 1800.
15. ACM S214. Curr's improvements were introduced into the Hesley Colliery, Chapeltown, which came under direct estate management in 1790. In 1800/01, the output of hard and small coal amounted to: 23,351 tons at Sheffield Park Colliery, 17,106 tons at Manor Colliery, and 44,538 tons at the Attercliffe Colliery.
16. ACM, S214.
17. ACM, S214.
18. B. Trinder, *The Industrial Revolution in Shropshire,* 1973, pp. 133-134.
19. M. Dunn, *An Historical, Geological, and Descriptive View of the Coal Trade of the North of England,* Newcastle upon Tyne, 1844, p. 146.
20. NEIMME, Buddle-Atkinson Collection, Volume 15. DRO, NCB/JB/366.
21. R. A. Mott, 'Old Sheffield Collieries', *Sheffield Telegraph,* 23 September, 1933, Newspaper Cuttings Relating To Sheffield, Volume 27, p. 47.
22. DRO, NCB/JB/345, 358, 359.
23. Dunn, p. 50-51.
24. DRO, NCB/JB/370-373.

Acknowledgements

I am grateful to His Grace the Duke of Norfolk E.M., C.B., C.B.E., M.C. and the Director of Sheffield Libraries for permission to quote and reproduce documents from the Arundel Castle Manuscripts in Sheffield Archives.

6. John Watts, Lambert Street: A Surviving Sheffield Company with over 200 Years' History

by Peter Machan

I ALWAYS APPROACH LAMBERT STREET with some anxiety, unsure whether I will be met by the sight of a bulldozer presiding over a heap of dusty rubble, the unhappy fate of so many of the nineteenth century inner city cutlery factories in the last few years. So far my anxieties have been relieved, as, each time I pass that way, little seems to have befallen the premises of John Watts, except that another chunk of the decorative plasterwork has fallen from the facade onto the irregular stone paving slabs in the street, and patches have appeared to repair yet another hole in the roof (Figure 1). Not that many people seem to be aware of what I regard as this gem of a survival of our city's industrial and social past and Lambert Street is not a well known thoroughfare, even though it is one of the oldest streets in the city. It runs for about 150 yards, sloping gently down the hillside from Scotland Street to West Bar, and today the rear of the modern premises of West Bar Police Station occupies all of one side, dwarfing the series of five frontages which make up John Watts's premises on the opposite side of the narrow street. Today there are no other buildings on Lambert Street, and no one lives there. The factory premises themselves are extremely dilapidated but the elegant plasterwork wording on the frontage proclaiming

JOHN WATTS, ESTABLISHED 1765. MANUFACTURERS OF CUTLERY AND OTHER SPECIALITIES, STAMPERS, PIERCERS AND METALWORKERS. SAFETY RAZORS, SCISSORS, SKATES ETC.

gives a strong hint of a former faded glory.

Behind this frontage lies a series of five courtyards, the pattern in which they were laid out in the mid-eighteenth century still clearly discernible. They are a jumble of early nineteenth century cottage properties and outbuildings which have been converted to a greater or lesser degree to office, workshop or warehouse accommodation, all

Figure 1. The frontage of John Watts's premises, Lambert Street. *The Author*

of which are interconnected by a warren of walkways, passages and stairways. Behind these lies a series of larger light engineering workshops equipped with large numbers of presses, drilling and milling machines, many of which are identifiable from a series of superb photographs taken of the factory in the early 1900s (Figures 2 and 3). Although the engineering shop still operates with a small workforce producing a range of products, the principal of which is the grinding wheel dresser, made to the pattern of the Huntington Company, Ohio, (a mundane product when compared to some of the extraordinarily elegant products which formerly came from the factory) much of the older cottage property is now abandoned (Figure 4). There are several particularly interesting shops on the second and upper floors of the building which were formerly used as cutlers' workshops and still retain much of the materials and tools used in this trade. One of these workshops still retains the benching along both walls and down the centre of the small room which supports the adjustable spindles to hold the dollies and glazers which were powered by leather belts from the shafting below the benches. All this, together with a unique pair of belt driven drills, is still complete. In a tiny room off this, originally a bedroom, a typical grinder's horsing still stands facing the tiny casement window. The extensive offices are similarly fascinating, with eye-catching arrays of advertising knives in glass topped mahogany cabinets and dusty ledgers in brown paper parcels on every shelf. Nothing whatsoever has been done to modernise the factory and there is an almost Dickensian air to some parts of it. The original accounts office, now a cluttered storeroom, is still furnished with the original high desks and stools. So little has been discarded that a wealth of documentary material has survived with which to piece together the history of this fascinating survival.

The firm of John Watts has not always occupied the present premises and indeed John Watts himself was not associated with the company until it was almost a hundred years old. A hand written document in the director's office charts the main events in the firm's history, tracing its founding to 1765, when Michael Shaw established himself as a maker of clog clasps and dog collars in West Bar Green. The earliest Sheffield trade directory, Sketchley's, records this fact in 1774, so we have no reason to doubt this date. It was to be the manufacture of clog clasps which would be the mainstay of the company until it diversified its product range in the 1890s. Only the earliest directory entries refer to the production of dog collars and the connection between these apparently unrelated products is unclear. One suggestion is that these were studded collars for fighting dogs and that the studs would be stamped and shaped and then fixed into leather in the same way as clog clasps would be fixed. The firm passed to Michael Shaw's son, John, in 1790, and in 1800 was in the hands of his brother-in-law, Joseph Wilson, whose daughter, Harriet, married Brian Bates. Bates is registered as being the sole proprietor of the firm from 1833 to 1853, when he entered into partnership with John Watts.

The manufacture of clog claps is not a trade which has been generally regarded as a part of Sheffield's industrial history but throughout the nineteenth century there were a number of companies which depended on this. White's Directory of 1833, for example, lists nine clasp makers and eight makers of clogs and pattens, half of whom were located in West Bar and Shalesmoor. The development of the clog trade has generally been associated with the growth of the woollen and cotton industries in the nineteenth century but clearly the humble clog was being produced in the West Bar area of Sheffield from the eighteenth century. The 1851 census returns for the five courtyards on Lambert Street now occupied by Watts's list no less than eight

Figure 2. John Watts, Machine shop *c.* 1904.

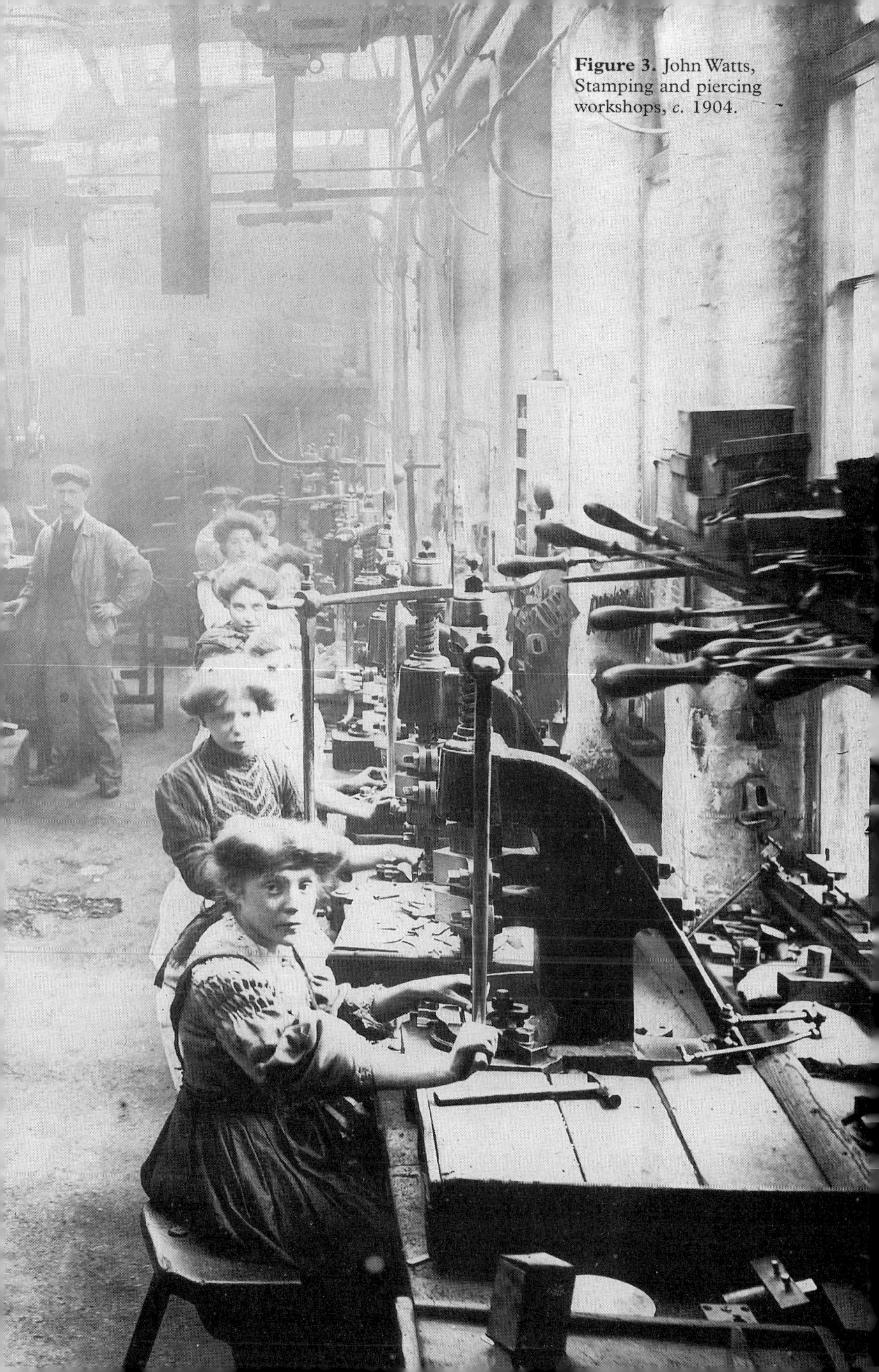

Figure 3. John Watts, Stamping and piercing workshops, *c.* 1904.

Figure 4. The rear of Court Seven at John Watts's, 1995. *The Author*

people describing themselves as clogger, boot maker, boot closer and cordwainer. The trade is well represented in these returns throughout the nineteenth century, and continued into recent living memory. Many people will remember Dalton's shop on Shalesmoor with its sign saying 'Boot and Clog Makers' above the door.

On the wall of the director's office at John Watts's is a framed, hand written letter, which is the earliest surviving document in the firm's history. It is a list and valuation of all the tools, stock and equipment in the workshop at the time of the sale of the company to Joseph Wilson in 1800. This lists tools for cutting and stamping sheet metal into the shape required for the clasps, including a heavy two armed fly press valued at £10, rollers, dyes, stamps and a 'willing boy' stamp, which is a tool often formerly used in silversmithing to hammer flatware. The inventory goes on to list glazers and polishing equipment and large stocks of clasps, both finished and in process of manufacture. This is interesting in that the list shows a workshop layout which would be immediately familiar to anyone working in a light metal-working workshop into modern times in Sheffield. The clasps themselves were simple items consisting of two parts, one of which hooked into the other, which would be fixed on the top flaps of the clogs. They were produced, however, in an enormous range of patterns and materials. The basic quality claps was made in a black japanned finish with the more expensive clasps being made in polished brass. These were available finished in a wide range of designs, as shown in the catalogue of Watts's 'Celebrated Clasps and Toe Plates, Cloggers and Shoemakers' Tools' printed in 1921, (Figure 5), and bodies such as police forces and fire brigades would order their own designs featuring shields and coats of arms.

Although production of clog clasps continued at the firm until at least the Second World War, there is little on the premises today which survives to tell of this former product. This is because the present management, when approached in the 1970s by the Colne Valley Museum in Golcar, donated any surviving material to help equip their reconstruction of a West Riding clogger's workshop. This donation consisted mainly of two large glass-fronted cupboards containing hundreds of boxes of clasps and plates, box labels and the printing blocks from which the catalogue had been printed. These had all come to light when a rough partition in a cutler's workshop had been removed. The Golcar museum also features displays of samples of clog clasps made by Watts's major competitor in the early 1900s, James Horsfield of Paradise Street, Bradford. Competition between the two firms was obviously fierce for in November 1899 Watts's took action against Horsfield's in the High Court to prevent the firm from advertising its products using the same letter and number product codes. Not surprisingly they were granted an injunction against Horsfield's which stated that:

> *The Plaintiff (John Watts) has not only sold for many years, clasps and toe plates, but for all practical purposes he may be considered as being the only manufacturer of these products!* [1]

Clearly, then, the firm had been based on the production of clog clasps and had built up its trade in these until, by the late nineteenth century, it held an unsurpassed position in this small market.

Until the 1870s the firm occupied premises in other locations than their present buildings in Lambert Street, although in Joseph Wilson's time, between 1817 and 1835, the works were situated in Lambert Street, on the opposite side of the road from today's factory, in buildings long since demolished. From 1835 until 1872, however, the business was back in premises on West Bar Green, at numbers 103 and 105. This was, in fact, very near to the present building, because the census enumerator's return for

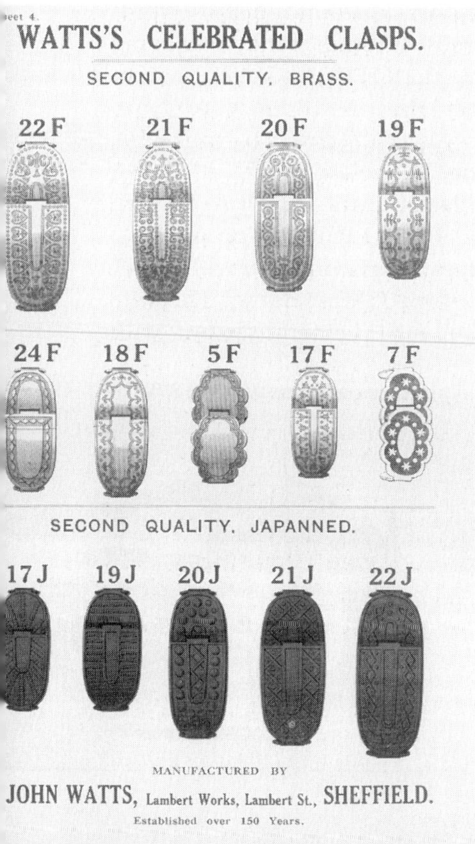

Figure 5. Sample page from Watts's catalogue of clog clasps and toe plates, 1921.

1871 lists the yard at the bottom left hand corner of Lambert Street as 'Bates Yard'. Very fortunately a trade card, complete with a beautiful illustration of this building, has survived from the 1870s, (Figure 6), and Robert Leader in *Reminiscences of Old Sheffield* records the following conversation:

> *You are familiar with the palisaded house at the bottom of Lambert Street, now occupied by Mr Watts, clasp manufacturer in a business carried on there for many years. Long ago it was the residence of Capt. Chisholm. The workshops behind have long been used by coffin makers, and there is a story of an escaped debtor from Scotland Street finding secure refuge in one of these ghastly structures!* [2]

Brian Bates was one of the many in-migrants to Sheffield, as the census records for 1841 reveal that he was born in the small Norfolk village of Buxton, some eight miles north of Norwich. An impressive framed Victorian studio photograph of an elderly bewhiskered gentleman in one of the firm's offices is reputed to be of Bates but nobody now seems quite sure. The name John Watts appears first in the records in the 1851 census in which he is listed as the third child of John and Mary Watts, coffee house keepers of Bridgehouses. John, then aged 21, is described as a whitesmith and his brother Robert, one year older, as a blacksmith. All the members of the family, except the youngest son, Thomas, aged ten, were born in Lound, near Retford, in Nottinghamshire. Like many hundreds of families they had come to seek their fortune in the town during the 1820s, and about half of the people listed as living in West Bar in 1851 were from Nottinghamshire. Unlike most, John was destined to make his fortune, or at least a comfortable living. His relationship with Brian Bates is unclear but their partnership lasted until 1863, after which date the trade directories list John and Robert Watts as proprietors. Subsequent census returns reveal the family's rise in fortune. In 1861 John was living at the company premises at 105 West Bar with his wife Elizabeth, two children, Mary and John, and a 'general servant' with

Figure 6. Tradecard showing the West Bar premises of John Watts, 1870s.

the delightful name of Charlotte Able. By 1871 they had five children and were living at 175 Burngreave Road, a fashionable area at the time, and by 1889 the family were living at Lea Wood, No. 138 Burngreave Road, an imposing, detached Victorian villa which still stands today. The partnership between John and his brother Robert was to last only a few years, for the trade directories of 1868 record that Robert had set up on his own behalf making clasps in premises on Netherthorpe Street. Clearly he did not prosper and he rejoined his brother in Lambert Street some time in the 1890s. It was during the 1870s and 1880s that John guided the firm through an enormous expansion of its product range and the acquisition of the premises on Lambert Street.

Lambert Street was one of those developments which extended the limits of the old town in the early eighteenth century. It is recorded on Ralph Gosling's famous town plan of 1736 as being on the edge of current development (Figure 7). In fact Gosling clearly marked out the plot of land between Lambert Street and Furnace Hill as being in three separate strips, with buildings on Lambert Street, a strip of garden plots behind these and separate plots behind these and Furnace Hill as yet undeveloped. The full deeds, dating back to 1728, to each of the separate plots which the Watts factory now occupies still exist.[3] They present a fascinating sidelight on the development of Sheffield at that time. From the earliest deeds we learn how the street got its name, for in each of them a lease is granted to Edward Lambert, 'Linnendraper of Manchester'. Edward Lambert was uncle to Matthew Lambert, a prominent figure in the town who became a member of the Town Trust and Assistant Town Collector to Joseph Broadbent. Matthew was also by trade a linen merchant, with

Figure 7. Extract from Ralph Gosling's map of Sheffield, 1736.

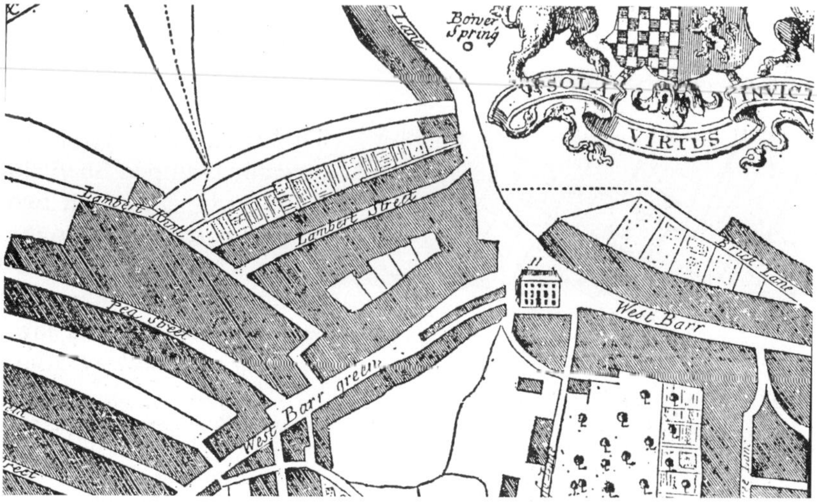

premises in Market Place. Ralph Gosling was his neighbour there. Each of the deeds begins in a similar way, describing the areas as:

> *A spot, piece or plot of ground on Skargell Knowle near West Bar, now staked out, and the use of the well intended to be made at the expense of Joseph Broadbent and other tenants, and the use of the thoroughfare to be made through the close.*

The Broadbents are remembered as having established one of Sheffield's first banks in 1778, as having developed most of Paradise Square and living at the Banker's House on Hartshead. The early development of Lambert Street was thus closely bound up with the affairs of the town's most influential citizens. The deeds give an indication that from these earliest developments the street had an industrial character. In the documents relating to Court Five, for example, there is a lease dated December, 1760, which lists 'The land and two houses, three smithies and other buildings which Broadbent had built on it.' In a lease on Court Four, John Broomhead, son of Robert Broomhead, deceased, cutler, leaves to Hannah his mother, 'all his shares in his father's house on Lambert Street, tools, business etc, for £100'. The early trade directories confirm this impression. Sketchley's 1774 Directory lists seven cutlers on Lambert Street, as well as a scissor maker, a file maker, a razor maker and three button makers. Subsequent directories list a similar range of typical Sheffield trades, and although we have little real information, we have an impression of a typical Sheffield street of artisans, some more well to do than others, but none reaching the depths of poverty which the occupants of Lambert Street were to experience in the following century.

The five courtyard properties which now comprise the Watts factory were acquired by the company in the late nineteenth century, the first in 1872. Detailed plans of them first appear in the Ordnance Survey Town Plans of 1853 (Figure 8). These plans show a series of typically cramped Sheffield courtyards, each with two properties fronting onto the street which are back-to-back with others facing the rear. Between these a low, narrow passageway gives

Figure 8. Extract from the 1853 O.S. Town Plan sheets showing the numbering of the courts in Watts's premises on Lambert Street.

access to a cramped flagged yard into which smaller cottage properties, privies and workshops protrude. Most of the cottages consist of only two rooms. A number of these buildings still exist in a hardly altered state today. We have no record of the actual date at which they were erected, but the granular nature of the locally hand-made bricks would suggest that some of them were by no means new in 1851, and I would suggest that some parts of the site were built in the eighteenth century. By using the census returns and the trade directories it has been possible to piece together a detailed picture of life in these courtyards throughout the nineteenth century, and in doing so it soon becomes clear that by the 1840s this had become one of the poorest areas of the town, providing mean lodgings for some of the poorest families of unskilled labourers who were attracted to the town in large numbers. It was only the families who lived in the more prestigious houses fronting the street who appeared in subsequent ten yearly returns. All the other occupants seem to have been more or less transitory. After 1841 the Sheffield trades no longer feature as the majority of occupations of these people. Increasingly they describe themselves as simply labourer and the number in domestic service increases. The population in these five small courtyards increased to an extraordinary density of 160 in about 20 houses between 1851 and 1871. Nearly 50 per cent of these residents were born outside Sheffield, half coming from the surrounding counties and the other half from Ireland. In the 1851 census returns five of the men gave their occupations as railway workers, so it is not improbable that they had been amongst the gangs labouring on the notorious Woodhead Tunnel during the previous ten years.

Doctors Haywood and Lee, the authors of the Sanitary Report of 1848, confirm the impression that there was a particularly strong Irish presence in this area, and make no effort to conceal their prejudices on this account:

> *On examining this district we found the back lanes, and many of the smaller streets, densely inhabited by the lower orders generally, including a great number of Irish, whose quarters are commonly filthy above the average. The narrow lanes and courts are of the worst possible description, being exceedingly close, tenanted by profligates of all descriptions, the houses are often dilapidated and badly supplied with air and light. Many of these serve as lodging houses in which congregate vagrants of every kind. The yards present the usual appearance, being unpaved, the soil often saturated with drainage and very filthy from accumulations of night soil and rubbish.* [4]

The census records certainly show that there was overcrowding in these Irish households of an almost unimaginable degree. In 1851, for example, there were seven occupied cottages around Court Six. Of the 48 people listed as living in these only four adults had been born in Sheffield. Three cottages were occupied by Irish immigrants. In No. 3 lived John Kennedy, a railway worker, with his wife, two children and five lodgers; at No. 5 was James McDonald, with his wife, young son, mother-in-law, brothers, and a lodger, whilst at No. 7, 48 year-old Michael Caffrey, also a railway worker, shared the two room cottage with his wife and four children, his two brothers and his sister-in-law, and seven lodgers; an amazing total of 16! By 1861 another two of the cottages in this court were occupied by Irish families and a number of people had set themselves up as 'lodging house keepers', five of the houses in the surviving Watts block being listed as lodging houses. By 1881 the number of people resident in the five courts was falling, due mainly to the fact that Watts's was progressively converting them to industrial use, and by 1891 there were no residents in Court 6 and the proportion of occupants of Irish descent fell to only two per cent. The only Irish left were two bricklayers living in the lodging house at No. 51.

There were other foreign immigrants, however, who must have contributed to Lambert Street an incongruous cosmopolitan air. For the final thirty years of the nineteenth century the names of Italian immigrants weave a colourful thread through the documentary records. The first listing of an Italian family appears in 1871, when Andrew Cuneo, his wife Maria and their six children, together with their son-in-law, are listed at number 41. The family was not new to Sheffield because all their children had been born here. Their occupations are particularly striking, because all the family except Maria and the baby were listed as 'musician'. Clearly, however, this talented family could turn its hand to meet circumstances, for in the directories from 1876 they are described as ice-cream makers. The musical theme was to continue, however, with Viltura and Conguela Spinia, their two children and three relations, recorded in 1881 in Court 19, all as musicians, and Guiseppe Lucchesi as a plaster figure maker. Unfortunately I have not yet been able to trace any further details of the contribution Italian musicians made to Sheffield's social scene, but there is clearly a fascinating story waiting one day! The Cuneos, incidentally, prospered as ice cream makers and continue to do so today.

As with all stretches of Sheffield streets, one of the properties, at least, is sure to have been a licensed property at some time. In the case of our five courtyards it was No. 51 which was described as a beer house in various directories from 1839, although it seems to have been occupied by a series of persons with a bewildering series of occupations. Thomas Cooper is described as beer house keeper in 1839, as a policeman in the 1841 census return, as a whitemetalsmith in a directory of the same year and as a filesmith in 1851. In 1871 the property appears under the name of *The Red Lion* kept by Oliver Bostock, whose occupation is confusingly listed as blacksmith, but the most curious entry of all appears in 1881 when the census recorded at this address a Daniel Gillow, a fish curer, and his wife, Elizabeth, from Kentucky in the USA.

Alongside the bewildering pageant of occupants of this short stretch of street, the courtyards continued to provide premises in which a number of small manufacturers carried on their trades. Craftsmen in the traditional Sheffield trades still worked in the little smithies and workshops in corners of the yards. There were, at various dates, pen and pocket knife cutlers in Courts Four and Five, file makers in Courts Five and Eight and scissorsmiths in most of the courts. These people needed little equipment, were self employed and worked at a bench in what was little more than a shed, but the premises of George Gill, listed as 'Fine Scissor Maker, Norbury Works', were far more substantial, consisting of the fascinating three storey building surviving in Court Seven. James Marsh, at No. 37, was another substantial manufacturer, producing the pressed black paper cases for razors and spectacles throughout the nineteenth century. Behind his house, in Court Five, Henry Bussey and Thomas Taylor established businesses as cabinet makers in the 1860s. This was clearly part of an ongoing tradition of working in wood in this street, for, as we discovered earlier, there had previously been the premises of coffin makers at the bottom of the street.

John Watts purchased the first of these properties, Court Six, in September 1872. The company was expanding for in 1876 White's Directory records that production was taking place at Soho Wheel and Bridge Street as well as Lambert Street and West Bar. In November 1879 Court 5, with its joiner's shop, had been added to Watts's properties and during the 1880s the directories begin to list a rapidly extending range of products. By 1884 the firm was producing steel skates and graining combs as well as their clog clasps, and by 1895 they described themselves as 'Manufacturers of pen and pocket knives, safety razors, graining combs, stampers and piercers'. The other three courtyards which now comprise the Watts factory were purchased in 1892, 1910 and 1916, and the progress of this development was illustrated in a superb series of engravings of the works which appeared in a series of catalogues which illustrated the growing range of products. The first engraving, depicting the premises in 1892 or 1893 (Figure 9) shows that the first courtyard, Court Six, had been extensively altered, the cottages having been cleared and glass roofed workshops built along one side and the rear. Numbers 41 and 43, fronting the street, had been adapted to create office and warehouse space, which remains largely unaltered, and the passageway widened. The scale of the premises, as is usual in these illustrations, has been much exaggerated by depicting the horses and people in tiny proportions. The next illustration, from a scissor catalogue of 1903, (Figure 10) depicts a considerably extended factory with the addition of Courts Five and Seven, and shows more of the original buildings still in place in these two courts. The three storey block to the rear of Court Seven had been George Gill's scissor workshop, and is today one of the most interesting surviving features of the whole site. By 1912, when the splendid final illustration of the works was published (Figure 11), Watts was on the crest of a wave, expanding rapidly to produce a great range of products for the discerning Edwardian gentleman. The factory premises were virtually complete, only Court Four being purchased after this and little was done to alter this in any way. The plasterwork lettering was in place and Court Eight had been entirely covered over with glass roofs to create more modern production spaces. This same illustration was being reproduced on all catalogues and lists, complete with the horses and wagons and vintage motor, until 1939.

Much of this expansion took place under new management. John Watts died in 1895 and the business passed to his son, John Robert Watts, who set about a programme of acquiring other related companies. Some of these, such as Gill's had already been manufacturing on the site. By 1902 Watts had added the trademarks of at least eight other companies to its own, Alfred Brittain and John Casson, both steelmakers,

Figure 9. Engraving of the Watts premises on Lambert Street from their 1892 Specialities catalogue.

Figure 10. Engraving of John Watts's premises from the 1903 scissor catalogue.

The Manhattan Cutlery Company, Thomas Wilton and John Newton, cutlery manufacturers, and Frederick Ward and Co., manufacturers of table and pocket cutlery, whose trademark, B4*ANY, Watts was to use on all its finest tableware, and at this stage the company opened a London office in Victoria Street. A valuation of the assets of the company carried out in July 1896 lists the stock of clasps and toe plates as worth £874 with another £1,145 worth of raw materials and part finished stock but already the value of the cutlery stock was £1,630, with £1,348 owing.

If this expansion had started with branching into such mundane articles as graining combs it was not long before far more exotic products were coming through the factory gates, a selection of which were beautifully illustrated in the 'List of Specialities', a wholesale price list issued in 1892/3. The coloured illustration on the cover showing the 'Watts Patent Champagne and Cigar Knife' in action opening a champagne bottle sets the tone and reflects the market at which these products were aimed. The quality of such products as 'The Watts Patent Sporting Knife', with its seven gadgets including cartridge extractor, was reflected in the wholesale prices which began at 100s.

Figure 11. Engraving of John Watts's premises from their 1912 catalogue. This illustration was used in all their catalogues up to 1939.

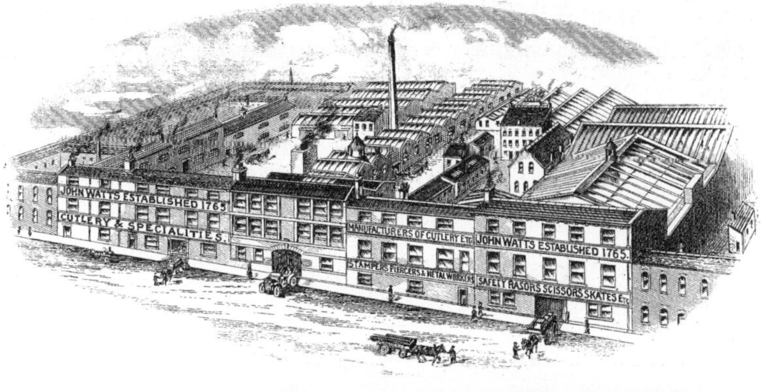

per dozen for the basic nickel plated steel scales and rose to 180s. per dozen for ivory scales. Here were combination knives for the sportsman, the angler, the smoker and the cyclist which would put any of today's Swiss Army knives to shame. Here also were button hooks, can openers, nail clippers and railway keys, as well as a truly remarkable looking selection of ice skates, but the most interesting pages are those which describe their range of safety razors.

In the company office is a framed exhibit of a razor with a guard accompanied by a patent drawing of the design of this. The exhibit is titled as follows:

> *This is an example of the first safety razor ever made. It was manufactured in the Watts factory in Sheffield in the year 1875 under the John Marks patent specification.*

The razor consists of a frame enclosing a section of a long (cut throat) razor which was held in place by a screw clip and which could be removed and fitted into a handle for stropping. The Watts 'Improved Safety Razor' illustrated in the price list, is almost identical to this, but the claim that this was the first to be produced cannot be substantiated since there were well documented examples of frame-backed razors going back to 1828, and several designs, disparagingly termed pig scrapers, were available in the latter half of the nineteenth century. It may well be the case, however, that the Watts safety razors were the first to reach a general market. Several trademarks were used by Watts's on their razors which illustrate the progress in shaving technology. 'The Ideal', 'Mignon' and 'Service' (Figure 12) models were introduced by 1893, 'The Mikado' in 1894, 'The Eclipse' and 'The Leader' and 'The Presto', which was the first to use a single edged wafer blade, in 1910. Gillette had only started to manufacture razor blades in their new factory in Leicester in 1909 and the companies of R. S. Mitchell and John Watts were the first Sheffield firms to follow suit. By the 1920s the firm was producing four patterns of blades, including 'The Mirror', a double edged blade in stainless steel, and 'The Gleaner'. On the gable wall of the factory facing West Bar can still be traced the faded lettering 'Home of the Gleaner Blade'. The production of razors was to prove extremely lucrative because in June 1915 Watts's won the contract to supply the army with frame backed razors at the rate of 20,000 per week until late 1918. One unique feature of the factory survives from the era of razor production. This is the remarkable six foot wide gallery which overlooks the machine shop on all four sides. It has high wooden barriers and a faded notice hanging on a nail certifies that 'this razor gallery has been authorised by the factory inspectorate for the use of 25 workers'. It is dated 1937. Originally this is where the razor grinders, the élite of their trade, would sit hunched over their wheels, high up here under the glass roof for maximum light. The story is still told in the factory of how John Watts would insist that the men came to work unshaved and that he would watch as they shaved with one of their own razors.

The firm continued to extend its product range, and some of the items which it developed early this century continued to be produced to recent times. The 'Historical Knife', for example, is one that many people will remember from school days. First produced in 1902 for the coronation of Edward VII, it had all the dates of the kings and queens of England embossed on the scales. Several versions were produced to celebrate royal events. It was quickly appreciated that pocket knife scales could hold an advertising slogan, and the company produced these for companies all over the world. The Presto Egg Topper is another device which was patented early this century by Watts's and is still produced. As well as products manufactured on the premises many others were either made using an outwork system or factored from other firms. These practices were almost universal in Sheffield. A hand illustrated ledger which survives in the office lists a huge range of 2,500 such items and gives an unusual insight into their origin. The shocking revelation is that many of the products which appear in the beautifully produced tableware and cutlery catalogue of 1912 were actually factored from producers in Birmingham, London and Solingen, Germany, all of whom were Sheffield's great rivals.

The products which were to set this company apart from all others in the city, however, were not originally metal but wood. It is not clear when Watts's started making quality furniture, but as we have seen, there were cabinet makers in the premises when they were purchased and the

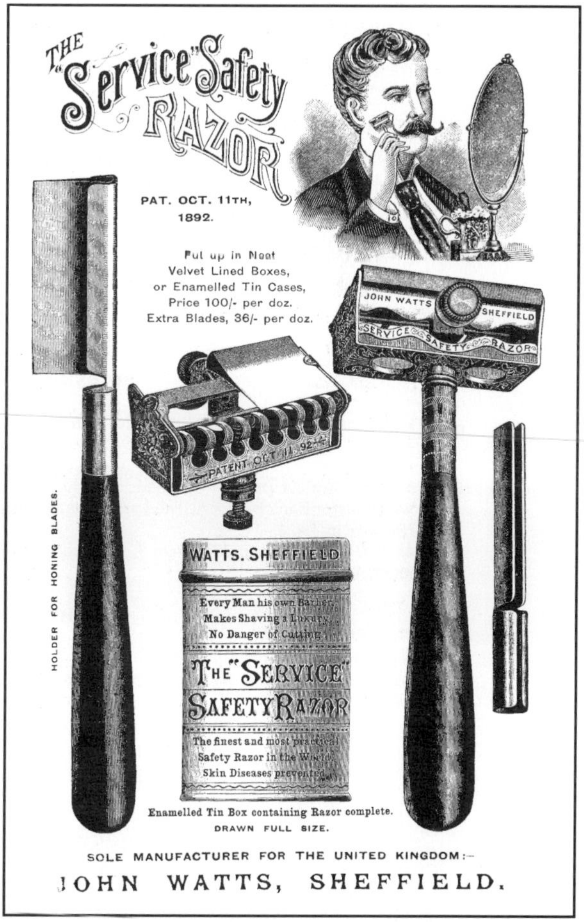

Figure 12. Illustration of the John Watts 'Service' Safety Razor from their 1892 'Specialities' catalogue.

large area of the covered courtyard of Court 8, acquired in 1910, has always been used for furniture production. The extensive catalogue of 'Wardrobes and other Specialities' dates from 1915 and there are photographs in the early 1900s series which show furniture production. All the Watts furniture incorporated a considerable amount of hardware in the form of patent fittings which could be easily produced by their existing machinery. The bulk of sales were of tie and trouser presses, which amounted, in the 1930s, to almost half of Watts's total revenue. Again the names coined for the various models, 'The Legal', 'The Imperial', 'The Empire' and 'The Victor' reflect the market at which they were aimed. The 1929 wardrobe fittings booklet has an illustration and explanation of how the Watts patent wardrobe fittings could be used in the cabins of luxury liners. There is a common belief in the factory that the Watts factory produced the fitted furniture for the first class cabins on board P&O liners.

The factory was damaged by enemy action in the war but by then tastes were changing. John Watts died in 1939 and although the family retained an interest in the firm they no longer had a managing role. A works manager was appointed, but with little investment and an oversized workforce, crisis followed crisis in the 1950s and 60s at the end of which Ron Bishop, a man well versed in the ways of the Sheffield trades, coming from the cutlery family of R. Bishop, Rockingham Street, took over as managing director. He slimmed down the premises, the workforce and the product range and, despite setbacks of a serious fire and recessions which have seen most other firms go to the wall, the company of John Watts looked set to continue into the next millennium under the leadership of Ron's son, Michael Bishop. Recent developments in the firm, however, may finally herald its demise. Judging by its past resilience, however, it may just be a new start.

Notes and References

1. A framed newspaper article recording the case is preserved in the manager's office.
2. Robert Leader, *Reminiscences of Old Sheffield, its Streets and its People*, Leader and Sons, Sheffield, 1876, p.128.
3. There are six packets of deeds relating to these properties. They are held by the National Westminster Bank but were listed and collated by the late Mary Walton for the National Register of Archives in 1974.
4. James Haywood and William Lee, *Report on the Sanitary Condition of the Borough of Sheffield*, Sheffield 1848, p.28.

Acknowledgements

I would like to thank all the staff at John Watts for all their help and encouragement and the staff at National Westminster Bank for their assistance in viewing the deeds.

7. Ecclesfield's Literary Connection

by Chris Morley

'...HEROWORSHIP IS NOT A NATIONAL WEAKNESS amongst us...'[1] So spoke the Reverend Alfred Gatty, the then vicar of Ecclesfield, to a meeting of the Literary and Philosophical Society of Sheffield in 1858.

Since that time the British have changed their attitudes towards literary connections. Today we have 'Bronteland', 'Herriot Country', Stratford upon Avon, etc., etc., to which crowds flock in their hundreds to attempt to experience for themselves the life and environment of the respected authors connected with those places. Places they leave, at the close of their visit, clutching mementoes and souvenirs, possibly in the fond hope that something of the personage they have come to admire and commemorate will transfer to themselves.

Ecclesfield has, so far, escaped the fawning crowd of hero-worship. In one way this is a pity for had it been so, today we would have had a greater respect for the associated buildings in the village, and a more serious and dedicated attitude to their preservation and conservation. True, we would see a host of knick-knack kiosks and shops foisting upon the gaping visitors useless trivia, but, on the other hand, the village may also have a learned and popular interpretive study centre for the research and enjoyment of both children's literature and local history.

The reason for this is that in 1839, on an autumnal September day, there arrived in Ecclesfield the Rev. Alfred Gatty and his wife Margaret (Figures 1 and 2). He to assume the role as vicar of the parish, a task he undertook for the next 63 years, and his wife to expand upon a literary career she had begun whilst still an adolescent. The Gattys made a lasting impression upon South Yorkshire, leaving an indelible mark in several spheres of cultural activity, but remaining

igure 1. Rev. Alfred Gatty, D. C. Maxwell, *Mrs Gatty ıd Mrs Ewing*

Figure 2. Margaret Gatty. C. Maxwell, *Mrs Gatty and Mrs Ewing*

reticent upon the subject of their own lives. The Gattys were avid letter-writers, letters that reveal endearing and charming intimate aspects of their lives, and both Margaret Gatty and their daughter, Juliana (Mrs Ewing) had important literary careers and literary connections but not one member of the immediate family wrote a full-length biography or autobiography. Alfred Gatty's book, *A Life at One Living* (1884)[2] contains - in his own words - 'no allusion to either my domestic or my spiritual life', and Margaret, before her death, begged 'that the partial affection of relatives and friends might never lead them to swell the voluminous list of modern biographies by a record of her life...'[3] Alfred Gatty, it is true, began a biographical draft but progressed no further than a few closely written sheets of manuscript; Juliana (Mrs Ewing) wrote a memoir of her mother because 'it might seem ungracious to withhold so much information about her [mother's] own mental training and processes of work ...'[4] Juliana's sister, Horatia (Mrs H. K. F. Eden), edited a collection of Juliana's letters and issued a memoir ('a list of her stories ... and to tell, as far as I can, what gave rise to them in my sister's mind').[5] It was left to a Gatty granddaughter, Christabel Maxwell (née Ward), the daughter of Undine Marcia Gatty, to attempt a more detailed account of the lives of Margaret Gatty and her daughter Juliana: her book *Mrs Gatty and Mrs Ewing*, is a delightfully written piece of research born of the enquiring, enthusiastic family history explorer. [6]

Rev. Alexander John Scott, DD

Margaret Gatty was the daughter of the Rev. Alexander John Scott (see Figure 3), famed for being the Chaplain on the *Victory* at the Battle of Trafalgar, and in whose arms Nelson died.

The Reverend Scott was one who did not, for himself, seek fame or fortune from his association with England's hero. Indeed, he was a reclusive and very private person, although he did not fear to be heard when undertaking campaigns for which he had strong feelings. He became a naval chaplain in 1794, and saw service in the Mediterranean, where he first met Nelson, and in the West Indies. This was followed by being Private Secretary and Chaplain to Admiral Sir Hyde Parker in the Baltic Campaign against the Danish fleet, and becoming more closely connected with second-in-command, Nelson. For his

Figure 3. Rev. Alexander Scott, DD, by Siegried Detler Bendixen. The original painting is in the National Maritime Museum, Greenwich.

services during that campaign, Nelson recommended Scott to the Governors of Charterhouse for a preferment to a living administered by that body, and he was appointed to the parish of Southminster in Essex. Scott returned to Jamaica in April 1802 where his usefulness as an interpreter was sought by Admiral Sir John Duckworth, then in charge of the West Indies Fleet. Aboard the frigate *Topaz* Scott was sent upon an intelligence gathering mission around the Caribbean, and it was during this tour, whilst taking exercise upon the ship's deck, that he was struck by lightning, and severely injured. Consequently he returned to London, where, during the winter of 1802-03, he made a slow, but not complete, recovery from his injuries.

Nelson, too, was in London that winter, often visiting Scott, and during the spring of 1803 invited him to complete his recuperation as chaplain at sea. Scott, however, decided to take up the living at Southminster, but upon the occasion of his first visit to that small Essex town was bitterly disappointed. The parish and the church were run-down and neglected, and the vicarage was a dirty, verminous abode. Much work and expense were needed for repair and restoration, and this, Scott, did not feel up to. He decided to take Nelson's offer of employment, and was duly appointed by the Admiral, now commander-in-chief Mediterranean, to be his personal secretary and chaplain on the *Victory*.

Nelson's brief and fatal appointment, and also Scott's brief association with the *Victory* and the Battle of Trafalgar are too well documented to repeat here. Suffice it to say that from that point on Scott was to be a 'Nelsonian Champion', and he spent much time and effort unsuccessfully attempting to ensure that the Admiral's personal wishes regarding dispositions for the future well-being of Lady Hamilton, and the admiral's daughter, Horatia, were carried out by mean and meagre government ministers and officials.

Following Trafalgar, Scott retired from the sea, and collecting his immense collection of books culled from his voyages and visits to foreign lands, returned to his old college at Cambridge to gain a Master's degree in Divinity. However, during his residence there he caused embarrassment to the governing body by reasons of his age, in comparison to the other students, his scholarship, and his fame, and they found no other alternative than to waive the Master's degree aside, and the Reverend Scott was awarded the degree of Doctor of Divinity by Royal Mandate.

Following the accident aboard the *Topaz*, Scott was left with a permanent and awkward limp, a partially destroyed, shattered and disfiguring upper jaw, the loss of all his front teeth, a premature greying of his hair, and a serious nervous disposition and a stutter. His mind and faculties were, however, unimpaired. He was a brilliant linguist and familiarised himself with a variety of dialects and vernacular tongues. He had studied art and architecture, was a popular teacher of mathematics and mechanics to young naval officers, and was a keen natural historian, and a competent musician. To the public at large he managed to disguise his nervousness by adopting the guise of an absent-minded, book-loving recluse.

Upon his return to Southminster, Scott set about and, by bullying and cajoling, effected a restoration of the parish church and a refurbishment of the vicarage, a project that was not completed until 1817. Against the wishes of her parents, he married, in 1807, Mary Francis Ryder, the daughter of Thomas Ryder, of Hendon, Middlesex, and the resident Registrar of Charterhouse. The couple went to live in a recently built vicarage at Burnham-on-Crouch, a parish adjoining that of Southminster, to which Scott had been appointed curate. His income was by now about £250 a year. The Scotts and Ryders became reconciled when it became demonstrably clear that the marriage was no gold-digging association, and a close family relationship was further cemented following the births of daughters Horatia in 1808 and Margaret on 3 June 1809. The arrival of a son, George Alexander, in November 1810 was a difficult birth, and his sudden death, in the following March, was a blow from which Scott's wife, Mary, never recovered. She died on 11 September 1811, her twenty-sixth birthday.

For the next five years or so, the sisters were to spend the summer months with their father at Burnham, and their winters at their grandparents' homes at Hendon or in Charterhouse. Their education in academic studies was undertaken by their father, who was a devoted and keen exponent of universal education, and by their grandparents and relatives. At an early age they could read and speak several languages, were well versed in mathematics, were interested in natural and applied sciences, were accomplished musicians, and were probably much better educated not only than any contemporary females, but also many males.

In 1816, Lord Liverpool recommended Dr Scott to the Prince Regent for the living of Catterick in North Yorkshire, and for appointment as a Royal Chaplain, so it came about that Scott could carry on as vicar of Southminster whilst holding the living of Catterick. His income now rose to about £1,650 a year, and Scott and his daughters moved north into the Catterick vicarage at Scorton leaving a competent curate to take care of Southminster and Burnham-on-Crouch.

Margaret's first venture into print came in 1829 when a few poems, translated by her from Italian and German, appeared in a literary journal, the *Bijou*, and it is from this time that she began to correspond with more renowned authors of poetry and prose, and to have short pieces of translated material accepted by other publications.

The Scott sisters' first acquaintance with Ecclesfield came in 1825 when they visited their late mother's brother, the Rev. Thomas Richard Ryder, the then vicar, who had succeeded Uncle William Ryder to the living. Frequent visits were made by Dr Scott and his daughters thereafter, and it became a convenient stopping place on the regular monthly visits made to Southminster and to the Ryders at Hendon, providing an especially welcome respite during winter journeys.

Dr Scott visited Ecclesfield in late June 1840 to attend the christening of his first granddaughter, Margaret, the child of his daughter Margaret and Alfred Gatty. His journey from the north had been made by stagecoach, and as he had planned to travel onwards to Southminster he decided, upon the recommendation of other guests present at the occasion, notably Alfred's aged parents, to extend his stay by a few days until a reservation could be made for him to continue to London via the recently opened railway from Rotherham to London. He returned to Ecclesfield in July, intending to continue to Catterick during the first week in August by coach. This was not to be. Upon his arrival at Ecclesfield, Scott was suffering from a slight fever, a draughty situation occupied in the railway carriage being blamed for the malady, and, because he had enjoyed such a pleasant and comfortable journey previously, he had packed his travelling cloak and warm clothes in his trunk, being, therefore, lightly clad. The fever intensified, and no amount of careful nursing, nor leeching and medication by a noted Sheffield doctor alleviated his condition and distress. Alexander John Scott, Doctor of Divinity, and Chaplain in Ordinary to Her Majesty Queen Victoria, vicar of Southminster, and vicar of Catterick, died in his daughter's arms shortly after midnight on 25 July 1840. The remains of the man in whose arms Admiral Lord Nelson died lie in the Gatty family vault in Ecclesfield Churchyard. Margaret later wrote of her father:

> *My father was a literary man, a fine musician, and a recluse. The world called him eccentric, and concluded him to be disqualified for society; but, although he had lived a very quiet life ever since I could remember anything, seeing but few people except old friends from a distance, no-one really knew whether this arose from his disliking company.*

A London bookseller described Dr Scott as follows:

> *I was always glad to see his white head and rosy face, and to have a little talk with him about books and the trade, though it wasn't always easy to catch what he said, for he spoke quick and not very distinct. But he was a pleasant old gentleman, and talked to a poor man as politely as he would to an admiral. He was very well known in the trade ...*[7]

It obviously required time and several meetings to appreciate the true qualities of Scott. A typical first impression of him has been recorded by the Rev. Benjamin Newton, rector of Wath in North Yorkshire, who wrote in his diary, following a visit to the Bedale Club on the 22 October 1817:

> *...present Dr Scott, a new member, late chaplain to Lord Nelson who died aboard the "Victory" in his arms. He appears a gentlemanly man who has seen much of the world but seems to have an idea he is sent here to inform the natives...*[8]

Margaret Gatty

Margaret's first literary efforts, translations from Italian and German poets into English poetry, appeared in the *Bijou*, a literary annual, in 1829 and in 1830. They were to spark off correspondence between Margaret and several other contributors, which in turn led to the submission of her work to other periodicals. However, it was not until during the winter months of 1841-42 that, in co-operation with her husband, she turned to a serious attempt to gain monetary reward for her writing. With the papers and correspondence of her father to hand they jointly wrote a biography of the Rev. Alexander John Scott. After a disappointing rejection from their chosen publisher - because there was not enough about Nelson in it - they decided upon the strength of 242 subscriptions to publish it privately. The book came out in June 1842 to very favourable reviews.[9] Margaret gained her first individual success in 1851 with the publication of *The Fairy Godmothers*, a book of fairy tales she had written for the amusement of her own children. Bell & Co. agreed to publish it at their own expense in return for which Margaret asked for no other payment than a copy of Dr Johnston's *History of British Zoophytes.*[10] The second edition of *The Fairy Godmothers* (1858) was rewarded by a similar payment - a copy of *The History of British Sponges and Lithophytes,* also by Johnston! The year 1855 saw the first edition of *Parables from Nature* appear, published at the Gattys' expense. Thereafter, Margaret produced a new book annually, sometimes illustrated with her own drawings. One of her most popular children's books, *Aunt Judy's Tales*, appeared in 1859, and during the years 1859 and 1860 Margaret supervised the autobiography of the Rev. Dr Joseph Wolff which was taken down by herself and her daughters at his dictation.[11]

Earlier, during the winter of 1848-49, Margaret had spent some months recuperating from an illness at Hastings where a local physician she was consulting encouraged her to become interested in the study of seaweeds as an aid to her recovery. And so began an intensive study of the subject in which she became an acknowledged expert specialising in zoophytes - plant-like animals such as corals, sea anemone, sponges, and aquatic invertebrates, Bryozoan (or Polyzoan). Henceforth, family holidays were spent collecting, cleaning, drying, identifying, and illustrating seaweeds. It was a task in which all the family, and family servants, assisted, culminating in 1863 with the publication of *British Seaweeds* in two volumes, a serious work intended to combine scientific accuracy with the minimum of technicality. Illustrated by 80 coloured plates containing 384 figures, each with a detailed though clearly understood description, the book was soon recognised as an important seaweed manual by both amateur and scientist.

In 1866 Margaret Gatty became editor of a monthly magazine for young people, *Aunt Judy's Magazine,* a task she loved although it was to consume a great deal of her time. One of the more significant outcomes of the periodical was the endowment of Aunt Judy's Cots at the Hospital for Sick Children in Great Ormond Street, London; by 1894 35 cots in all had been endowed at a cost of about £1,000 a cot with contributions coming from subscribers as far afield as Russia and India.

Margaret Gatty's last two books, *Sundials* and *A Book of Emblems,* were published in 1872, the former being the result of a lifetime's collection of sketches and associated mottoes to be found on sundials.

Since 1863, Margaret Gatty had suffered from ill-health. Her right arm and hand became disabled, and, after she had taught herself to write with her left hand, the disability transmitted also to her left-hand side. Her work continued, however, with the able assistance of her daughter, Horatia, until the disease slowly robbed her of the use of arms, legs, and speech, giving her intense and almost intolerable pain. Until the last, the vigour of her brain and her mental awareness were untouched and she died on 4 October 1873 in the vicarage at Ecclesfield.

Margaret Gatty was principally a children's writer but one who, unlike her contemporaries, told tales from a child's viewpoint. The 'morals' contained in them were unconventional for that time and contain much simple scientific teaching. Not for her were there early death-beds, or irretrievable pathetic happenings. But what was she really like? Dr William Harvey[12] described her as being:

> *slight, tallish, and intellectual looking and withal quiet; at least as yet nothing very mercurial has broken out. But there is evidently the mercury below the surface, and I can quite fancy her blazing up … when strongly excited.*

Unfortunately, we have little else to guide us, except for a photograph (see Figure 2), as to Margaret Gatty's character.

Alfred Gatty

The writings of Alfred Gatty are, in the main, concerned with local history, and it is in that connection that he is best known. His editing and updating of Joseph Hunter's monumental *Hallamshire: The History and Topography of the Parish of Sheffield,* published in 1869, with a further, revised, edition in 1875, is a permanent inspiration and source book for all South Yorkshire historians. His own work, *Sheffield: Past and Present* (1873) is dedicated to Sir John Brown and Mark Firth and members of the first Sheffield School Board, 'with the hope that it may help the rising generation to appreciate the history of their native town'. He presented several papers on historical and cultural subjects to local societies, papers that show a great depth of knowledge and studious research by their author. Little known to the general public are his poetical and lyrical works, his first volume being published in 1833 when he was twenty years of age.[13]

Alfred Gatty was born in London, quite close to the Bank of England, on 18 April 1813. His father was a solicitor practising in the City, who was in his fifty-third year at the time of his son's birth. His mother, too, was past the normally accepted childbearing age being in her fiftieth year. During his infancy Alfred lived with maternal relatives near Hasland, Chesterfield, until, shortly following his seventh birthday, he was enrolled as a boarder at Dr Pinkney's Preparatory School, Temple Grove, East Sheen, on the edge of Richmond Park, a school at which he was very unhappy, and from where he made at least one, unsuccessful, attempt to run away to sea. In January 1825 he was sent to Charterhouse, again as a boarder even though it was but a short distance from his home. Charterhouse too, was not to his liking, and after only twelve months' residence he was dispatched, following a moving approach to his mother, to a private tutor at Ramsgate - for the sake of his health! In 1826 he went to Eton, a school where he was much happier and from which he progressed to become articled to a solicitor at Stony Stratford. After only a month in a dry-as-dust musty office, he left, to return home to a very different atmosphere. His father's health had broken down, and the law practice had been left in the hands of assistants who had been making speculative investments that came to nought. Gatty senior, after selling the practice, his London home, and family property in Cornwall, had just sufficient to provide for an income, a home in Sevenoaks, the means of paying off the debts of his law practice, and a small amount to provide for Alfred's attendance at Exeter College, Oxford, to read for a BA degree. On leaving Oxford Alfred was ordained at Ripon Cathedral by Bishop Longley and took up the curacy of Bellerby, a chapel-of-ease in the parish of Spennithorne in the North Riding of Yorkshire, settling in lodgings at Leyburn.

At a supper party Gatty was introduced to the Rev. Alexander Scott, Vicar of Catterick, and so impressed was Scott that he invited the young curate to pay him a weekend visit and to preach at sunday service. This was the first of several visits Gatty paid to the Catterick vicarage, and there he met, and fell in love with Scott's daughter Margaret. The couple were married by Bishop Longley at St Giles-in-the-Fields on the 8 July 1839. While on honeymoon in Edinburgh they were informed that Margaret's uncle, Thomas Ryder, the vicar of Ecclesfield, had died, and that the vacant living was being offered to Alfred, an offer that was accepted.

Juliana Horatia Ewing (née Gatty)

Juliana Horatia was the second daughter of Alfred and Margaret Gatty, born on 3 August 1841 at Ecclesfield. At the age of three and a half she was described as being: 'pure flaxen in hair ... pretty but small in bones and ... short. She has the softest and handsomest eyes ... can read very nicely ...'[14]

The Gatty family grew apace. Margaret (1840) was their first born - always called Mo in the family but Madge in more formal times; then Juliana (Julie), then Alfred Alexander (1843, but who died when he was but two months old); then Reginald Alfred in 1844; Horatia Katharine Frances (Dot) in 1846; Alfred Scott Gatty in 1847; Undine Marcia (Diney) in 1848; Stephen Herbert in 1849; Charles Tindal Gatty in 1851 with the aid of chloroform, and finally the Gattys' last child, Horatio Nelson, born in 1855, but who did not survive infancy.

Margaret undertook the education of her children during their formative years, with the 'polishing off' of the boys, prior to their attendance at boarding school, being taken care of by the Ecclesfield curates. For the amusement of the children their mother made up and told them stories, tales that were to be written and published for the benefit of a larger audience. As Juliana grew older it was she who took over as the provider of amusement for, and organiser of, childhood games and pastimes, and in doing so assumed the role of 'Aunt Judy', a name bestowed upon her by her brothers, and later immortalised as the kindly, story-telling character when her mother's *Aunt Judy's Tales* were published.

Juliana's first published tale, *A Bit of Green*, appeared in Charlotte Yonge's *The Monthly Packet* magazine in July 1861, and her first book, a collection of stories, was published in 1862 by Bell.[15] In the December 1865 edition of *The Monthly Packet* appeared *The Brownies,* the tale of two brothers who, like elves, so long as they were unseen and unheard, would carry out all the housework, and whose name, and the theme of the story, was adopted by Lord Baden-Powell in 1915 as the name for the junior section of the Girl Guide Movement, replacing the earlier 'Rosebuds' name.

Compared to her siblings Juliana (see Figure 4) was small, sharp-featured, frail in health, very highly strung, and easily tired by any physical exertion. On the other hand, she had a most charming manner, was generous to a fault, had a lively loveable character, and put the utmost effort into the task in hand. She established and ran the village lending library, and was also an invigorating Sunday School teacher and parochial visitor; her fault was that she never knew when to stop and take breath, and would carry on until she collapsed with fatigue.

Figure 4. Juliana Horatia Ewing. C. Maxwell, *Mrs Gatty and Mrs Ewing*

She met Alexander 'Rex' Ewing in November 1856. He was then twenty-six, a very personable young man employed in the Commissariat Department of the Army, a relative of the Bishop of Argyle and the Isles, and composer of the hymn tune *Jerusalem the Golden*. For the next ten years he held postings abroad, returning to England in 1866, and he then became a frequent visitor to the Ecclesfield vicarage, where it soon became clear that the visits were not to the family but to Juliana. Alex was unaware of her exhaustion following his visits; nor did he know of the weakness of her constitution, nor did she allow him to know. Initially, her parents opposed their courtship on the grounds that it would be unfair to impose upon a man a wife who could not lead the sort of life he was committed to in his chosen

Figure 5. Captain and Mrs Ewing and Hector in Canada. C. Maxwell, *Mrs Gatty and Mrs Ewing*

career, and they discouraged any further, deeper association. Eventually, worn down by persuasion, they relented and allowed the engagement to be announced in November 1866. In April 1867 Alex received a posting to Canada and he and Juliana were married on the 1 June, sailed for Halifax, Nova Scotia on the 8 June, and landed on the 17 June 1867, to be stationed in Fredericton, New Brunswick, where they were to live until their return to England in the autumn of 1869 (Figure 5).

Juliana's authorship continued throughout her stay in Canada from where she regularly sent manuscripts for publication in *Aunt Judy's Magazine*, chief among them being the series of *Mrs Overtheway's Remembrances,* and the early stories of *Old Fashioned Fairy Tales*. Alex transferred to the Army Pay Department in 1870 and was posted to Aldershot where the couple were to live in quarters. Further stories and books issued from Juliana's pen, and such became her popularity that her publishers commissioned illustrations from eminent draughtsmen. Illustrations for *A Flat Iron for Two Farthings,* by Mrs

Allingham, were praised by Ruskin; and Cruikshank and Caldecott were to make more memorable, and today collectable, copies of *Aunt Judy's Magazine*. Also from her Aldershot days came the first of Juliana's stories based upon soldiers and soldiers' families, *The Peace Egg*.[16] Her contribution to the November 1873 edition of *Aunt Judy's Magazine* was a short memoir of her mother, Mrs Gatty, and it has been said that the inspiration for her story of Madame Liberality resulted from this painful task.[17] From 1875 Juliana took to assisting her sister Dot as joint editor of the magazine, she continuing to live and work from Aldershot, and her sister from Ecclesfield. A new posting for Alex to Manchester in 1877, was followed by a move to York in 1878, and, six months later in March 1879, to Malta. Juliana's attempt to follow Alex to Malta resulted in a breakdown of her health, and she was forbidden to travel overseas. She returned to live at Ecclesfield and spent varying amounts of time with other relatives and friends until Alex returned home.

Her professional relationship with Randolph Caldecott stems from about this time and is wonderfully portrayed in a series of letters, especially the one regarding pictures to accompany her story *Jackanapes*, describing her young nephew William - sister Margaret's son William Smith of Barnes Hall, riding the family pony Robin.[18] Through her brother Charles, she met Ruskin and was much influenced by him and his ideas leading to her taking on the overtaxing burden of supervising her own publications and the commissioning of the illustrations and engravings for her stories. In the meantime *Aunt Judy's Magazine* had run into troubles. In 1882 its publication had been taken over by David Bogue who brought new ideas and sought to make a profit - in only one of the previous sixteen years had it made a profit. However, the venture was a lost one and Bogue went bankrupt with the magazine afterwards struggling on for only a further couple of years.

Alex returned to England in 1883, and they were stationed at Trull near Taunton in Somerset. The majority of Juliana's letters, from this time on, are devoted to gardens and gardening topics, and she wrote a series of 'Letters' upon the subject for the final editions of *Aunt Judy's Magazine*. Early in 1885 she was diagnosed as suffering from an unknown form of blood poisoning and she was confined to bed in almost constant pain. Dot came to nurse her, and at the same time assisted her sister with the correction and finalisation of several unfinished pieces of work. After three weeks of confinement Juliana was taken to Bath, to be more convenient for the expert medical care she needed, and where she was subjected to two surgical operations. They were unsuccessful, and Juliana Ewing died, at Bath, on 13 May 1885 from a deep seated cancer. She is buried in the churchyard at Trull in Somerset.

It has been written that Juliana wrote 'more about children than for children'; and that she had deep integrity, delightful invention, a fastidious choice of language, and an absolute avoidance of vulgarity. All she wrote was civilised and mature.[19] Marghanita Laski said of her work:

> *She was not 'Victorian' - as based upon Charlotte Yonge's proprieties - the children in her stories belong to every age; their interests do not date them, dressing up, and dogs, and gardens are as popular as ever they were. But the greatest of all Mrs Ewing's merits ... is the emancipation of the child from the adult world and adult moral responsibilities. The adults in children's books have always presented the author with a problem, and the common twentieth-century technique of making the children seem to exist in an adult-less vacuum (Arthur Ransome's books for instance) is rather an artificial solution ... Mrs Ewing puts her children against a background of adults, but she treats her readers as equals, and freely makes fun of the adults' behaviour.*[20]

However, although she was an unqualified success with children during her lifetime and for long after, none of her books has become a classic.

The other Gatty children

Of the other Gatty children, eldest daughter Margaret (1840-1900) was to mother a family, the Smiths of Barnes Hall, all of whom were to contribute, in their own way, to the well-being of the district during war and peace.[21] The eldest surviving son, the Rev. Reginald Alfred Gatty (1844-1914) (Figure 6), was Rector of Bradfield, and later Rector of Hooton Roberts, and through his assiduous studies in field archaeology, contributed much to our knowledge of the ancient inhabitants of South Yorkshire,[22] and the second surviving son, Sir Alfred Scott Gatty, KCVO (1847-1918), attained the distinction of Garter King at Arms. Sir Stephen Herbert Gatty KC (1849-1922), the third surviving son, became an eminent law officer and Chief Justice of Gibraltar. The

Figure 6. Rev. Reginald Alfred Gatty. H. Armitage, *Early Man in Hallamshire*

youngest surviving son, Charles Tindal Gatty (1851-1928)(Figure 7), was a much published author, an artist, and a Fellow of the Society of Arts. Undine Marcia Gatty married the Rev. W. Ward, and their daughter, Christabel, wrote the only full-length published biography of the Gattys. Finally, Horatia Katherine (1846-1945), the third eldest daughter, edited *Aunt Judy's Magazine* from the death of her mother until its demise. She married T. B. Eden, and she retained the copyright of Juliana Ewing's works. She was the last of the Gatty children to die, in 1945.

Figure 7. Charles Tindal Gatty. *Catholic Church of the Holy Ghost, Yeovil*

Alfred Gatty, the father of the family, undertook the restoration and conservation of the church in Ecclesfield (Figure 8), and, at the same time, witnessed the building of eight churches and numerous schools in various parts of the old parish as the population grew and new ecclesiastical districts were created. He played no insignificant part in the family enterprise by his own literary research and output, as well as encouraging his wife and chil-

Figure 8. Ecclesfield parish church. *Chapeltown & High Green Archive*

dren. Alfred Gatty died on 20 January 1903, and he too is buried in the family vault in Ecclesfield churchyard.

The Gattys deserve a more lasting memorial, especially in the village of Ecclesfield, than that afforded by a family vault, the Gatty Memorial Hall, and a street name tucked away on a council estate.

Notes and References

1. From 'Literature and the Literary Character', a lecture delivered at the Music Hall, Sheffield, to the Literary and Philosophical Society of Sheffield, 14 September, 1858, published by Bell & Daldy, London, 1858, p.9.
2. Alfred Gatty, *A Life at One Living* (1884), Bell & Sons, London, and Robert White, Worksop.
3. Quoted by her daughter, Juliana Horatia Ewing, in a memoir of her mother entitled 'Margaret Gatty' and published in the 1894 edition of *Parables from Nature*, George Bell & Sons, p. xi.
4. Margaret Gatty, *Parables from Nature*, 1894 edition, p. xi.
5. Horatia, K. F. Gatty, *Juliana Horatia Ewing and Her Books* (1885 and revised 1896), SPCK, London.
6. Christabel Maxwell, *Mrs Gatty and Mrs Ewing* (1949), Constable, London.
7. Henry Mayhew, *London Labour and London Poor,* 1851-64, Volume 1, p. 296. See also Juliana Horatia Ewing's memoir of her mother in Margaret Gatty, *Parables from Nature* (1894), footnote on p. xiii.
8. C. P. Fendall and E. A. Coutchley (eds), *Diary of Benjamin Newton* (Rector of Wath) *1816-1818* (1933), quoted by B. Anthony Bac in *The English Parsonage,* John Murray, footnote on page 152.
9. A. and M. Gatty, *The Life of Dr A. J. Scott* (1842), Saunders and Otley.
10. George Johnston (1797-1855), naturalist. He was a surgeon at Berwick-upon-Tweed and editor of the *Magazine of Zoology and Botany.* He was the author of *Flora of Berwick*, 2 vols, 1829-31, *The History of British Zoophytes*, and other scientific works. Margaret Gatty corresponded with him and visited him between 1850 and his death in 1855, in connection with her interest in collecting and cataloguing seaweeds. She dedicated her first edition of *Parables from Nature* to him.
11. Joseph Wolff (1795-1862). He was born of Jewish parents at Weilersbach, near Bamberg, Germany. He converted to Christianity and studied at Vienna, Tubingen and Rome. He entered the Order of Redemptorists, joined the Church of England and studied Oriental languages at Cambridge. He travelled widely in Egypt, Mesopotamia and Persia, and journeyed through Central Asia to India. He also visited the USA. He was ordained priest in the Church of England in 1838 and became Rector of Linthwaite, Yorkshire. In 1843-45 he went to Bokhara to establish the fate of two English officers, Stoddart and Conolly. He returned to England to be vicar of the parish of Isle Brewers in Somerset.
12. William Henry Harvey (1811-1866), botanist, honorary MD and Professor of Botany at Dublin. He lectured in the United States and visited India, Australia and the South Seas. He published works on British and Australian algae and *Genera of South African Plants.* He supervised the proofs of Mrs Gatty's *British Seaweeds* and in honour of her reputation as 'a diligent explorer of British algae and Marine Animals' he named an Australian genus of algae, *Gattya pinella*, after her.
13. *The Fancies of a Rhymer* (1833), Davison Simmons & Co.
14. Letter written by Margaret Gatty in 1845 and quoted in Christabel Maxwell's *Mrs Gatty and Mrs Ewing*, p. 84.
15. *Melchior's Dreams and Other Tales (*1862), Bell & Sons, London.
16. Published in 1873 in the first edition of *Lob Lie-by-the-Fire and Other Tales,* Bell & Sons, London.
17. Christabel Maxwell, *Mrs Gatty and Mrs Ewing*, p. 194.
18. Michael Hutchins (ed), *Yours Pictorially: Illustrated Letters of Ralph Caldecott* (1976), Frederick Warne, London, pp. 75 et seq.
19. Marghanita Laski, *Mrs Ewing, Mrs Molesworth & Mrs Hodgson Burnett* (1950), Arthur Baker, London, p. 54.
20. Gillian Avery, *Mrs Ewing* (1961), a Bodley Head monograph, pp. 65-67.
21. David T. Smith, 'The Smiths of Yorkshire and Glen Sherr' (1961), *Transactions of the Hunter Archaeological Society,* Vol 8, parts 2 & 3.
22. Harold Armitage, *Early Man in Hallamshire* (1939), Sampson Low, Marston & Co., London.

8. Juliana Ewing, Children's Writer, and Ecclesfield's Countryside

by Melvyn Jones

THIS IS NOT A WORK OF LITERARY CRITICISM. It extends Chris Morley's general study of Ecclesfield's connection with the Victorian literary world by exploring the extent and the ways in which Juliana Horatia Ewing (née Gatty) drew literary inspiration and a kind of life enhancing elixir from the physical and human world in which she spent her first 26 years and which she revisited in her imagination and in person with such sympathy and strong affection for the rest of her life.

The Gattys of Ecclesfield vicarage

The Gattys, Alfred and Margaret, came to Ecclesfield in September 1839. After a curacy of less than two years at Spennithorne in the then North Riding, Alfred Gatty, with his new wife (they were married on 8 July 1839), had come to a very large parish covering 50,000 acres

Figure 1. Dr Alfred Gatty, in the vicarage garden in the 1890s, surrounded by members of Ecclesfield church choir. In his later years he was seldom seen without his skullcap, which was his trademark. *Shirley Kirk*

or nearly 78 square miles. Gatty was succeeding his bride's uncle. The new vicar was to see his large parish dismembered in his own long lifetime, first by its separation from Bradfield chapelry, which for all intents and purposes had been an independent parish with its own church from as early as the mid-twelfth century, and then by the creation of separate ecclesiastical districts at Wadsley, Oughtibridge, Chapeltown and High Green.

Alfred Gatty (Figure 1), born in London, the son of a solicitor, and educated at Charterhouse, Eton and Oxford, was the quintessential Victorian 'gentleman-parson', mixing easily with artisan, squire and the local aristocracy alike (he was a contemporary of Earl Fitzwilliam at Eton). He became a Doctor of Divinity and Sub-Dean of York. He was to remain at Ecclesfield until his death in 1903 at the age of 89. He recorded details of his long incumbency at Ecclesfield in his *Life at One Living* (1884). Dr Gatty published lectures and sermons, wrote *Sheffield: Past and Present* (1873) and contributed hymns, carols and historical essays to his wife's magazine for children. He is best known as the reviser and editor of the definitive editions (1869 and 1875) of Joseph Hunter's *History of Hallamshire* (first published in 1819).

Margaret Gatty was the daughter of the Rev. Alexander John Scott, Lord Nelson's chaplain at Trafalgar, and later vicar of Southminster in Essex and Catterick in the North Riding. Mrs Gatty, was multi-talented and had a much wider literary reputation than her husband. She was an 'exquisite calligraphist', an expert on sundials, a landscape artist, writer on natural history (she was an authority on British seaweeds), but above all a writer for children in which capacity she had a world-wide reputation and readership. She is best known for her *Parables from Nature* (five series, 1855-71) and her editorship of *Aunt Judy's Magazine* (from 1866 until her death in 1873). She was compared in her lifetime to Hans Christian Andersen.[1]

Dr and Mrs Gatty presided over a family of eight surviving children of rare talent. Their second daughter, Juliana Horatia, the subject of this essay, had an even greater literary reputation as a children's writer than her mother. She wrote more than 100 children's stories, most of them first published in her mother's magazine. Two of the Gatty sons were knighted: Alfred Scott Gatty (b. 1847), who was also an accomplished composer, became Garter King of Arms at the College of Heralds and Stephen Herbert Gatty (b. 1849) was a colonial high court judge.

The vicarage at Ecclesfield must have taken on at times the air of a writers' colony. In the late 1850s and 1860s, for example, Dr and Mrs Gatty were directing the publication of Dr Joseph Wolff's autobiography (1859-60); Mrs Gatty was writing her *Parables from Nature* series, and her *History of British Seaweeds* in two volumes (1863) and editing *Aunt Judy's Magazine* (from 1866); Alfred Gatty was revising Hunter's *Hallamshire* (published 1869); Juliana was writing a stream of children's stories after the publication of her first in the *Monthly Packet* in 1861; some of the other Gatty children were also writing short pieces for their mother's magazine and others took on editorial duties; and the whole family was involved in compiling its own 'in-house' magazine, which went under various names, the longest lasting being the *The Gunpowder Plot*.[2] Even one of the curates had been involved at a slightly earlier period: Jonathan Eastwood, who was curate from 1848-54, publishing his important *History of Ecclesfield* in 1862. In the case of *Aunt Judy's Magazine* last minute writing and editing was often done against the clock in order to ensure the mail train from Sheffield to London was not missed.

Figure 2. Juliana Horatia Ewing (1841-1885).

Juliana Ewing's formative years and the parochial round

Juliana Horatia Gatty (always known as Julie within the family circle) was born in 1841 (Figure 2). She was always a delicate child but from an early age took charge of activities in the nursery, being the chief storyteller and organiser of games and play-acting. She was the eponymous 'Aunt Judy' of her mother's later magazine. In her teens she played an important part in parish affairs, being, like her sisters, an unpaid curate. She organised a village library, held a young women's class once a week at the vicarage, and was an assiduous parish visitor, sometimes working until dropping from exhaustion. She was sometimes referred to locally as 'cayling Julie' (cayling = delicate, dogged by ill-health). She published her first story in 1861 at the age of nineteen.

In 1867 she married Captain (later Major and eventually Colonel) Alexander Ewing who had been a visitor to Ecclesfield vicarage since 1856.

Within days of their marriage they took ship to Canada, where Captain Ewing was stationed for two years at Fredericton, New Brunswick. In late 1869 they returned to England where they were successively posted to Aldershot, Bowdon in Cheshire and York. In 1879 the now Major Ewing was posted to Malta and then to Ceylon but Juliana was too unwell to accompany him. It is likely that she already had cancer. From 1883 until her death in 1885 at the age of only 43 the couple were stationed near Taunton in Somerset. She is buried in the churchyard at Trull, near Taunton, where there is a window in the church dedicated to herself and her husband.

In her lifetime, Juliana Ewing was compared to Lewis Carroll and Robert Louis Stevenson, was much admired by John Ruskin, and her books were printed by the tens of thousands. Baden-Powell took the name 'Brownies' for the junior branch of the Girl Guides from the characters in one of her stories. Today she is largely forgotten, her stories being thought to be too sentimental for modern tastes.[3]

Juliana's mother endured Ecclesfield, but would have liked to have been elsewhere; somewhere where she could collect seaweed in a mild climate. Margaret Gatty had spent her early years in the south of England, the first eight years of her life being divided between Southminster in Essex where her father held the living from 1804 until 1817, and her maternal grandparents' house in London. In 1817 the Rev. Scott accepted the Crown living of Catterick in North Yorkshire and the family moved north. As a young woman Margaret Scott spent periods away from the vicarage at Catterick, at the nearby home of the Earl and Countess Tyrconnel, in London and at Southminster. All her haunts were rural or metropolitan, and half of them were in the south. For all these reasons she never loved Ecclesfield, even though she lived there for 35 years. The family kept a 'confession book' in 1862 and one of the questions was 'In what place would you most like to live?' Mrs Gatty's answer was 'somewhere warm near the sea.'[4] In a letter written in 1863 she was more specific about her yearning for the south and her attitude towards her place of residence in the north on the fringe of the Pennines:

> *It makes me queer to hear of lovely gardens anywhere just now! Not but what I left the almond tree in full flower in the blessed South, and nightingales all but come to Sevenoaks. But my destiny never permits my being there in the time of singing birds. This cold harsh North is our fate.*[5]

Later the same year, when there were reports circulating in the neighbourhood that the family was about to leave Ecclesfield, she wrote a

Figure 3. Ecclesfield church and village under a cloudy sky. *Drawing by Juliana Horatia Ewing.*

letter scotching the rumours, but added, fatalistically, 'we shall fight on here if it is to be so.'[6]

Mrs Gatty's antipathy towards the place where she lived was not shared by her children. In the same confession book in which their mother had admitted that she would prefer to be living in a mild coastal location, the children all said 'home' or 'Ecclesfield' or 'Yorkshire'. Dr Gatty, child of the metropolis, said 'London'.

In the case of Juliana, this love of her local patch: the church, the vicarage and its grounds, the local countryside and the local people, was particularly strong (Figure 3). It not only fed her literary imagination throughout her life, it sustained her in illness, and time and again on the army postings with her husband in different parts of Britain and in Canada it manifested itself in bouts of homesickness.[7]

Juliana was educated at home in Ecclesfield by her mother. Part of that education was undertaken in the surrounding countryside. Long walks with nurse maids when young were replaced by country rambles, games in the local woods and fields and visits to nearby country houses.

Home thoughts from abroad

In 1867 Alexander Ewing was posted to the province of New Brunswick in Canada's maritime provinces. Juliana, his new bride, accompanied him and they were stationed at Fredericton until October 1869. This posting was a wonderful adventure for Juliana, discovering and exploring a new land, going on short trips upriver by canoe and across country in winter on snow shoes, sketching ceaselessly and writing letters home about the land and its people, especially the native Indians. But homesickness was never far below the surface.

In June 1868 she wrote to her family in England: 'Whatever I have been doing and thinking during the day, I almost invariably dream of Ecclesfield.'[8] At Christmas of that year there was the first talk of a new posting and thoughts of home again surfaced uncontrollably:

> *... I had had a sort of dim, wild, unlikely hope that the next change might be an order Home; and Ecclesfield just rushed over me so unbearably, that after hiding it two or three times when he came in with tea and things for me, I couldn't hold out - and when Rexie came in and began to talk about it, I broke down and had a "regular good cry". I knew it was very selfish for he thinks me quite Home enough - and in fact has no other ties and likes travelling, and prefers being abroad, and I fully expected him to be vexed, though keep it back I couldn't.*[9]

In 1869, a new posting became a reality, and Juliana hoped it would be back in England. During the New Brunswick summer when she wondered where their new home would be, she also thought of Ecclesfield and its familiar countryside:

> *in all this lovely weather - these moonlight nights, as I plan, and pack, or sing, or garden, at musical meetings or the early cathedral service - the hope that is so near and yet so far runs under everything, like a brook ... in the Shroggs.*[10]

As we shall see, the Shroggs, a small wood about a quarter of a mile from Ecclesfield vicarage, held a special place in her heart and was a lifelong inspiration (Figure 4).

Figure 4. Lee Shroggs Wood, Ecclesfield, Summer 1998. *Joan Jones*

Rest and recuperation

Major Ewing was posted to Malta in March 1879 and then to Ceylon, and Juliana, who was too ill to travel abroad, was separated for long periods from her husband until 1883. In between intense and exhausting periods of writing, dealing with illustrators, publishers and booksellers she spent increasing amounts of time recuperating among her family and friends in south Yorkshire where the familiar and loved landscape gave her intense pleasure. This is nowhere more evident than in a letter to her husband in January 1880:

> *... very dear to me are all your "tender and true" regards for the old home - the grey-green nest (more grey now than green!) a good deal changed and weatherbeaten, but not quite deserted - which is bound up with so much of our lives. ... Another chord of sympathy was very strongly pulled by your writing of the 'grey-green fields' and sending your love to them. No one I ever met has, I think quite your sympathy with exactly what the external world out-of-doors is to me and has been ever since I can remember. From days when the batch of us went-out-walking with the Nurses, and the round moss-edged holes in the roots of gnarled trees in the hedges, and the red leaves of Herb Robert in autumn, and all the inexhaustible wealth of hedges and ditches and fields, and the Shroggs, and the brooks, were happiness of the keenest kind - to now when it is as fresh and strong as ever; it has been a pleasure which has balanced an immense lot of physical pain ...'*[11]

In the autumn of 1881 she spent long periods in and around Grenoside:

> *All November I was sketching on the edge of Greno Wood, one and a half miles from here. Grenoside might be the birthplace of the dying man who offered to fly his future fellow angel for a sovereign. The men are terrible pigeon fanciers. It has a very rascally side - but oh! the beauty - the exquisite beauty of all the changeful play of the pretty doves that strut and rest on every cottage roof - and come and go against the dusky wood that girdles the whole hamlet at its back and upper side - the front of it looking down from a sandy height on to the misty valley and the top of Ecclesfield Church Tower! I used to get almost choked with the colour before my eyes, and the air up my nostrils, and my own incapacity to do the scene justice. Sandstone in sunshine is very beautiful - and the greenery-yallery of old stone roofs - whitewashed walls - a pea-green doorway ... all against the soft warm brown of the leafless wood behind - and a sky of leafless blue. Then "whoosh! cla!" and up rise a dozen spots of mother of pearl upon the roof - and one snow-*

> *white pigeon plays upon the air against the wood in a fashion to drive a painter mad - and a dauber desperate! quite desperate!!* [12]

Nor was she just a fair weather lover of the local countryside in spite of her regular bouts of ill-health. She loved the autumn in the woods, and stormy days and grey days ('that grey-green winter tone (for which I have a particular love)' [13], and the approach of winter and leafless and cold winter itself.

In March 1878 she wrote to her husband of a long walk she had taken round and about Ecclesfield and described a water colour she had in mind to attempt:

> *It has been v*[er]*y lovely today & I have been a fairly long walk. The view (if I could but remember it) was very effective. From the common - strongly marked lights on Church & vicarage & houses of the village - the leafless trees letting them show through so well, & the Grenohead outline of hill looking dark purple and showing them off so well! Wait a wee & I'll do him yet.* [14]

She wrote to Randolph Caldecott, the book illustrator, in November 1881 about the 'glorious November' at Grenoside 'amid the autumn fires of the red and golden woods, and the sandstone walls, and old women and bonny children gathering sticks after the equinoctial storms!!'. [15]

'The dear familiar scene': Ecclesfield's countryside and Juliana Ewing's writing

The remarkable thing about the countryside that inspired so much of Juliana's writing is its small compass. Many British writers, the great and the half forgotten, Victorian and of the twentieth century, 'serious' and popular, have derived great sustenance from the places in which they were born, brought up or lived their professional lives. Hardy had his Wessex, Daphne du Maurier her Cornwall, Francis Brett Young his Black Country, Catherine Cookson her North-east of England, and James Herriott his Yorkshire dales. As a well of literary inspiration and the source of a kind of natural health cure in times of loneliness and debilitating ill-health, Juliana Ewing drew on a stretch of countryside about two miles in extent from east to west and about a mile from north to south. It was essentially her childhood countryside which she re-visited in reality and in her imagination for the rest of her life. It contained for her both a set of general well-loved memories: fields, hedges, stone walls, trees, woods, streams, mossy banks, flowers, grasses and ferns, sandstone cottages, bridges, paths; and real places: Lee Shroggs Wood (most importantly), St Mary's church at

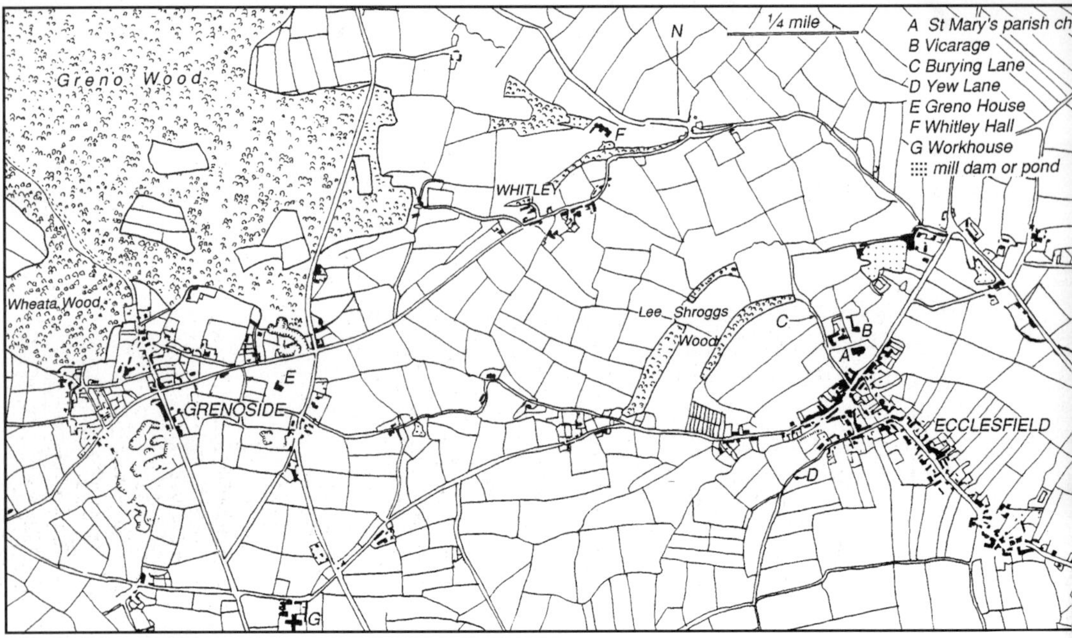

Figure 5. Ecclesfield's countryside featured in Juliana Ewing's stories.

Ecclesfield, the vicarage and its gardens, Ecclesfield Hall Farm, Whitley Hall, Greno House, Greno Wood, William Dronfield's wood-yard (Figure 5).

In the rest of this section eight stories are considered in which Ecclesfield village or the vicarage or the surrounding countryside have most obviously been used as a setting.

Melchior's Dream

Juliana's first three published stories *(A Bit of Green, The Blackbird's Nest and Melchior's Dream)* appeared in the magazine the *Monthly Packet* in 1861, the first when she was still nineteen. Her sister, Horatia, in *Juliana Horatia Ewing and Her Books* describes these as 'parochial' tales.[16] With the addition of five additional tales they were published in book form as *Melchior's Dream and Other Tales* in 1862. *Melchior's Dream* itself is an uplifting tale about the virtues of family life, set in a vicarage on Christmas Eve. The vicarage could be Ecclesfield (Figure 6). Paterfamalias is in his study writing his Christmas sermon, materfamilias is upstairs in her room with a headache, and the children – all ten of them – are bored, and the eldest wishes he were an only son. A visitor staying with them for the Christmas season, tells them the story to while away the late afternoon before the Christmas Eve supper. A few South Yorkshire dialect words are included betraying the author's Ecclesfield origins – Melchior in his dream forgets to 'mend' the fire, and the family have 'furmety' (a kind of porridge eaten with Christmas cake) and yule cake.

Figure 6. Ecclesfield vicarage, now demolished.

Significantly, Juliana's commonplace book contains a list of local dialect words and their meanings, presumably listed with a view to considering using them in her stories.[17]

The Yew Lane Ghosts

One of the additional stories in *Melchior's Dream and Other Tales* is *The Yew Lane Ghosts.* This again is set in a south Yorkshire village like Ecclesfield and is the story of a local bully getting his just desserts after frightening a boy on his way home after attending an evening class run by the rector's son, the hero of the hour. As in *Melchior's Dream* the setting appears to be Ecclesfield, with the author even using the real name of one of the village streets – Yew Lane – although its location is slightly changed (Figure 7). Her description of the lane suggests a long and intimate knowledge of it.

> *Yew Lane – cool and dark when the hottest sun lay upon it – a loitering place for lovers – the dearly-loved play-place of generations of children on sultry summer days...*[18]

The story also contains, again like *Melchior's Dream*, its share of local expressions and dialect words, most notably the expression 'to loose'

Figure 7. Yew Lane, Ecclesfield, in about 1900.

with the meaning of some occasion ending and the participants leaving the venue: 'It must be dark now before school looses'.

Mrs Overtheway's Remembrances

Cottages on the edge of the woods at Grenoside form the setting for the first part of *Mrs Overtheway's Remembrances* first published in *Aunt Judy's Magazine* in five parts between 1866 and 1868. The first part of the tale, entitled 'Ida', which sets up the rest of the sequence of stories, concerns the circumstances in which Mrs Overtheway, the storyteller, makes the acquaintance of her neighbour the orphan, Ida. The introduction is effected as a result of Ida getting through a hole in her garden fence and going into the wood beyond to pick a bunch of primroses for Mrs Overtheway, an elderly neighbour she has seen from her nursery window but never met. The setting is typical Mrs Ewing: an overgrown hedge, an old and grey stone water trough, gurgling water, rich mosses, blue sky, a wood, birds in song, a brook, a steep bank, and primroses.

Writing to her husband in Malta in early 1880 from Greno House she recalled how she had used Grenoside as the setting for 'Ida'.

> *Harry Howard drove me up yesterday. It was just as much as I could bear; but I lay on the sofa till dinner, and went to bed at eight, and although my head kept me awake at first, I did well on the whole. Breakfast in bed, a bigger one than I have eaten for three weeks, and since then I have had an hour's drive. The roughness of the roads is*

Figure 8. Moss and lichen encrusted wall, Grenoside. *Joan Jones*

Figure 9. Water trough in Bower Lane, Grenoside, Autumn 1998. *Joan Jones*

unlucky, but the air divine! Such sweet sunshine, and Greno Wood, with yellow remains of bush and bracken, and heavy mosses on the sandstone walls, and tiny streams trickling through boggy bits of the wood, and coming out over the wall to overflow those picturesque stone troughs which are so oddly numerous, and which I had in my head when I wrote the first part of 'Mrs Overtheway'. [19] (see Figures 8 and 9)

An Idyll of the Wood

An *Idyll of the Wood* was published in *Aunt Judy's Magazine* in 1867 and is interesting in that it was written in Fredericton in Canada. 'Tell us a story' say the children at the beginning of the tale, 'a sad one, if you please, and a little true.' It is the story of a thrush that is taken from its native wood by town boys, sold to a sailor and taken in a cage on a long sea voyage during which it escapes and perishes when in sight of land. It is clearly a story inspired by her own recently completed Atlantic crossing and the associated homesickness. The thrush's song in its native wood sounds like Juliana thinking of her Ecclesfield countryside and her local wood:

Joy! Joy! Fresh water and green woods, ambrosial sunshine and sunflecked shade, chattering brooks and rustling leaves, glade, and sward and dell. Lichens and cool mosses, feathered ferns, and flowers. Green leaves! Green leaves! Summer! summer! summer! [20]

The Land of Lost Toys

This story, which first appeared in *Aunt Judy's Magazine* in two parts in 1869 and subsequently in book form in *The Brownies, and Other Tales,* is set in Shroggs Wood, the small wood a quarter of a mile from Ecclesfield vicarage. The storyteller, 'Aunt Penelope', tells of her stroll into a wood she had played in as a child:

If I have a stronger predilection than my love for toys, it is my love for woods, and, like the other, it dates from childhood. It was born and bred with me, and I fancy it will stay with me till l die. The soothing scents of leaf-mould, moss, and fern (not to speak of flowers) – the pale green veil in spring, the rich shade of summer, the rustle of the dry leaves in autumn, I suppose an old woman may enjoy all of these, my dears, as well as you. But I think I could make "fairy jam" of hips and haws in acorn cups now, if any child would be condescending enough to play with me...I strolled on in leisurely enjoyment, and at last seated myself at the foot of a tree to rest. I was hot and tired ...The tree under which I sat was an old friend. There was a hole at its base that I knew well. Two roots covered with exquisite moss ran out from each side, like the arms of a chair, and between them there accumulated year after year a rich though tiny store of dark leaf mould. We always used to say that fairies lived within, though I never say anything go in myself but wood-beetles. There was one going in at that moment. [21]

Aunt Penelope is invited inside – into the land of lost toys. Juliana's vivid imagination had no doubt been working on what fairy tale world might exist inside the holes at the base of the trees in Shroggs Wood since her early childhood. In the letter to her husband of 11 January 1881, quoted above, she makes specific mention of her childhood memories of 'the round moss-edged holes in the roots of old trees' (Figure 10).

Figure 10. Holes at the foot of a beech tree in Shroggs Wood, Summer 1998. *Joan Jones*

Our Field

Her memories of the pastures and meadows in which she played with her brothers and sisters are the basis of *Our Field*, first published in *Aunt Judy's Magazine* in 1876. Her sister, Horatia, in *Juliana Ewing and Her Books*, recalls that Juliana organised the excursions and childhood games there:

> *She invented names for the spots that we most frequented in our walks, such as "The Mermaid's Ford" and "St. Nicholas". The latter covered a space including several fields and a clear stream, and over this locality she certainly reigned supreme, our gathering of violets and cowslips, or of hips and haws for jam, and our digging of earth nuts were limited by her orders.* [22]

Our Field, which is the story of exhibiting wild flowers, grasses and mosses at a village show to pay a dog licence, is a veritable cornucopia of wildlife. In the space of eleven pages she manages to make reference to blackthorn, oak, holly, elder, dog rose and hawthorn; cowslip, violet, bluebell, ox-eye daisy, earth nut, meadowsweet, mallow, cock's-foot-grass, fox-tail grass, shivering grass and fern; feather moss, hair moss, pincushion moss and scale moss; wren and lark and freshwater shrimp; and mushroom and rush.

Her brother Charles sent a copy of *Our Field* to John Ruskin. In a letter to her husband Juliana told him that she was 'proud to hear he [John Ruskin] says its *[sic]* not a mere story – it's a poem. Great praise from a great man!'. [23]

We and the World

This is one of Juliana's longer stories, published in *Aunt Judy's Magazine* between November 1877 and October 1879, and is a tale for boys contrasting the world of the family with experience of the wider world. The early chapters, dealing with the home and school life of the two brothers Jem and Jack (the storyteller) is full of exciting or funny set pieces – the funeral of a miser, stealing walnuts, accompanying the beekeeper to his hives on the moors, the rescue of a skater in the mill dam, the return from imprisonment of the man who is to become their schoolmaster, running away from the cruel regime in a boarding school – all but the last set in a thinly disguised Ecclesfield and Bradfield (where her brother, Reginald Alfred, was rector from 1869 to 1880). The track from the vicarage towards Shroggs Wood, for example, becomes the path to Walnut Farm (the miser's house and later their first school Walnut Farm Academy):

> *Walnut-tree Farm was an old house that stood some little ways from the road in our favourite lane – a lane full of wild roses and speedwell, with a tiny footpath of disjointed flags like an old pack-horse track. Grass and milfoil grew thickly between the stones, and the turf stretched halfway over the road from each side, for there was little traffic in the lane, beyond the yearly rumble of the harvesting waggons, and few foot-passengers, except a labourer now and then, a pair or two of rustic lovers at sundown, a few knots of children in the blackberry season, and the cows coming home to milking.* [24]

It was a track that was to re-appear in Daddy Darwin's Dovecot about four years later.

The local setting of the first part of the story is emphasised by the use of local dialect words and expressions in the dialogue between village characters such as dodder (to tremble), fettle (to see to, to make good, clear up), loppered (sour), 'see thee' (look here!), 'hissen' (himself), 'yon' (that ... over there), and even the modern sounding 'chuff(ed)' (pleased).

Daddy Darwin's Dovecot

One of Juliana's best known and best loved stories, it was first published in *Aunt Judy's Magazine* in 1881, and is set, fair and square, in the local countryside where the author had spent a great deal of time walking and sketching at the time of its composition. It is the story of a workhouse orphan (there was, of course, a workhouse at Grenoside to which the author was a regular visitor before her marriage); about his apprenticeship to an old man who breeds and shows doves; about the theft of the doves and their subsequent retrieval (based on a local event); about the growing relationship between the old man and the boy; and about the love of the boy for his neighbour's daughter. The setting is the Ecclesfield countryside, peopled by Ecclesfield 'types', speaking the local dialect, and including, as a minor character, the parson's daughter as parish visitor and balancer of the parish charities accounts.

Juliana persuaded Randolph Caldecott, one of the leading book illustrators of his day, to illustrate the book version published by SPCK the same year. Caldecott responded by producing sixteen line drawings, an illustrated cover/title page and, most famously, a full page, coloured frontispiece.

The frontispiece (Figure 11) is one of the best known of Caldecott's illustrations for Juliana (he also collaborated on *Jackanapes and Lob Lie-by-the-Fire*). Part of the fame of this illustration lies in the fact that, so accurate is the portrayal of the scene, local readers were convinced that Caldecott had been to Ecclesfield to draw it and they knew the exact spot where the artist had set it. The scene portrayed in the illustration forms the preamble to the story in which two old 'gaffers' or 'standards' as they were known locally, set the scene:

> *Summer's afternoon. Early in the summer, and late in the afternoon; with odours and colours deepening, and shadows lengthening towards evening.*
>
> *Two gaffers gossiping, seated side by side upon a Yorkshire wall. A wall of many colours, glowing redder and yellower as the sun goes down; well cushioned by moss and lichen, and deep set in rank grass on this side, where the path runs, and in blue hyacinths on that side, where the wood is...*
>
> *Continuing the path, a stone pack-horse track, leading past a hedge snow-white with may, and down into a little wood, from the depths of which one could hear a brook babbling. Then up across the sunny field beyond, and yet up over another field to where the brow of the hill is crowned by old farm buildings standing against the sky.* [25]

Figure 11. The frontispiece to *Daddy Darwin's Dovecot* (SPCK, 1881) by Randolph Caldecott.

Figure 12. The view today looking from the edge of Shroggs Wood towards Whitley. *Joan Jones*

The scene is unmistakably on the edge of Lee Shroggs Wood looking towards Whitley (Figure 12). In November she wrote to Caldecott to tell him of her 'delight and gratitude for the Gaffers' and to convey her appreciation of the skill with which he had depicted 'the scene and all its local colour'. She went on:

> *In the latter you have been quite marvellously successful. It would amuse you to hear how many people 'hereabouts' know the exact spot in 'Shroggs' wood where you must have sat to sketch the dear familiar scene – or at least that I must have made a rough sketch and sent it to!* [you]. *An enthusiastic Yorkshireman, a young coal owner... delivered a sort of lecture to me on the subject the other day! He walked over here and complained that he had been hunting about the neighbourhood of 'the Shroggs' for the precise point of view and not quite hit it. 'But one knows the gaffers, of course. They're Yorkshire, and Yorkshire of this district.' The exclusion of the other ridings amused me much.* [26]

Conclusion

Juliana Ewing made full use of her experience of people and places to feed her literary imagination, not least her experiences as an army wife. But it was her early life in a crowded south Yorkshire vicarage and her love of the local countryside which she came to know so intimately during her childhood and early adult years, that affected her most deeply. It made her homesick when she was away from it, she wrote lyrical letters to her husband about it when they were apart, she sketched it and painted it all her life, and she incorporated scenes and people from it in some of her best loved stories.

Why, then was she so happy to leave her beloved Ecclesfield and travel abroad and live on army stations in various parts of England? The answer is simply that she had met her perfect man and wished to share her life with him wherever he was posted, no matter what the sacrifices she would have to make. Shortly before her marriage in 1867 she confided in a friend:

> *It is only fair to say I have found a double of myself – and that it feels like the addition of a few new faculties – a large accession of strength & a sort of mental companion, footman, courier, lady's maid, lover & attendant geni all rolled into one!!!!!!!!!!!!* [27]

But that did not stop the homesickness, nor did it prevent her from expressing it in her stories. At the beginning of the *The Peace Egg*, the story of a soldier's wife (from Yorkshire) disowned and disinherited by her father for marrying the soldier and then reconciled through the performance of a mumming play by her children, unknowingly before her father, the narrator expresses sentiments very much shared by the author:

> *And yet, as years went and children came, the Captain and his wife grew tired of travelling. New scenes were small comfort when they heard of the death of old friends. One foot of murky English sky was dearer, after all, than miles of the unclouded heavens of the South. The grey hills and overgrown lanes of her old home haunted the Captain's wife by night and day, and home-sickness (that weariest of all sicknesses) began to take the light out of her eyes before their time.* [28]

What better then than to leave Juliana Ewing in a corner of a favourite bit of her local countryside, in the final years of her life, surrounded by admirers, as she described it to her husband:

> *...I have sketched up to-day, but it was cold and sunless, so I did some village visiting. I am known here (Grenoside), bye the bye as 'Miss Gatty as was'! I generally go about with a tribe of children after me, like the Pied Piper of Hamelin! They are now fairly well trained to keeping behind me, and are curiously civil in taking care of my traps, pouring out water for me, and keeping each other in a kind of rough order by rougher adjurations!*
>
> *"Keep out o't leet can't ye?"*
>
> *"Na then! How's shoo to see through thee?"*
>
> *"Shoo' gotten t' Dovecot in yon book, and shoo's got little Liddy Kirk and thy moother wi' her apron over her heead, and Eliza Flowers sitting upo't' doorstep wi' her sewing – and shoo's got t' woodyard and Maester D.* [William Dronfield, clog sole maker] *smooking his pipe – and shoo's gotten Jack."*
>
> *"Nay! Has shoo gotten Jack?"*
>
> *"Shoo 'as. And shoo's gotten ould K. sitting up i't' shed corner chopping wood, and shoo's bound to draw him and Dronfield's lad criss-cross sawing."*
>
> *"Aye. Shoo did all Greno Wood last week, they tell me."*
>
> *"Aye. And shoo's done most o' t' village this week. What's shoo bound to do wi' 'em all?"*
>
> *"Shoo'll piece 'em all together and mak a big picter of t' whole place"* [29]

Notes and References

1. For fuller details of Mrs Gatty's life and literary output, see Christabel Maxwell, *Mrs Gatty and Mrs Ewing,* (Constable, 1949) and *In Memorium,* an appreciation of Margaret Gatty by Juliana Horatia Ewing in *Aunt Judy's Magazine,* 1874.
2. The family's manuscript magazines, *Anon, Le Cache, The Winton Wag* and *The Gunpowder Plot,* complete with very competent pen and wash drawings by Juliana Ewing and less competent ones by her brother Alfred Scott Gatty, have survived (Sheffield Archives, H.A.S. 76).
3. For a recent local critique of her work see Stephen McClarence's article in the *Sheffield Star,* 21 June 1991, on the 150th anniversary of her death.
4. Quoted in Christabel Maxwell, *Mrs Gatty and Mrs Ewing*, Constable, 1949, p.17.
5. Maxwell, *Mrs Gatty and Mrs Ewing,* p.17.
6. Maxwell, *Mrs Gatty and Mrs Ewing,* p.18.
7. Juliana was not the only one who was homesick upon leaving Ecclesfield. Christabel Maxwell, daughter of Juliana Ewing's younger sister, Undine Marcia (b. 1848), recounted that when her mother went to live in Australia (she married the Rev. W. Ward) 'she was bewildered and homesick and her heart hankered after a peal of church bells and the glimpse of grey stone walls under a cloudy sky.' (Maxwell, p.19).
8. Maxwell, *Mrs Gatty and Mrs Ewing,* p.18.
9. Maxwell, *Mrs Gatty and Mrs Ewing,* p.18.
10. Maxwell, *Mrs Gatty and Mrs Ewing,* p.176.
11. Letter to her husband, 11 January, 1880, in Horatia K. F. Eden, *Juliana Horatia Ewing and Her Books* (with a selection of her letters)., SPCK, *c.* 1886, pp. 216-17.
12. Maxwell, *Mrs Gatty and Mrs Ewing,* p. 225.
13. Letter to her husband 11 January 1880, in Horatia K. F. Eden, p.217.
14. Unpublished letter to her husband, 2 March 1878, Sheffield Archives, H A S 61/37.
15. Letter to Randolf Caldecott, 23 November 1881 in Michael Hutchins (ed), *Yours Pictorially: Illustrated Letters of Randolf Caldecott,* Frederick Warne, 1876, p. 84.
16. Horatia K. F. Gatty, *Juliana Horatia Ewing and Her Books,* SPCK, 1887, p.12.
17. Sheffield Archives, H A S 78, pp. 65-67.
18. Juliana Horatia Ewing, *Melchior's Dream and Other Tales,* SPCK, 1862, pp.199-200.
19. Letter to her husband, undated, (January 1880?), in Horatia K. F. Eden, p. 216.
20. An *Idyll of the Wood* in *Aunt Judy's Magazine,* 1867, p. 259.
21. Mrs J. H. Ewing, *The Brownies and Other Stories,* Dent, 1954, p. 161.
22. Horatia K. F. Gatty, *Juliana Horatia Ewing and Her Books,* p.9.
23. Letter to her husband, 19 September 1879. Sheffield Archives H A S 61/161.
24. *Aunt Judy's Christmas Volume,* 1878, p.12.
25. Juliana Horatia Ewing, *Daddy Darwin's Dovecot,* illustrated by Randolph Caldecott, SPCK, 1881.
26. Hutchins, *Pictorially Yours,* pp. 83-84.
27. Sheffield Archives, H A S 68/21, undated letter 1867.
28. *The Peace Egg,* SPCK uniform edition, n.d. p.14. The story was first published in *Aunt Judy's Magazine* in December 1871.
29. Letter to her husband, from Grenoside, 30 November, 1881 in Horatia K. F. Eden, p.251.

Acknowledgements

I wish to thank Chris Morley, who knows much more about the Gattys that I do, for putting me on the right track. Acknowledgements are also due to the Hunter Archaelogical Society for permission to quote from the Ewing Papers in Sheffield Archives. Last but not least I wish to thank Mrs Joan Scott Swann (née Smith), a grand-daughter of Juliana Ewing's eldest sister, Margaret, for her generous gift to Chapeltown and High Green Archive of a copy of Christobel Maxwell's *Mrs Gatty and Mrs Ewing,* which renewed my interest in the life and work of Juliana Ewing.

9. Regulating an Industrial Township: Religion, Politics and Leisure in Attercliffe, *c.*1851-81

by Andrew Walker

THIS ARTICLE SEEKS TO EXPLORE the extent to which the nature of the social and cultural life of Attercliffe, a manufacturing township in Sheffield's east end, was determined by its working-class inhabitants. By examining the religious, political and leisure activities of Attercliffe's inhabitants an attempt will be made to assess whether imposed outside 'social control' strongly influenced their behaviour or if the township's residents were able to determine themselves what took place within their own community. The term 'social control' is usually employed to indicate the imposition of opinions and habits by one class upon another.[1] Initially, however, the nature of house ownership will be examined.

In many industrial communities, particularly in the textile and mining towns of the later nineteenth century, a large number of employers owned much of the property in which their labour force lived. Inevitably, as a consequence, the degree of control such employers enjoyed over their workers was significantly greater than that exerted by non-residential property-owning manufacturers. The advantages of this residential property ownership were perhaps most obvious during industrial disputes when an employer could simply evict striking workers from their homes.

In Attercliffe, however, despite the proximity of vast steel and engineering companies (see Figure 1), both within the township, such as Brown, Bayley and Dixon and outside it in neighbouring Brightside, the extent of residential property ownership by the large employer seems to have been minimal. According to the Attercliffe Rate Books for 1851-2, the largest property owner within the township appeared to have been Francis Huntsman, who owned at least 39 houses in Worksop Road and Swallow Row, near to the steel works which bore his family's name. Huntsman's property ownership had increased further ten years later when at least 100 houses belonged to him.

Huntsman, however, appears to have been an exception. Few other large employers in the township seemed intent on providing accommodation for their workers on a large scale. William Jessop, whose

Figure 1. Attercliffe in 1903 as depicted on the 25 Inch Ordnance Survey map, Sheet 295.01.

works had a rateable value five times that of Huntsman in 1867 had less than one fifth as many houses in his ownership.[2] By 1881, whilst the Huntsmans were recorded as owning some 90 residential properties in Attercliffe, in addition to their small works, in contrast John Brown, whose works in the township had a rateable value of £6,893, employing over 1500 men, owned just 17 houses.[3]

Indeed, throughout the period of the study, the pattern of residential ownership within Attercliffe revealed a prevalence of small property owners with very few owners of large numbers of houses being present in the area, the most conspicuous exception being the Huntsman family. This pattern of ownership appears to have been common to Sheffield as a whole. Surveying the fortnightly minutes of the New Works and Plans Subcommittee of the highway committee in the Borough Council minutes, Peter J. Aspinall discovered that between 1864 and 1900, 'almost two thirds of all applications refer to projects of less than five houses.'[4]

A survey of the new house building projects in rapidly-growing Attercliffe between 1865 and 1869 revealed that of 45 developers listed, only fourteen had submitted plans for more than five properties.[5] Thus, many of the landlords of Attercliffe's residential accommodation were comparatively small. The rent they received was an important means of supplementing their income. Many of these landlords were resident in the community and therefore, to an extent, accountable to their tenants, especially if they were engaged, as many small property owners were, in the competitive retail trade. This depended on goodwill amongst customers. Consequently, there were pressures on such landlords to provide accommodation which was acceptable to potential tenants.

Religion

A common means by which members of the middle classes sought to exert influence upon the working classes was through the use of religion. Considerable evidence exists within Attercliffe which appears to substantiate this claim. Many employers encouraged evangelism in their works. John Brown, one of the district's most influential employers, in an address to his workmen in 1858, praised the success of the Bible Society in selling amongst his employees 84 copies of the Bible at 21 shillings each.[6] Four years later, the *Sheffield Independent* reported the Bishop of Oxford's visit to the works of John Brown, where the bishop 'exhorted his hearers to turn their attention to religious subjects ...'[7] Similarly, in a report on the actions of representatives of Sheffield Church Scripture Readers' Society of

1858, it was noted that,

> *In some manufactories they had opportunities of conversinng with workpeople. 30,000 or 40,000 tracts had been distributed, not indiscriminately, but carefully and with regard to the applicability of the tract to the party.* [8]

To many members of the middle class a continual source of anxiety remained their fear of the nonbelieving members of the working classes. The apparent hopelessness of his task prompted John Earnshaw, the vicar of Christ Church, Attercliffe (Figure 2), to distribute a pamphlet throughout his parish entitled 'An Address to the Inhabitants of Attercliffe'. In it, he wrote accusingly that:

> *two-thirds, three-fourths, or, in the estimation of many, a much larger proportion of you live in entire neglect of everything that can be called religion.*

His thundering address concluded explosively:

> *God knows, I would willingly take you with me but you will have it otherwise. You cannot say now that you have not heard of the fatal danger of your course ... you have made your choice and it is sin, Satan, the wrath of God and the torments of Hell !* [9]

Figure 2. Christ Church, Attercliffe, *c.* 1905. *Sheffield City Libraries, Local Studies Library*

Such pamphlets, far from enticing working class families into churches, may have had quite the reverse effect. In 1867, a conference was held in Sheffield examining the issue of low church attendance amongst the working classes. One significant cause identified

> *was the want of sympathy among the clergy. They held themselves aloof from working men, hitherto they had not been seen in the homes of the working classes.*[10]

A number of Attercliffe nonconformist ministers appeared to adopt a rather different approach to their potential congregations from Earnshaw, with rather more positive results. The strength of nonconformity in Attercliffe reflected that in Sheffield as a whole. According to two religious censuses, one conducted in 1851 throughout the country and the other, commissioned by the *Sheffield Independent* thirty years later, and confined to the borough of Sheffield, attendance in Sheffield's nonconformist chapels exceeded that in its established churches on both occasions.[11] A correspondent in the *Sheffield Independent*, commenting on the 1881 religious census figures and the revealed strength of nonconformity, wrote that, 'the Established Church is the church of the minority and not the Church of England.'[12] Both censuses, however, reveal the vast amount of church attendance across the denominations which characterised Victorian society. As E. R. Wickham has observed, in both 1851 and 1881, 'one in three who could do so attended a place of worship on an average Sunday.'[13]

By examining the history of one dissenting chapel in Attercliffe, for which records are available, the factors underlying nonconformity's success in the community will be considered, as will the extent to which the church was used in any way to exert a form of social control upon its congregation. The history of Zion Congregational Chapel (Figure 3) reveals the importance of the resident minister (Figure 4) in determining a church's success. Upon John Calvert's arrival at the chapel in 1857 as pastor, there was much disarray with internecine disputes in progress and a very low attendance. Calvert transformed the fortunes of the

Figure 3. Zion Congregational Church, Attercliffe. *Sheffield City Libraries, Local Studies Library*

chapel. According to the chapel's historian, P. Hopwood, within a year or two of Calvert's arrival, 'the almost entirely deserted old chapel began to put on a new appearance as large congregations at times overflowed into the aisles.'[14] Calvert's style was far removed from the aloofness which marked the characters of some establishment religious figures. He declined to adopt the title 'reverend' and was described as 'greatly beloved' and 'infinitely tender' by members of the congregation, whom he served for 38 years. 'Criticus', a journalist who wrote a series of descriptions of local places of worship for the *Sheffield Post* in 1873 and 1874 emphasised the empathy Calvert appeared to have with his congregation:

Figure 4. Rev. John Calvert (b. 1833), Minister of Zion Congregational Church, Attercli[ffe] 1857-1895. *Sheffield City Libraries, Loc[al] Studies Library*

> *There is nothing of the roaring lion about him. He does not deal in thunder and lightning. He is earnest and enthusiastic but it is in head and heart, not in his hands and feet. As a pastor Mr Calvert is earnest, diligent and successful. His congregation is widely scattered ... Many of his materials were rough and unpromising but I question if there is in this district a minister who has made his mark so deeply on the working population.* [15]

As 'Criticus' observed, Zion Congregational Chapel was very much a working-class place of worship. Rules for its membership were devised in church meetings. To be elected a member of the church, an individual's application had first to be approved by the pastor and then an interview was arranged with two existing members of the church. If candidates satisfied these church members then they were received into fellowship. Such a process enabled the strict church discipline to be maintained. Individuals' lapses from approved standards of behaviour were punished either through a suspension for a specified time period or through excommunication. Reasons for individuals' punishments were listed in the Zion Church records. Fornication and other forms of 'inconsistent behaviour' were invariably punished by excommunication. Behavioural lapses resulting from excessive drinking were also regularly punished, usually by means of a member's suspension.

Membership of Zion Congregational Chapel brought with it then strict regulations about behaviour as well as demanding a high degree of religious commitment: every member was expected to attend Sunday services, Monday evening prayer meetings, Wednesday night services and monthly Friday night church meetings. The rigorous standards expected of Zion's membership undoubtedly met with the approval of members of the middle classes concerned at the growth of the industrial East End of Sheffield, but the discipline expected of Zion's congregation was not imposed as a form of social control from above. It was very much a self-disciplinary device, designed, implemented and imposed upon Zion's largely working class congregation by the church's members themselves.

Attercliffe's Methodist Reform chapel, the township's third most populous place of worship in 1881, also involved the congregation heavily in its government.[16] 'Criticus' remarked that on his previous visit to Attercliffe's Methodist Reform Chapel, a 'forger at one of the works' was the preacher. On the occasion of his more recent visit, the preacher was a 'steel melter at Messrs Sanderson Brothers Ltd.' 'Criticus' reported that 'There was an excellent congregation consisting chiefly of working people, their wives and families.'[17]

The importance of the Sunday School has been the focus of much debate amongst historians interested in the concept of 'social control'. Historians such as E. P. Thompson have regarded such institutions as important agencies by which means middle-class sponsored ideals such as time-work discipline, and the 'moral rescue' of the poor could be implemented.[18] Evidence discovered relating to Attercliffe's Sunday Schools appears in part to support E. P. Thompson's thesis. Newspaper reports of Sunday School treats or annual gatherings invariably spoke of the educational and spiritual nature of the events, at which the involvement of members of the middle class was often prominent. For instance, the scholars of Attercliffe and Grimesthorpe church schools , totalling some 550, met for their annual gathering in June 1857 when, according to a contemporary newspaper report,

> *An excellent sermon was addressed to them by Rev. W. Ramsden-Smith, rector of Hulcott, Bucks. ... the children went from church to the school room where they were refreshed by an abundance of good plum cakes and tea, furnished by the benevolence of the ladies of the congregation ... After tea they were addressed and questioned by the Rev. J. Blackburn; and the day's proceedings concluded with the favourite and loyal anthem of 'God Save the Queen'.*[19]

Appeals to patriotism were a common feature of Sunday School gatherings. At the Whitsuntide meeting of the East End's Sunday schools, some 5000 children met in June 1867. As the *Sheffield Independent* noted, 'Three cheers were called for the Queen and the assembly responded with such fervour and heartiness as to make us fancy that the teachers gave lessons in loyalty ...'[20]

Nevertheless, though such appeals to loyalty undoubtedly met with the approval of the middle class readers of the *Sheffield Independent*, the vast majority of those involved with the running of such Sunday Schools in Attercliffe were themselves resident in the township and often, as in the case of the teachers at Zion Chapel, members of the working classes.[21] Sunday Schools offered some children the opportunity to learn to read and write, before the provision of compulsory education, and, quite contrarily to the social control function many have attributed to Sunday Schools, Kenneth Thompson has suggested 'the learning and organisational abilities developed in Sunday Schools could be used in working class radicalism.'[22] Evidence from Attercliffe supports this claim. The large working class congregation of Zion Chapel quite clearly was made aware of political situations through the teachings of the church: at a Zion Chapel Sunday School meeting of over 500 members in 1862, for example, according to the *Sheffield Independent* 'In the course of the evening a petition to the English Government praying that the American situation might be referred to arbitration was numerously signed.'[23]

Although throughout the period under study concern was continually expressed by various Attercliffe church leaders about the large number of non-church goers in the township, nevertheless the strength of fellowship particularly amongst the nonconformist chapels such as Zion Chapel and the Methodist Reform Chapel was especially impressive. What characterised much of the religious worship practised in Attercliffe was the high degree of working class involvement, ranging from teaching in Sunday Schools and preaching, to active participation in decision-making, such as the election of new members, clergy and the drafting of regulations. Of significance in the development of religion within the township of Attercliffe during the period was not the subtle implementation of middle-class determined forms of social control but, with the exception of the Roman Catholic church, built in 1867 with much financial assistance from the Duke of Norfolk,[24] the marked absence of middle class and aristocratic religious involvement. Unlike neighbouring Brightside, where John Brown financed the construction of All Saints Church[25], in Attercliffe the vast amount of religious building which took place was undertaken at the expense of the inhabitants.

Politics

Both in Attercliffe's religious and political activities, the larger steel manufacturers seemed to play a limited role within the settlement. No doubt, as 'Criticus' wryly observed, this had much to do with large manufacturers' predilection for residences on the west side of Sheffield. Writing of his experiences in Attercliffe, 'Criticus' noted:

> *When I was there before I could not help thinking how different was the place where people made money to the place where they spent it. At Attercliffe everything seems to speak of work ... This is the place where our merchant princes made the money with which they built those stately homes in fashionable Ranmoor, rich sounding Sharrow and lofty Broomhill.* [26]

Employers' involvement in the Attercliffe community tended to be left to the small and medium sized manufacturers, many of whom remained resident in the township despite its 'tall chimneys, black buildings, black faces and black smoke.'[27] The participation of such employers in the life of the community was most evident in the sphere of local politics. The saw manufacturer Samuel Jackson was for instance elected a councillor for the township in 1848.[28] The Vestry Minutes of the township also highlight the important role played in its development by resident manufacturers. Throughout the period names of manufacturers in the light trades and owners of small- and medium-sized steel works recur in the Vestry Minutes in capacities such as overseers of the poor, or as members of the Board for the Repair of the Highways. A battle with the Sheffield Canal Company over responsibility for the maintenance of the main Sheffield-Rotherham road through the district in 1845, for example, was spearheaded by a vestry-appointed committee comprising the Attercliffe manufacturers George Hill, William Makin, Samuel Jackson and Francis Huntsman.[29]

The extent of such manufacturers' influence in the local government of Attercliffe remained considerable throughout the period of study. However, the influence wielded through the machinery of local politics by these manufacturers was the subject of dissatisfaction amongst other members of the community. As one speaker at a vestry meeting held immediately before a local election in 1858 commented:

> *The business of selecting candidates has hitherto not been done by the people but by persons meeting in the snug at the 'Horse and Jockey' and was then immediately brought before the people to be confirmed. The working classes must have representatives of their own order whose interests were identical to theirs.* [30]

Throughout the period under study, the inhabitants of Attercliffe sought firstly to have their political voice heard and latterly pressed to have their political questions answered satisfactorily by potential representatives. The political independence of Attercliffe's inhabitants was manifested, with the extension of the franchise, both at local and national levels. The 1867 Attercliffe ward contest between John Moseley and Henry Wild, a leather merchant and the ultimate victor, was described in the *Sheffield Independent*, where the degree of interest in the township was emphasised:

> *upwards of 1100 burgesses voted ... In fact it is a long time since there was such an exciting day at Attercliffe, but it is much to the credit of the inhabitants that beyond a little good humoured hustling in front of the polling place there was up to 4 o'clock no disorderly conduct on either side which could be considered a breach of the peace. Cabs, spring carts and other conveyances, each bearing a conspicuous label denoting the candidate for which it had been engaged, were flying about in all directions.* [31]

In his survey of nineteenth-century Blackburn, Patrick Joyce revealed through an inspection of the town's poll books the close coincidence between the voting preferences of employers and their employees. He also stressed the importance of the brewers' influence in political decision-making in working-class districts.[32] The influence of the brewers was evident in the 1874 national election campaign in Attercliffe. Reporting upon Attercliffe on polling day the *Sheffield Post* noted that 'Here almost every public house had Roebuck placards.'[33] Two candidates standing against the reactionary Roebuck were the more progressive liberal candidates, Mundella and Chamberlain. While Roebuck was evidently the favourite of the brewers, in Attercliffe the strong nonconformist interest stood behind Mundella and Chamberlain, the latter of whom 'addressed a crowded meeting of his supporters in the Zion School Room, Attercliffe,'[34] where his speech 'was very able and enthusiastically received. A resolution adopting Messrs Mundella and Chamberlain as liberal candidates was unanimously passed.'

Although Chamberlain was narrowly defeated, the election of Mundella alongside Roebuck suggests that the large East End steel employers' political influence over their workforce was by no means as strong as the owners of Blackburn's cotton mills.[35] Mundella had been a director of John Brown and Company, but, as he explained to a meeting in Attercliffe, he had retired because

> *he was an advocate of arbitration between master and workmen and when one party would not arbitrate he considered that party wrong and he could not honestly sit on a board that refused to arbitrate.* [36]

That such a champion of steel workers won the popularity of Attercliffe's workers was by no means surprising, but that overt support for such a candidate was shown at public meetings within the township was a little more so, and suggests that the employers' political influence over their workforces in the township was indeed slight.

Leisure

An area in which some social commentators of later nineteenth-century Britain have argued the bourgeoisie was successful in influencing working-class lives by imposing middle class values was the sphere of leisure. The slogan 'rational recreation' was much employed by members of the middle class. As Peter Bailey has observed, by offering superior counter-attractions to popular recreations, the reformers sought to introduce the working class 'to the satisfaction of mental recreation, thus immunising them against the contagion of the pub and the publican, and the animal repression of sensuality.'[37]

From reports in the *Sheffield Independent* it seems that the inhabitants of Attercliffe were subjected by employers to various types of rational recreation. As Bailey has intimated, the employers' motives in so doing were rarely altruistic but were prompted by attempts to instil a degree of discipline in the workplace. Among the principal proponents of rational recreation was the large firm of Sandersons which, in 1858, to some of its workers, 'furnished tickets for a journey to Manchester and admission to the Arts Treasurers' Exhibition with money for refreshments whilst there.' The *Sheffield Independent's* report of the trip concluded that

> *such consideration is not without its effect on the workmen whose temperate habits, consequent reliability and skill in workmanship will bear comparison with any in the trade.* [38]

Encouragement of rational recreation amongst its workers also led Sandersons to hold an annual horticultural show for its employees.[39] The encouragement of such rational recreation necessitated a degree of prosperity amongst the workforce since evidently to enter such a contest the employees needed access not only to leisure time to tend their entries but also ground - either a back garden or an allotment - upon which to grow them.

A vehicle for proselytisation which met at least with the tacit approval of many employers in the drive for rational recreation was the temperance movement. According to the *Sheffield Independent*, the fourth annual report of the Sheffield Temperance Society, in 1867, referred to

> *the gratifying success which had attended the efforts of Mrs Ward and Mr Taylor, the two agents of the society who were promulgating its principles by house to house visitations in some of the poorer districts. Their labours had resulted in the reclamation of a large number of drunkards, many of whom had joined Christian churches. Mrs Ward had succeeded in obtaining 380 pledges and Mr Taylor who had done much good by visiting workmen while at their employment had induced 350 persons to sign the pledge.*[40]

The link between temperance and religion was evident at Attercliffe where, for instance, a successful temperance society was attached to Zion Chapel. At the society's second annual soirée in 1862, it was reported that 200 members were present, of whom 100 were members of Zion Chapel. The chapel's minister, John Calvert, was, however, rather dubious about the influence the temperance movement's champions had upon the working classes. The *Sheffield Independent* reported Calvert's speech to the annual meeting of the Sheffield Temperance Society in 1867 where he noted that:

> *There was much prejudice against the temperance movement. But he was sorry to say that for much of this prejudice temperance men themselves were to blame for their overbearing manner and want of sympathy towards their opponents with which they advocated their principles at public meetings, repelling instead of conciliating others who were disposed to throw their influence on their side.*[41]

In such circumstances reports of poor attendance at temperance society-organised events for the non-converted members of the working classes were not surprising. One such poorly attended temperance gala was held at the Botanical Gardens on Monday 16 September 1867. The *Sheffield Independent* reported that there was not 'anything like a good attendance.'[42]

The success or otherwise of the temperance movement in Attercliffe is perhaps best gauged by examining the number of public houses and beerhouses in the township over the period under study. According to *White's General Directory* of 1841, 22 retail outlets existed in the township for the sale of beer, rising to 39 in 1865[43] and 69 in 1883.[44] Although this three-fold increase appears dramatic, the population of the township rose over the same period at more than twice this rate, increasing from 4,156 in 1841 to 26,965 in 1881.[45] Nevertheless, the influence of the public house and beerhouse in the later part of the period remained the focus of much middle class and respectable working class concern, and the listings in the directories may well have masked an increase in the size of beerselling outlets or underestimated their number.

Much of the concern attached to the public house by 'respectable' members of the community was not about the problem of drink *per se*, but related to the associated culture of the pub. The warmth and comfort of the pub, as many commentators have observed, contrasted sharply with the living conditions of many working men and so regularly attracted them from their homes. The culture of the pub, it has been claimed, was based upon gambling and violent recreations such as pigeon shooting and rabbit coursing, much to the dismay of the advocates of rational recreation. Reports of illicit gambling in Attercliffe pubs[46] and an Attercliffe publican's sponsorship of pigeon shooting with accompanying betting amongst spectators[47] formed part of the background against which John Calvert spoke to a meeting of Sheffield ministers on the subject of popular recreation in 1873. According to a report in the *Sheffield Post*, Calvert remarked that

> *a craving for amusements and a general rush after them had become a prominent feature of our times ...Handicapping and horse racing were the visible manifestations of a ramification of poisonous influence and pernicious arrangement constantly at work in thousands of workshops and homes.*

Beneath the report of Calvert's speech, the *Sheffield Post* noted that

> *an interesting discussion followed ... it was agreed that it is not the work of the Church to create or provide amusement any more than business, but that it rests upon her to enforce the principles which should regulate both...*[48]

The rational recreation evident within Attercliffe at the time of this meeting of Sheffield ministers reflected the clergymen's general views. In the main, the activities which characterised this rational recreation, though often run under the auspices of Attercliffe's church and chapels, were the exclusive domain of the township's workers and their families. Little evidence exists suggesting the successful direct imposition of rational recreation from above and from outside the township.

Reports of societies meeting in Attercliffe were contained in local newspapers, particularly from the 1860s onwards when, as Calvert had identified, many workers were beginning to enjoy more leisure time. Attercliffe's Christ Church football team caught the attention of newspaper reporters in 1871 when the 'friendly spirit' of the team's games was invariably highlighted.[49] Gardening was an activity popular with working class men who had access to cultivable land. Attercliffe winners in the Sheffield Floral and Horticultural Society shows, together with Sanderson Brothers' successful horticultural shows for its employees, testified to the hobby's popularity.[50]

Significantly, little evidence could be found regarding the existence in Attercliffe of societies formed specifically for women. It seems they were expected to remain in the home whilst their husbands pursued their recreational activities elsewhere. Where women's societies did exist they appeared to function as a reinforcement of the belief that the married women's role was to service the family: Attercliffe Methodist New Connexion's 'Ladies' Sewing Meeting' group typified such societies.[51]

One of the most active centres of rational recreation and self help in Attercliffe was Zion Chapel. Members of this church tirelessly raised money for a number of societies for their collective spiritual and educational improvement: a school library with 490 'good and useful books' was established and a 'magazine society and literacy mission' was instituted, the aim of which was 'to supply the area with wholesome reading.'[52] The inculcation of the doctrine of self help was revealed by the founding of a Provident Society formed by church members in 1864, into which members paid three halfpence weekly and received two and sixpence a week when sick. Three years later, a Penny Savings Bank was established by church members which, in 1873, boasted 800 accounts.[53] Similar institutions such as sick and burial clubs were instituted in many firms, often by the employees themselves.[54]

Summary and conclusions

It seems, then, that the degree of social control imposed upon Attercliffe's largely working class population by members of the middle classes was by no means substantial. Influence over employees outside the workplace was not wielded to a great extent by employers through the ownership of residential property, nor, it seems, from the 1874 election campaign in Attercliffe, did they exert considerable political influence over workers eligible to vote.

The larger employers in the township, by moving outside the township to pleasant residences on the western side of the city, did not involve themselves directly in the life of the township in which many of their employees lived and worked. The smaller employers however, of whom there were a large number in Attercliffe, were active in the running of the community, particularly and most conspicuously, through their participation in local government, either on the borough council or through the holding of such offices as overseer of the poor, or by being a member of the influential highways committee.

However, the extent to which the smaller employers and other resident members of the middle class in the community enjoyed influence over the working class members of the township must not be overemphasised. John Calvert, for example, stressed the unprofitable effect overbearing evangelists had upon working class people in the fight against intemperance. The existence of at least 69 beer retail outlets in the community in 1883 revealed how far temperance campaigners still had to travel if they were to succeed in their mission to rid Attercliffe of drink.

The presence in the township of a large group of respectable working class citizens by the end of the period under study, it seems from the evidence available, was not the consequence of some form of social control imposed from above by morally superior members of the middle class. Respectability was a notion with which many members of Attercliffe's community were familiar. 'Respectable' members of the township's working class initiated the foundation of burial and sick clubs both in their churches and places of employment. They participated prominently in the running of the township's burgeoning nonconformist chapels, choosing ministers and drafting strict codes of conduct for themselves and fellow members, with still sterner punishments for transgressors.

Although respectability and rational recreation had many champions in Attercliffe, nevertheless some members of the township still adhered to the worship of Saint Monday and participated in a drink-orientated culture. As the American consul in Sheffield remarked, often 'the husband, knowing that there is no comfort for him at home resorts to the nearest dram shop for refreshment.'[55] Yet even in some public houses attempts were made to uphold respectability. William Hague, a churchman and former overseer of the poor and a member of Attercliffe's Board of Guardians, on his 85th birthday reflected upon the respectable nature of two public houses in Attercliffe, the *Blue Bell* and the *Queen's Head* (Figure 5). Hague remembered that the landlord of the *Queen's Head*, who died in 1879

> *was very particular in the regulation of his customers and the conduct of his house and would not have a drunken man on the premises. If a man was known to use bad words ... he would be fined for the first offence, 3d, for the second offence, 6d, and if he were fined three times he was expelled.*[56]

Evidently the commentator, 'Vulcan', writing in the *Sheffield*

Figure 5. The Queen's Head, Attercliffe. *Sheffield Newspapers*

Independent was right to observe of the working classes that 'there is not that unanimity amongst them which one might be led to expect from a number of men similarly circumstanced.'[57]

Overall, the evidence collected about Attercliffe strongly reinforces F. M. L. Thompson's attack upon the notion of social control. It was, Thompson asserted,

> *unwarrantably condescending to the humble and anonymous masses to suppose that they were incapable of cultural development except as a result of instruction or coercion from outside ... There is plenty of evidence that the respectable working classes wished to be respectable, not because some middle class pundit told them to be so, but because they liked it and disapproved of shiftless and sluttish ways ...* [58]

The evidence examined regarding Attercliffe suggests not only that the degree of middle class control in the community was minimal but also powerfully illustrates the important influence the township's largely working class population had upon the development of the social and cultural life of the community.

Notes and References

1. F. M. L. Thompson, 'Social Control in Victorian Britain', *Economic History Review*, 34, 1981, p. 190.
2. Attercliffe Rate Book, 1861-2. Francis Huntsman's steel works had a rateable value of £206 10s. William Jessop's works, plus seventeen houses, was valued at £1066.
3. Attercliffe Rate Book, 1881-2.
4. P. J. Aspinall, 'The Internal Structure of the Housebuilding Industry in Nineteenth Century Cities', in J. Johnson and C. Pooley, eds, *The Structure of Nineteenth Century Cities*, New York, 1982.
5. Sheffield Town Council Minutes, 1865-9.
6. *Sheffield Independent*, 9 January 1858.
7. *Sheffield Independent*, 3 May 1862.

8. *Sheffield Independent,* 2 October 1858.
9. J. Earnshaw, *Address to the Inhabitants of Attercliffe,* in Local Pamphlets, Vol. 14, Sheffield Local History Library.
10. *Sheffield Independent,* 10 May 1867.
11. E. R. Wickham, *Church and People in an Industrial City,* London, 1957; 1851 religious census figures, p. 109; 1881 religious census figures, p. 148.
12. *Sheffield Independent,* 29 November 1881
13. Wickham, *Church and People,* p. 108.
14. P. Hopwood, *The Gates of Zion,* Sheffield, 1948, p. 72.
15. *Sheffield Post,* 7 June 1873.
16. Hopwood, *The Gates of Zion,* p. 89. The 1881 religious census figures for Attercliffe were given. Zion Congregational Chapel had 380 worshippers in the morning and 504 in the evening; the Parish Church had 303 and 479; and the Methodist Reform Chapel had 241 and 236.
17. *Sheffield Post,* 3 January 1874.
18. E.P. Thompson, *The Making of the English Working Class,* London, 1963, pp. 397 and 414.
19. *Sheffield Independent,* 14 June 1851.
20. *Sheffield Independent,* 11 June 1867.
21. Hopwood, *The Gates of Zion,* p. 97.
22. K. Thompson, 'Religion, Class and Control', in R. Bocock and K. Thompson, (eds), *Religion and Ideology,* Manchester, 1985, p. 143.
23. *Sheffield Independent,* 2 January 1862.
24. *Sheffield Independent,* 4 December 1867.
25. *Sheffield Independent,* 6 February 1869.
26. *Sheffield Post,* 3 January 1874.
27. *Sheffield Post,* 3 January 1874.
28. *Sheffield Independent,* 4 November 1848.
29. Christ Church, Attercliffe, Vestry Minutes, 27 February 1845.
30. *Sheffield Independent,* 23 October 1858.
31. *Sheffield Independent,* 2 November 1867.
32. P. Joyce, *Work, Society and Politics,* Brighton, 1980. See especially ch. 6, pp. 201-39.
33. *Sheffield Post,* 7 February 1874.
34. *Sheffield Post,* 31 January 1874.
35. *Sheffield Post,* 8 February 1874. Roebuck polled 14,193 votes; Mundella gained 12,858; and Chamberlain attained third position with 11,053 votes.
36. *Sheffield Post,* 7 February 1874.
37. Peter Bailey, *Leisure and Class in Victorian England,* London, 1978, p. 177.
38. *Sheffield Independent,* 21 January 1858.
39. *Sheffield Independent,* 20 September 1862.
40. *Sheffield Independent,* 1 May 1867.
41. *Sheffield Independent,* 1 May 1867.
42. *Sheffield Independent,* 17 September 1867.
43. Kelly's Post Office Directory, 1865.
44. White's General Directory, 1883.
45. *Victoria County History of Yorkshire, Volume Three,* London, 1913, pp. 544-5.
46. *Sheffield Independent,* 31 May 1873.
47. *Sheffield Independent,* 2 January 1873.
48. *Sheffield Post,* 19 April 1873.
49. *Sheffield Independent,* 17 January 1871.
50. *Sheffield Independent,* 1 September 1858.
51. *Sheffield Independent,* 30 December 1867.
52. Hopwood, *The Gates of Zion,* p. 100.
53. Hopwood, *The Gates of Zion,* p. 99.
54. Parliamentary Papers, *Trade and Industry Depression,* 1, Vol. XXI, 1886, p. 351.
55. Edward Young, *Labor in Europe and America,* Philadelphia, 1875, p. 403.
56. *Sheffield Independent,* 22 May 1909.
57. *Sheffield Independent,* 26 June 1858.
58. F. M. L. Thompson, 'Social Control', p. 196.

Acknowledgements

I would like to record my thanks to Professor David Hey, for his comments on an earlier draft of this article, and to the staff of Sheffield Archives and Sheffield Local Studies Library.

10. An Illustrated History of Izal

by Joan Jones

Legend has it that the germicidal 'magic' of coal tar, which dripped from the Thorncliffe coke ovens, was first noticed when the cuts and sores on the hands and arms of the coke oven workers miraculously healed.

ON THE 27 FEBRUARY 1893, Mr T. C. Newton, Chairman of Newton Chambers & Co Ltd, announced to the shareholders, 'As to the Oil Works at Chapeltown, the Company has a trade secret which we believe will be ultimately valuable.'[1] The trade secret was Izal. At the next annual meeting he told the shareholders, 'In the future Izal will be one of the most profitable things the Company will deal in.'[2] His prophecy came true. Within a year or two of its discovery Izal was receiving remarkable tributes to its value as a non-poisonous disinfectant and antiseptic liquid. This, allied to a very rigorous and imaginative promotion and marketing strategy, kept Izal at the forefront of the sales of household, institutional and industrial disinfectants for the next 70 years.

The firm of Newton Chambers was established in 1793 at Thorncliffe, near Sheffield and by the end of the nineteenth century was a complex industrial enterprise employing several thousand workpeople (Figure 1). The founders were George Newton and Thomas Chambers, then partners in the Phoenix foundry in Sheffield, and Henry Longden. In December 1793 they signed a 21 year lease from Earl Fitzwilliam of Wentworth, for land at Thorncliffe. The purpose of the lease was to build an ironworks and to mine coal and ironstone. In fact they mined ironstone until the 1880s and coal until nationalisation in 1947. Pig iron was made at Thorncliffe until 1942. In the nineteenth century the range of products was staggering:

Figure 1. Newton Chambers letterhead of 1897 showing the firm's coal mining, coke-making, iron manufacturing and chemical interests. *Tony Ellis*

anvils, bedsteads, brewing pans, chimney pieces, clothes posts, footscrapers, guttering, irons, kitchen boilers, spittoons, spouts, wheels, etc. From 1815 the Company was involved in heavy castings such as beams, forge hammers, rails for waggon roads and furnace doors. About this time they also began to manufacture gas lighting plant and later gasworks plant. In 1860 the firm acquired Chapel Furnace, later the site of the Izal Factory. This factory produced the famous Thorncliffe Patent Cooking Range and a wide selection of piping, grates, palisading, stable fittings and light castings for the hardware trade. In the last two years of the First World War, three bays of the light casting shop at Thorncliffe were converted into a munitions factory and over two million shell cases were manufactured. After the War, as a contribution to the 'Homes for Heroes' drive and, in the face of a brick shortage, the firm made cast iron houses. In the 1930s Newton Chambers became a major manufacturer of excavators and, during the Second World War, of Churchill tanks. Their engineering enterprises were important to the end and the firm is well remembered for them. However, experiments into the distillation of coal, from 1883, also brought world-wide fame.[3]

Discovery, development and launch

In 1881 Newton Chambers & Co was established as a limited liability company. The Newton and Chambers families still retained virtual control together with Mr George Dawson (who married Thomas Chambers' great grand-daughter) and Dr Edwin Drew (who had married George Newton's grand-daughter). George Dawson set up a plant at the firm's Rockingham Colliery in order to extract benzol and sulphate of ammonia from coal. Mr Arthur Marshall Chambers and Dr Edwin Drew were interested in the other branch of coal chemistry, the production and refinement of tar acids, particularly the carbolic range.

These two directors were influential in the appointment, in 1885, of an exceptionally talented analytical chemist called Jason Hall Worrall (Figure 2). He proved the high calorific value of coal gas and it was subsequently used instead of coal for firing the works' boilers. He then experimented with the liquid product and the oil. At an early stage paraffin wax was extracted from the oil and was later successfully marketed. The oxidised portion of the oil was repeatedly distilled until a germicidal oil was produced. This oil was insoluble in water and the next stage was to mix it with an emul-

Figure 2. Jason Hall Worrall.
Thorncliffe News

sifying agent so that it disseminated and dispersed perfectly through any fluid (Figure 3). He then conducted experiments to verify its effectiveness against sheep scab (many of the experiments taking place at Beauchief Abbey Farm in Sheffield) and it was marketed as a sheep dip under the name 'Noxona'. It was also exported to New Zealand under the name 'Acaricide'. The trade name 'Izal' was registered in 1893, the germicidal oil previously being marketed as the 'Thorncliffe Patent Disinfectant'. It is sometimes said that the name Izal is an anagram of Liza, J. H. Worrall's favourite sister, but there is no direct evidence to support this belief.[4] It is more probable that the name Izal was invented by the first advertising agent to be employed, T. B. Browne. It was chosen because it was short, easily remembered and lent itself to effective typography and artistic treatment.

At this time the product left the works in 40 gallon casks and was packed in green bottles in half pint, pint and quart sizes by Newholmes, manufacturing chemists in Sheffield. H. E. Elliott, writing for the *Thorncliffe News*, the Company newspaper, in the 1940s, interviewed John Austen, the managing director of Newholmes, who recalled obtaining the pale green bottles from Rotherham. He said that the bottles were capped with parchment and tied with thin twine before dispatch to customers.

The first advertisement for Izal appeared in 1893 - a whole page in *The Times* - on Monday 21 August. The firm agreed to spend £5,500 between May and September 1893, on advertising Izal and £500 on advertising Noxona.[5] Other full page advertisements appeared such as the one shown in Figure 4 from the *Illustrated London News*.

The seal of approval for Izal was provided by reports from distinguished members of the medical profession. On the 1 July 1893, *The Lancet* published a long report of tests carried out by Dr Bruce Clarke, assistant surgeon at St Bartholomew's Hospital, London. He used Izal for:

the soaking of sponges, the impregnation of dressings, the steeping of ligatures and sutures, and also for the disinfection of his hands; in all these respects the results were as satisfactory as possible.[6]

Figure 3. This photograph, entitled 'The pyrotechnic dispersal of Izal in water', was taken a split second after one drop had been poured into a beaker of water. It was taken by Howard H. Briddon and was accepted for the International Photographic Exhibition in 1949.

The *British Medical Journal* of 17 February 1894, reported on experiments carried out by Professor E. Klein, the leading bacteriologist of the day. Klein confirmed 'Izal's germicidal properties and its relative freedom from toxicity and corrosive action.' The results of the experiments were summed up as follows:

> *Exposure for five minutes to Izal in the strength of one in 200 completely destroys the vitality of the microbes of diphtheria, typhoid fever, fowl cholera, swine fever, glanders, cholera of suppuration, of erysipelas, of scarlatina, and other non-sporing pathogenic and non pathogenic species.*[7]

In the same year, in *Vratch*, the leading medical journal of Russia at that time, Dr N. A. Blagoveshtchensky, of Moscow, recorded his experiments with Izal. His reports confirmed those of Professor Klein as to its antiseptic and disinfecting properties. Many others including Dr W. Robertson, surgeon to the Ear and Throat Hospital, Newcastle-upon-Tyne, Mr Nathan Smith, veterinary surgeon from Grantham, Sheridan Delepine, Professor of Pathology at Owen's College, Manchester and even 'an eminent Romanian surgeon from Bucharest' spoke highly of Izal's remarkable powers.[8]

By 1895 Izal was not just available as a disinfectant emulsion but also in a number of preparations - Izal toilet soap, Izal medical soap, Izal soft soap, Izal soap in almond scented tablets, Izal ointment, Izal tooth powder, Izal lozenges, Izal embrocation, Izal disinfecting powder and sawdust. Prices, however, were far beyond the reach of the ordinary worker - a 4oz bottle of Izal emulsion cost 1s 6d. It was, of course, highly concentrated - one or two tablespoons were recommended for a twenty gallon bath! Izal emulsion was for domestic and personal use as well as for medical and surgical use. In the opinion of its manufacturers Izal was:

Figure 4. Izal advertisement from the *Illustrated London News*, 16 June 1894.

an excellent soap for ordinary toilet purposes. It is fragrant and refreshing, and the habitual use of it will keep the skin not only clean but healthy, smooth, and supple. The use of Izal soap is a protection against the bites of insects; it soothes itching of the skin, 'prickly heat', 'sunburn', 'heat bumps', etc. Izal soap does not irritate the tenderest skin, and its use may be recommended in all cases of redness, blotchiness, or scaliness of the face or other parts. It subdues eruptions, and removes pimples. The secret of a fine complexion is a healthy skin; this is ensured by the use of Izal soap. Price, 1s 6d per box.[9]

In 1898 the firm signed a contract with Dr Thresh for the manufacture and use of his ingenious machine for disinfection with Izal. These machines can be seen in Figure 5. They were mobile steam boilers in which clothing could be sterilised by boiling in an Izal solution. The high cost of Izal meant that Newton Chambers needed massive advertising campaigns. Numerous booklets and leaflets were printed and distributed including a small 80-page book called *Izal: Its Nature and Properties* which detailed the tests carried out by Clarke and Klein as well as testimonials from other doctors, veterinary surgeons, medical officers, etc. Leaflets appeared on the use of Izal - for bark diseases *(Bark Diseases of Hevea Brasiliensis)*, with dogs *(Dogs: Their Health and Hygiene)* and with cows *(In the Dairy)*. A leaflet entitled *The Izal Rules of Health* by Dr Andrew Wilson advocated that Izal should be used for:

cholera, typhoid fever, chicken pox, whooping cough ... as a cure for worms ... consumption ... malaria, perspiring feet, baldness (a solution of Izal applied night and morning to the bare patches has frequently the effect of causing a fresh growth of hair) ... use in the stable, kennel,

Figure 5. Thresh Disinfectors *c.* 1900.

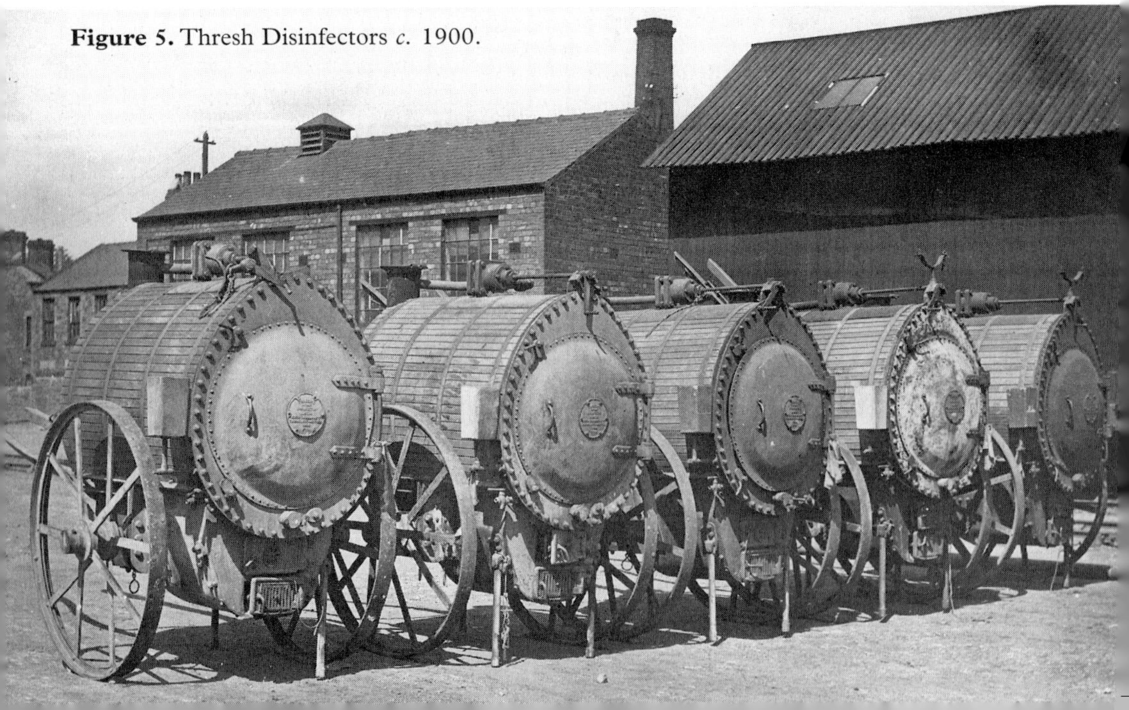

poultry yard and aviary.[10]

In June 1894 the firm decided to paint the word 'Izal' on 150 new railway waggons. During 1895 samples of Izal were delivered to homes in Southport and Newcastle-upon-Tyne from horse-drawn vans. The samples consisted of a gift box with a 4oz bottle of Izal emulsion, a tin of Izal powder and a tablet of soap. They targeted 'houses of the £40 class and over.'[11]

In 1896 Newton Chambers appointed Joseph Godber as commercial manager of the Chemical Works at Thorncliffe with special responsibility for the sale of Izal and its companion product, Noxona. He began a world-wide campaign to get Izal noticed and adopted by government departments and medical authorities 'with missionary fervour'.[12] He concentrated on raising it in the public esteem as an antiseptic of astonishing strength and versatility. He exerted himself especially to get the medical profession and sanitary authorities throughout the country to conduct more stringent tests of germicidal power, knowing that the sterner the test the more likely Izal was to shine in competition with other disinfectants of the day. He was a perfect salesman for this purpose. No-one could fail to be impressed by his zeal, his earnestness, the thoroughness of his study of the entire field of disinfection, and the conviction his sincerity carried. At the same time he dealt with manufacturing problems, difficulties of supply, both of raw materials and finished products, severe competition, technical problems of bottling and packing, and within a few years with overwhelming demand from the military authorities for use in South Africa. At one stage in the Boer War he was confronted by the War Office with a plain demand for either his full output or his total plant.[13] Toilet paper, as a means of advertising Izal, was being issued to Manchester Corporation at this time and Figure 6 was drawn by Walter Newton Drew (son of Dr Edwin Drew) for toilet paper being sent out to South Africa.

Before the Boer War was over, Joseph Godber went out to South Africa and opened agencies in Cape Town, Port Elizabeth, Kimberley, Johannesburg and Pretoria. He also opened agencies in West Africa and Egypt shortly afterwards. He toured Canada in 1902 and India in 1904. He opened agencies in Bombay, Calcutta, Madras and Rangoon

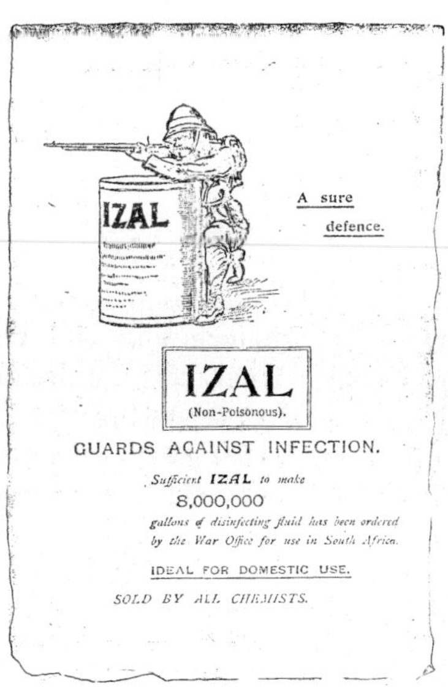

Figure 6. A piece of toilet paper designed to advertise Izal during the Boer War.

before going on to Malaya and the Far East. He also made a trip to the United States of America. Under his supervision the bottling and packing of Izal was undertaken at Thorncliffe and sales received a great boost. He was succeeded in 1922 by Harold West.

Expanding product range and market penetration

Jason Hall Worrall retired from Thorncliffe in 1910 after 25 years of research and experiment. His successor was Meredith Wynter Blyth who, at one time, had worked with Professor Klein at St Bartholomew's Hospital as consulting chemist and bacteriologist. He remained at Thorncliffe until his death in 1931, having it is said, 'carried Izal and Izal products as far as the laboratory could take them.'[14]

During the late Victorian period, public authorities were becoming very health conscious and new public conveniences were being built with great zeal. It became the practice of Newton Chambers to give away free toilet paper to authorities who placed large orders for Izal Germicide for disinfecting lavatories. The paper was strong tissue, four inches square, in cut leaf form with a hole in the top right hand corner for ease of hanging on a nail. It was printed with slogans advertising Izal, which was not the only disinfectant around. Newton Chambers placed annual orders with John Miller & Co Ltd, Glasgow, for ten million 'pieces'. Soon other authorities began to participate in the scheme and a small charge for the paper was then made.

After the First World War, there was a drive to improve health and housing standards. New legislation was introduced which made it compulsory for all new houses to be provided with water closets. This created a big demand for toilet paper and in 1922 a decision was taken to sell Izal toilet paper and the cheap supplies to local authorities were dropped. Packets of 500 sheets were sold at 4s 6d per dozen and rolls at 6s per dozen. These early sheets and rolls do not appear to have been treated with Izal. However, in February, 1928, it was stated that 'Izal is incorporated in this paper making it the most antiseptic toilet paper available'. The sheet size was now seven inches by five inches and the printing was done in green. There were six differently designed sheets and each featured two 'Health Rules' - all, of course, recommending the use of Izal.

When Harold West took over as commercial manager of Newton Chambers' disinfectant and tar distillation business in 1922, he had already been abroad for the company on two occasions - to the Far East and to South Africa - 'revising, confirming, extending, or adjusting the pioneering arrangements of Joseph Godber.[15] Harold

West was a 'natural salesman with an astonishing flair for presenting and publicising his wares. He had the 'selling touch' and ... Newton Chambers felt the benefit'.[16]

By the 1930s the range of Izal products had grown. In addition to those mentioned earlier there were now Izal perles (for internal use) and Izal lint, wool and gauze - the last three impregnated with one per cent Izal germicide. There was also development in the wood preservation and stain field, called Noxo. This product was for protection against noxious insects, moulds and bacteria and was recommended as being specially valuable in the treatment of hen houses, cattle sheds and pig pens. About 1932 a variation of Izal germicide, was introduced for soil sterilisation under the name Sterizal. This was sold as a liquid and a powder. Another product at this time was Newton Chambers' tip dressing for use on local authority waste tips.

In the mid-1930s the firm entered the insecticide field with Zaldecide, used in slum clearance operations. An interesting paper survives from September 1936 on which an Izal sales representative made notes following a visit to Eton College. He was seen by a Mr Fisher, who he remarked was 'aged and difficult to talk to'. Mr Fisher was very concerned about 'the boys' rooms in the old part' being 'infested with bugs'. The representative showed him Zaldecide but Mr Fisher was concerned that 'the smell would be sure to create suspicion'. The representative noted that 'utmost secrecy is essential as they are scared of anyone knowing there are bugs at Eton'. Mr Fisher confided that:

> *the present method is to get the room vacant somehow and clean it thoroughly even behind the panelling, but they have difficulty to get the rooms vacated. They have even pretended Scarlet Fever etc.*

He went on to say that:

> *Viscount Lascelles' room was infested and as Princess Mary chose his room for its view of the Castle and River they dare not ask him to vacate it, so they took a slate off the roof, so the rain poured in, and they suggested three days vacation whilst it was repaired and the room thoroughly dried!'*[17]

Mr Fisher wanted a thorough disinfection with Zaldecide next vacation and temporary measures too. I wonder if Zaldecide did the trick!

In 1936 the first part of the new Izal factory was completed, situated on Station Road, Chapeltown, on the site of the former Chapel Furnace. Izal medicated rolls and interleaved packets began to be produced. The range of products now included Izal mints, Izal shaving cream, Izal dog shampoo, Newcol powder and disinfectant, Izal floral essence for spraying cinemas (no more bug huts!) and Izal paper handkerchiefs (Figure 7). In the mid-1930s a decision was made to launch another disinfectant, less expensive than Izal emulsion, which would meet the needs of the working class. The new product was a black sanitary liquid called San Izal.

Again, every opportunity was seized to promote sales. A book was published in the early 1930s called *What to do if it's catching* (Figure 8). It cost a shilling and was bought by thousands of mothers who, before protective vaccinations, had the problem of measles and whooping cough to deal with. A less conventional way of promoting Izal was employed in 1924 when W. Heath Robinson, the cartoonist, was invited to the works and commissioned to produce a series of illustrations purporting to depict the Izal process. These drawings formed the basis of a 16-page booklet, *Thorncliffe Visited.* They also featured on rolls of medicated toilet paper. He noted the occasion as follows:

Figure 7. The Izal Medicated Handkerchief. *Sheffield Archives TR 444*

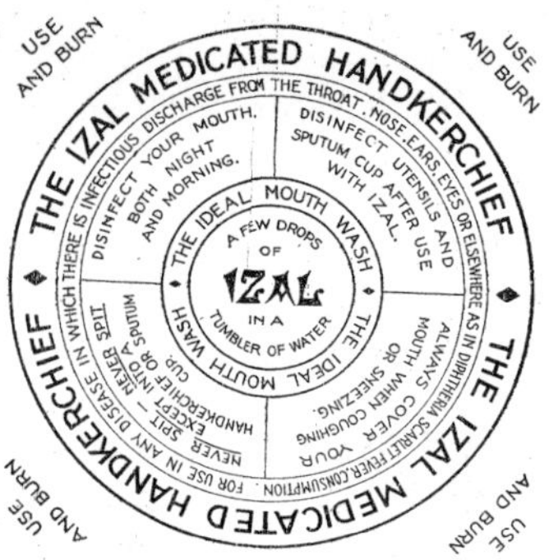

TAKE THESE PRECAUTIONS DAILY YOURSELF AND SEE THAT YOUR FAMILY DO THE SAME—GENERAL HEALTH WILL BENEFIT.

WASH HANDS WITH IZAL SOLUTION—two teaspoonfuls to a basin of water—to sterilise the skin and kill germs after touching anything suspected of bearing illness germs or anything an illness carrier or sick person has used. This precaution removes the most common cause of the spread of minor ailments. Make your family observe this rule and do it yourself too, especially after working or travelling or shopping.

BRUSH TEETH WITH IZAL SOLUTION. Three drops to a tumbler. Helps to keep gums firm and healthy. Soak the brush well before use in this solution. The toothbrush is exposed to germs and all kinds of infection when not in use, so sterilise your brush before putting it in your mouth.

CLEANSE WOUNDS WITH IZAL. Bathe wounds and abrasions with warm Izal solution — 3 drops of Izal to a tumbler of quite warm water to which a large pinch of salt has been added.

GARGLE WITH IZAL. A clean throat is a joy. Keep yours healthy by gargling night and morning with three drops of Izal in a tumbler of water to which a large pinch of salt has been added.

I visited the works of Messrs Newton Chambers & Co Ltd at Thorncliffe near Sheffield. I studied their coke ovens and the methods whereby the valuable by-products are extracted from coal. A ton of coal could be seen taken from the mine at one end of the process, and at the other, a tube of shaving cream or bottle of mouthwash. It was miraculous. I have often thought of suggesting a scheme to them for reversing the process and reconverting the by-products back into coal again, in case of over production.[18]

One of his illustrations can be seen in Figure 9.

In 1932 the Green Cross Trade Mark was registered and used - initially on the toilet roll wrapper. Two years later the words

Figure 8. A page from the book, *What to do if it's catching*, outlining how Izal can protect a family from disease.

'Medicated with Izal Germicide' appeared for the first time.

In addition to publications there was the great Nursery Rhyme offer on the Izal medicated toilet rolls where members of the public were invited to send in rhymes and prizes were won. From 1936 until the outbreak of war, the sheets of toilet paper were printed with potted nursery rhymes such as:

Mary had a little lamb,
It's fleece was full of germs,
She put it in an Izal bath,
And now it's full of perms.

Jack and Jill climbed up the hill -
Today we call it hiking,
An Izal bath as an aftermath
Was greatly to their liking.

Pussycat, Pussycat, where have you been?
I've been to London to see the queen,
What did she say to you when you got there?
She said, 'I use Izal everywhere'.

Humpty Dumpty sat on a wall;
Humpty Dumpty had a great fall,
All the Queen's nurses used Izal, and then
Soon had poor Humpty quite better again.

In addition to printing rhymes on the rolls, small slips were inserted in the rolls with illustrated nursery rhymes on them and children were

Figure 9. One of W. Heath Robinson's illustrations from *Thorncliffe Visited.*

IZAL IN MALARIAL SWAMPS.

Figure 10. Advertisement which appeared in the *Rotherham Advertiser*, 4 November 1939.

encouraged to collect a full set which could be sent to Thorncliffe and exchanged for a book called *Rhyme Time*. The scheme was so popular that a special department was set up and a second book was produced called *More Rhyme Time*. During the war the scheme was wound up due to a paper shortage.

With unceasing energy the chemicals department at Thorncliffe continued to publicise its products in newspapers, magazines, exhibitions, films, radio competitions and literature of all kinds. Films included *Cleaner Milk*, offering useful suggestions for dairy hygiene, and *The Prey of the Spray*, in support of Zaldecide. The latter film had a supplement of interest to entomologists and biologists, dealing with the life history of the bed-bug and the cockroach. For those living in the south of England a commercial on Radio Normandie might be heard -

Is everybody happy?
Is everybody well?
You will be, if you use San Izal.[19]

During the Second World War there continued to be promotion of the Company's products as shown by the advertisement (Figure 10) from the *Rotherham Advertiser*. Rhymes were still used to advantage (Figure 11). Even Hitler appeared on the toilet paper! (Figure 12).

Figure 11. Rhymes in newspaper advertisements in 1941.

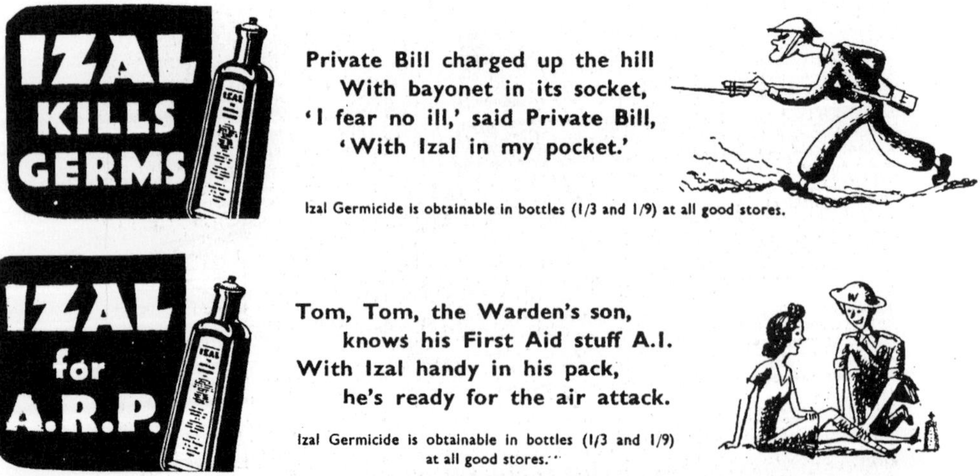

Figure 12. A piece of wartime toilet paper.

Post-war competitive world

In 1949 considerable extensions to the Izal factory were opened with the now customary panache. Sir Samuel Roberts, Chairman of the Company, Sir Harold West (Managing Director) and Mrs Newton Drew arrived for the opening ceremony in a 1906 vintage car. Sir Samuel Roberts presided and Lady Roberts performed the opening ceremony. A lunch was provided in the Newton Hall for local dignitaries, local authority representatives and other guests. The building had been designed by Husband & Co, Sheffield and built by Henry Boot & Sons Ltd using reinforced concrete. On this spacious site (Figure 13) the reeling and medication of Izal toilet paper took place (Figure 14), the mechanical packing of San Izal and the bottling of the recently-launched Zal Pine Disinfectant. There was a large canteen, kitchen, staff dining rooms, a lecture hall, packing rooms, warehouses and a 3-storey office block. A special exhibition was mounted for the occasion entitled *The Producer at Work and Play*. It showed not only the products of the Company but also something of the social and recreational life of Thorncliffe (see Figure 15).

Zal Pine Disinfectant was a success from the outset. 'Its clear, golden appearance, its fragrant pine odour, its non-poisonous and non-staining qualities soon won the acclaim of the housewife'.[20] It was initially sold in two sizes of bottle domestically and in one gallon and larger sizes industrially. The bottles and labels were redesigned by Christian Barman and Milner Gray in 1954 and a family size added in 1959 and a giant size in 1965. New legislation in 1963 caused the

Figure 13. The Izal factory, between Station Road and Arundel Road, Chapeltown. *Roncraft*

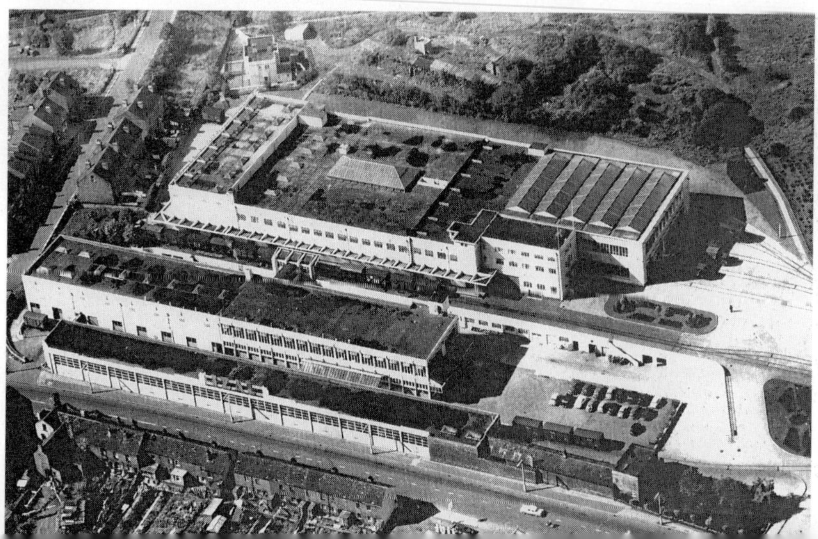

word 'antiseptic' to be dropped to avoid paying purchase tax and increasing the price for the consumer. At the same time Nicholas Products took a similar decision about Lifeguard but Reckitts took the opposite decision about Dettol.[21] Zal led to the demise of Izal Germicide which was withdrawn in 1957. When the first British Commercial Television programmes were transmitted, Newton Chambers advertised Zal and three films of 30 seconds were prepared. The first one was transmitted between 7.00 and 8.00 p.m. on Tuesday 27 September 1955. A series of newspaper advertisements was also launched, which incorporated a 'human interest' story which anticipated by forty years the story-line TV coffee advertisements of the 1990s.

By the end of the 1950s a number of new products had been introduced including the Polly Kitchen Roll, the Poppet Dishwasher, K2R Spot Lifter and in 1960 Izal Soft Tissue. In the industrial field Zalpon was launched in 1951 at a press conference at the Savoy Hotel in Leeds. Zalpon was said to be 'a new way of washing' particularly suitable 'for schools, factories, office blocks and other buildings with communal wash-places.'[22] The Zalpon system employed a new form of soap and a new type of dispenser. The original dispenser had taken four years to develop. The inventor was Mr H. W. S. Churchill and Christian Barman was the designer. The dispenser consisted of an

Figure 14. The reeling of paper in the Izal factory. *South Riding Estates*

Figure 15. The Izal factory employed a large number of female operatives who took part in many of the social and recreational activities offered by the firm. There were many lunch-time and evening classes specifically for the girls at the Izal factory ranging from keep-fit (on the roof of the new Izal factory) to demonstrations of fruit bottling. The classes were well-attended by the girls in their distinctive coats of leaf-green material, with short sleeves, collars and revers. The collar and cuffs were faced with biscuit-coloured material, matching the breast pocket bearing the Izal green cross in a diamond, embroidered in silk. The BBC programme 'Music While You Work' was relayed throughout the factory, supplemented on occasions by the girls' own favourite gramophone records. At Christmas the main machine rooms were decorated with streamers. Tableaux ranging from Nativity scenes to winter sports were created from waste paper, card and cotton wool, as shown above. Every suitable pipe, pillar and stanchion was bedecked and garlanded. Annual Christmas parties were also held for Izal factory employees and friends. In December 1952 over 600 attended. After games and novelty dances to Bob Lomas' Band, the highlight of the evening came with the 'Miss Izal' competition. The evenings were funded by money raised through social activities during the year. *Clarice Hyde*

inverted glass jar which contained the translucent, lavender-perfumed, olive-green coloured, washing cream. Below the jar was a chromium-plated lever which, when pulled, delivered the cream into the palm of the hand - only a minute amount was needed! The following month a large part of the Izal stand at the British Industries Fair at Olympia was devoted to Zalpon. There were numerous modifications to the dispenser, including replacing the glass jar with a plastic container, over the next few years and the introduction of two barrier creams.[23]

In the late 1950s Bowater Scott launched the Andrex soft toilet tissue. Its effect was not immediately noticeable because of a general upsurge in demand for toilet paper. However, by the 1960s, massive slum clearance and rehousing schemes were under way and occupants of new houses with, perhaps, a pink bathroom, wanted pink toilet paper and Andrex was the only one to meet this demand. Izal responded by launching its own soft toilet tissue but 'Bowater Scott complained that the wrapper of the Izal roll was far too much like theirs and insisted on its withdrawal. This was done but it was costly and time consuming.'[24] Mr Shaun Waide, the General Manager of that time, commissioned Pritchard Wood to undertake some market research into consumer attitudes. 'These showed that the Izal Medicated Roll had very loyal consumer support ... due to the fact that medication gave it a unique selling proposition.'[25] Experiments were carried out into medicating the soft paper but it was not suitable for the technique. The research also revealed that consumers preferred the soft tissue because it was 'soft' and it could be used for other purposes such as nose wiping. Izal decided to launch a 'softer than soft' roll that was lanolised for extra softness. The results were disappointing from the outset and in spite of advertising on TV and in popular women's journals Izal Lanolised Soft Tissue never equalled the impact of Izal Medicated Tissue and it was discontinued. The sales of Izal Medicated Tissue, however, remained buoyant throughout the 1960s and 1970s.

In May 1960 Newton Chambers & Co Ltd acquired Ronuk Ltd, a company based at Portslade in Sussex, manufacturers of floor and furniture polish. In 1962 the Kent Floor Machine business was bought and Newton Chambers began to manufacture floor polishing and cleaning machines. To promote their image further, a film called *The Threatening Veil* was made in 1967 dealing with the dangers arising from the existence of dirt and dust. An accompanying book entitled *Dangerous People* was written by Elizabeth Gundrey, formerly Director of the Consumers' Association, and produced and published on behalf of Izal by Spectator Publications. Both were widely acclaimed and the book was reprinted the following year. Following the success of the film the decision was made to support it with a further film on the subject of floor maintenance. Filming took place during the summer of 1968 in a number of locations and Michael Aspel was used as the link man.[26]

In 1969 the Thawpit business was acquired whose products included, apart from the Thawpit Spot Remover, Doby Washing-up Liquid and a range of Delafine Bath Crystals and toiletries. By this time there were a number of new Izal products including Izal Bath Cleaner and Izal Antiseptic, both launched in 1968.

In 1973 Newton Chambers was taken over by the Central and Sheerwood Trust after a bid on the open market. Under its new chairman, Dr Francis Stringer, each part of the firm was made self-contained with the declared intention of selling it off. Between January and November 1973 Izal Ltd operated as a separate entity for the first and last time. In November of that year it was acquired by the Sterling-Winthrop Group. At the time of the take-over the Company made 137 products, from lavatory tissue through air freshening equipment to floor cleaning materials and equipment. The Izal factory as a production unit was closed in October 1981 and the site has been redeveloped by Hassall Homes. Some Izal products are still marketed by the Lever Group to industrial customers and by Jeyes to the general public.

Notes and References

1. Harold E. Elliott (*c.* 1958), *Thorncliffe: A Short History of the Newton Chambers Co Ltd and Its People,* Chapter XVIII, published in parts in *Thorncliffe News.*
2. Elliott, *Thorncliffe: A Short History,* Chapter XVIII.
3. Joan Jones and Mel Jones (1993), '*... A Most Enterprising Thing ...*' *An Illustrated History to Commemorate the 200th Anniversary of the Establishment of Newton Chambers at Thorncliffe,* Chapeltown & High Green Archive.
4. Elliott, *Thorncliffe: A Short History,* Chapter XVI.
5. Sheffield Archives (SA); Thorncliffe Records (TR) 456/1.
6. *Izal: Its Nature and Properties* (1895), Newton Chambers & Co Ltd, pp. 13-14.
7. *Izal: Its Nature and Properties,* pp. 6-7.
8. *Izal: Its Nature and Properties.*
9. *Izal: Its Nature and Properties,* p. 57.
10. SA/TR 444.
11. SA/TR 444.
12. Elliott, *Thorncliffe: A Short History, Chapter XXV.*
13. Elliott, *Thorncliffe: A Short History.*
14. R. W. Kelly (1974), *The Story of Izal,* unpublished typescript, Chapeltown and High Green Archive.
15. Elliott, *Thorncliffe: A Short History,* Chapter XXVIII.
16. Elliott, *Thorncliffe: A Short History,* Chapter XXVIII.
17. Copy of Sales Representative's Report (23.9.36) amongst R. W. Kelly's papers.
18. *Thorncliffe News,* October 1941.
19. Elliott, *Thorncliffe: A Short History,* Chapter XXVIII.
20. Kelly, *The Story of Izal.*
21. Kelly, *The Story of Izal.*
22. '*A New Way of Washing*', reprint of article by Newton Chambers Co Ltd, originally published in *Design,* July 1951.
23. R. W. Kelly (no date), *History of Izal Industrial Sales,* unpublished typescript, Chapeltown and High Green Archive.
24. Kelly, *The Story of Izal,* p.12.
25. Kelly, *The Story of Izal,* p.12.
26. Kelly, *History of Izal Industrial Sales.*

Acknowledgements

I am indebted to: the late R. W. Kelly for donating his typescripts to the Chapeltown & High Green Archive; Sheffield Libraries and Information Services for permission to quote from the Thorncliffe Records held in Sheffield Archives and to reproduce Figure 7; and Freda Casson for donating the advertisement from the *Rotherham Advertiser* (Figure 10).

11. Henry Bessemer: Sheffield's Radical Steelmaker

by Trevor Lodge

For as certain as the age of iron superseded that of bronze, so will the age of steel succeed that of iron.

Henry Bessemer addressing the Sheffield Meeting of the Institute of Mechanical Engineers in 1861 when describing his new process for making mild steel in bulk.

Introduction

SHEFFIELD'S STEELMAKERS OF THE LAST CENTURY were a conservative lot. Even by the time of the Great Exhibition of 1851, at which the manufacturers of all nations were urged to display their best industrial art and manufacturing technology, the town was still employing a century-old process exclusively to make cast steel. And the time consuming process Sheffield employed for making so-called 'blister steel' - the essential feedstock for its cast steel industry - was even older.

Yet within five years of the Great Exhibition Sheffield's steel industry was being challenged to its very foundation by a revolutionary process developed by an outsider who, to add insult to injury, had no previous steelmaking experience. Furthermore, this 'upstart' had the audacity to establish a business to exploit his process in Sheffield alongside some of the town's best known names in steel and engineering, obviously bent on defying their hostility head on.

Such was Sheffield's introduction to inventor and entrepreneur Henry Bessemer, who ultimately was described as the Father of the Steel Age. (Figure 1). Needless to say, following their confrontational introduction, he and Sheffield's orthodox steelmakers never really came to terms.[1]

The present article is by way of a belated tribute to Bessemer, and has been prompted by the centenary of his death, which occurred on 15 March 1998. Fortunately the anniversary was marked more formally with a two day metallurgical

Figure 1. Henry Bessemer in 1880, shortly after receiving his knighthood.

conference at Sheffield University organised jointly by the Institute of Materials and the Sheffield Metallurgical and Engineering Association. The Institute also published a commemorative volume written by a team of historical metallurgy specialists drawn from the UK, North America and mainland Europe.[2] Bessemer's influence was truly international.

There is not space here to consider the wider ramifications of the Bessemer steel industry. Rather, the narrative is confined to an examination of its initial impact on Sheffield, essentially during the first fifteen years or so of its commercial development in the town, and plotting the later fortunes of the company which Bessemer established in Sheffield to exploit his invention. Neither of these aspects has been adequately considered by previous steel historians.

The man

Bessemer's life was in the best tradition of those featured by Samuel Smiles in his 'Self-Help' series. In particular, the development of his steelmaking converter was a story of promise, disaster, rejection and ultimate success. A story in which one man's faith in his invention, despite all the technical set-backs and carping criticisms of his adversaries, would ultimately repay him with a fortune beyond his wildest dreams.

Born in 1813 at Charlton, near Hitchin in Hertfordshire, Bessemer was the son of Anthony Bessemer who, in the aftermath of the French Revolution, had to flee his skilled job as a designer of engraving equipment at the Paris Mint. Henry seems to have acquired his engineering and metal working skills from his father. Furthermore, he was very perceptive and clearly able to turn his skills to a wide range of outlets. These traits, coupled with his strong personality and an immense capacity for work, were the real basis of his future success.

The Bessemer steelmaking converter, which is central to the present account, was only one of Bessemer's many achievements. He had no fewer than 117 patents to his name, and was responsible for many inventions which were not covered by letters patent. As a skilled designer and draughtsman he actually designed most of the equipment described in his patents, and produced the detailed engineering drawings required for their construction.

His first successful commercial venture - he was barely 20 years old at the time - was based on a superior die metal he developed which reproduced fine embossed detail on cardboard and leather. A method he devised in the early 1840s for making artificial gold powder (actually bronze) for decorative lettering and japanning was a spectacular commercial success and would provide an income which allowed him to turn his attention to a whole range of new projects - including improved manufacture of malleable iron, which ultimately resulted in the development of the steelmaking converter.

The idea of constructing a simple solar furnace using 'burning glasses' had appealed to Bessemer for some years, and in the mid-1840s he attempted to produce some large lenses at relatively small cost. This work led to a technique which allowed large sheets of superior glass to be produced, and Bessemer sold this idea for £6,000 to Lucas Chance of the Chance Glass Company, which operated at Birmingham the UK's largest glassworks. Bessemer's attempts to establish a glassworks in London to exploit his ideas on plate glass production were still-born, essentially because he was unable to convince likely partners in such a venture of its potential future success.

In 1849, spurred on by a Society of Arts competition, Bessemer began work on designing a more efficient machine for extracting juice from raw sugar cane. The new machine was a complete contrast to existing equipment. Despite being much lighter, and therefore easily transported around the plantations, Bessemer's equipment gave a much higher yield of juice. He won the competition and had the satisfaction of being presented with the Society's gold medal prize by Prince Albert.

It might be inferred from his ultimate commercial success that Bessemer possessed astute business acumen, but the facts do not support this. A number of his earlier business ventures based on his inventions either came to nought or were short-lived - notably his sugar refinery on the Thames, his London glass works and his Greenwich steel works. And these were small beer compared with what would come later. In the 1870s Bessemer became consumed by a passion to ensure that his invention to eliminate sea-sickness was brought to fruition, and he unwisely continued to advance monies to keep afloat (quite literally!) the Bessemer Saloon Ship Company, a venture set up to build a prototype vessel incorporating his ideas. Following an accident when the vessel collided with Calais pier in 1875, the company went into liquidation and Bessemer ultimately lost £34,000 in the venture - an enormous amount in those days. The strain of the whole affair also brought about a nervous breakdown. As *Engineering* stated in his obituary notice, published on 18 March 1898, 'he was an inventor to the tips of his fingers'. He was certainly not a hard-nosed businessman.

Sir Henry Bessemer - he was knighted in 1879 - was a prolific inventor, but the contemporary world was not always ready for his ideas. For example, as an extension to his steelmaking converter, he proposed a method of casting the steel by pouring it between cooled rolls, which first solidified the metal and then proceeded to shape it. In effect he sowed the seeds for elementary continuous casting, a process that was a full century away. How prophetic he was!

But it is for his converter that he will be remembered. Abram S. Hewitt, one of the pioneers of the Bessemer process in the United States, emphasised its full significance when he said, 'the Bessemer invention takes its rank with the great events which have changed the face of society since the time of the Middle Ages.' [3]

In later life Bessemer received many honours and titles, national and international, in recognition of his achievements. One which he treasured highly was the Freedom of the City of London, granted him in 1880. (Figure 2). This more than dispelled the misgivings of his youth, after he had just moved to London and often mused, 'Shall I ever be known here?'

The Steel Converter

When the Crimean War broke out in 1853, Bessemer's thoughts turned to how he could best support his country's war effort. At this time ordnance accuracy was notoriously poor, as a result of smooth bore guns being employed, together with round shot. Bessemer devised a system of giving elongated (cylindrical) shells a spin about

Figure 2. Solid gold casket housing Bessemer's Freedom of the City of London scroll. The figure of Commerce on the rounded cover stands between a stack of pig iron and the steel converter. Vignettes on the side of the cover show a London North Western Railway locomotive and a steel clad ship. *Author*

their longitudinal axis to keep them on course without the need for rifling within the gun barrel, enabling larger shells to be fired with greater accuracy. The British Government in the form of Woolwich Arsenal pooh-poohed the idea but the French Emperor, Napoleon III, was only too ready to finance Bessemer's work. Bessemer then came up against a physical limitation which prevented existing guns firing his shells; their iron barrels were just not strong enough to resist the discharge. Consequently, his work had to be extended to finding a better metal for ordnance purposes. Cast steel made using Huntsman's crucible method, though widely employed by this time in Sheffield for cutlery and edge tools, was considered too costly for this particular application.

After eighteen months of experimenting to improve the quality of iron in his home 'workshop' at Baxter House in St Pancras (London), Bessemer hit on the idea of blowing air into molten pig iron in a crucible to burn away the unwanted elements present, essentially silicon and carbon. The result was a few pounds of soft malleable iron - sufficient to prove the technique, and encourage Bessemer to persevere. He then argued that the use of a refractory lined vessel with holes in the bottom (for blowing in air) would make a greater quantity of iron by the same principle. When such a vessel was tried the violence of the reaction which took place some minutes after the molten pig iron was first introduced into the vessel literally petrified everyone present. They were equally amazed some minutes later when the violence died down and the material remaining was found to be malleable iron. Bessemer, describing the incident later, spoke of the reaction as 'a veritable volcano in a state of active eruption'.

Encouraged by George Rennie, the noted civil engineer (to whom he demonstrated the process in private) Bessemer announced his invention to the British Association in Cheltenham in August 1856, his paper being entitled 'The Manufacture of Malleable Iron and Steel without Fuel'. His work was received with much scepticism - not surprisingly, since to make one ton of crucible steel by then existing techniques consumed some four tons of hard coke. Then, to make matters worse, a number of UK ironworks purchased licences from Bessemer to make malleable iron by the patented process but quickly reported it to be a failure, producing 'rotten' material which lacked ductility and broke up during rolling and forging. Bessemer was at a loss to explain this unexpected turn of events, and returned the licensees their money.

It took some little time for the chemists of the day to show that the problem was caused by the unwanted presence of phosphorus and sulphur - two elements found to a greater or lesser extent in the initial pig iron. For his experiments, Bessemer had used pig iron from Blaenavon Ironworks (South Wales), which was relatively low in these impurities, thereby unwittingly guaranteeing success! Very soon the addition of spiegeleisen (an alloy of iron and manganese) after blowing was found to improve the hot ductility by rendering the sulphur harmless. At the same time it reduced porosity in the final product, and introduced a small amount of carbon to the melt, resulting in a 'steely' product, rather than a malleable iron. Thus, provided low phosphorus pig irons were used the Bessemer process was capable of converting them into good steel.

The Lion's Den

Because of the bad publicity the Bessemer process received during this initial set-back there was still considerable prejudice from the establishment within the industry. There was only one option left to Bessemer, and he did not lack conviction when it came to making a decision. With several partners he purchased land on Carlisle Street, Sheffield, erected a works in 1858 and commenced production of Bessemer steel in an area of the country where he was most unwelcome. The business, styled 'Henry Bessemer & Company', was a partnership consisting of Henry Bessemer, his brothers-in-law Robert Longsdon and William Allen, together with William and John Galloway of Manchester. Bessemer's decision to invite the Galloways to join the venture was an inspired choice. Their old-established business at the Knott Mill Ironworks in Manchester was well versed in engineering matters, and Bessemer had previously entrusted them to construct machinery in connection with his sugar-refining work. They also became involved with his early experimental work on developing the steel converter, and never lost faith in Bessemer, despite the setbacks.[4] Their partnership involvement would be of mutual benefit. It was an effective way of Bessemer thanking Galloways for their earlier trust, and it gave the new steelmaking company access to vital mechanical engineering prowess. Thanks to the 'hands-on' experience of building and equipping the UK's first commercial Bessemer steelplant, the firm of Galloway Brothers soon became a world leader in the design and supply of Bessemer converters and ancillary equipment - blowing engines, rolling mills and so on.

An important role of the works established by Henry Bessemer & Company on Carlisle Street, Sheffield, was 'to serve as a pioneer works or school, where the process was for several years exhibited to any iron or steel manufacturers who desired to take a licence to work under [Bessemer's] patents.' Such potential licensees were also allowed to see their own iron converted satisfactorily before committing themselves.

Not only was the Bessemer steelmaking process radical. Because of its high output rate - it produced several tons of liquid steel every half hour - a radical approach had to be adopted to develop equipment to deal with such tonnages. The steel casting pit and bottom pouring ladle were just two such innovations developed at the Carlisle Street Works (Figure 3).

Bessemer was fully aware of the possible consequences of setting up the business in Sheffield and later wrote:

In thus opposing the old-established steel trade in its very midst, we ran the risk of 'rattening', or a bottle of gunpowder in the furnace flues, by which the workmen of Sheffield had earned for themselves an unenviable notoriety.

He was referring of course to the 'Sheffield Outrages', which were the culmination of politically motivated incidents involving restrictive trade practices and associated intimidations.

Bessemer never came to terms with Sheffield's ultra-conservatism. He commented that:

Sheffield wrapped itself in absolute security, and believed that it could afford to laugh at the absurd notion of making five tons of cast steel from pig iron in twenty or thirty minutes, when by its own system fourteen or fifteen days were required to obtain a 40-lb or 50-lb crucible of cast steel from pig iron.

Well, the local steelmakers might have been a conservative lot, but some of them began to see potential in the process - especially when Bessemer started to undersell them by some £15 per ton and selected

Figure 3. Early form of Bessemer converter plant, as installed at the Carlisle Street Works. The tilted converter (left) is tapping steel into a waiting ladle; the ladle on the right (shown in section) is teeming the steel into a mould set in a casting pit. In this example the ladle was manoeuvred by means of a hydraulically-operated radius-arm crane.

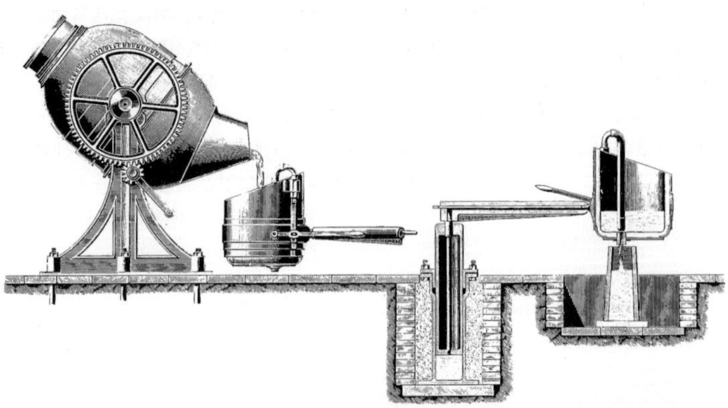

users of Bessemer tool steel reported the product to be indistinguishable from that made by the crucible process.

With the major problems solved, Bessemer presented a paper to the Institute of Civil Engineers in 1859, emphasising the role his steel could play in the constructional field - building railways, bridges, and so on.[5] This, in fact, was the direction in which his new mild steel industry quickly moved. As a result, the Bessemer process was never a serious threat to the established crucible steel industry in Sheffield; instead the two became somewhat complementary. The ones who would have real grounds for fearing the infant Bessemer steel industry as it found its feet were the wrought iron producers, as we shall see.

The First Disciples

Even as new outlets for Bessemer steel were opening, Bessemer remained somewhat obsessed with the idea of using it for ordnance. To this end he invited Colonel Eardley Wilmot of the government's Woolwich Arsenal in London to view the process in action at the partners' Sheffield Works. Wilmot was impressed with what he saw, and as he had separate business with John Brown and John Ellis of the neighbouring Atlas Works, he persuaded them to join him in his tour of the Bessemer Works.

Brown and Ellis saw a converter blow and were rapidly 'converted' themselves. This was a crucial moment for Bessemer, for these men were part of the Sheffield establishment who had previously shunned Bessemer, and were now publicly acquiescing to the merits of the process. Their Atlas Works was one of a new generation of giant iron- and steelworks established on the Don Valley flats east of Sheffield following the opening of the Sheffield and Rotherham Railway in 1838. John Brown & Company was already supplying the burgeoning railways with steel goods - Brown's conical spring buffer, patented in 1848, made him his first fortune - and here was an opportunity to increase business in this lucrative market.[6]

Charles Cammell of the nearby Cyclops Works quickly followed Brown's initiative by also taking out a licence. Cammell's earlier career had been 'on the road', working as a travelling representative for Ibbotson & Company of the Globe Works, an old established Sheffield engineering tool manufacturer.[7] He numbered several of the early railway companies, such as the Liverpool and Manchester Railway, amongst his customers, and his experiences had left him in no doubt of the business potential that existed for those prepared to supply goods to this 'new-fangled' railway industry.

Brown's Atlas Works was producing Bessemer steel and rolling it to rails by mid-1861; Cyclops was doing likewise before the end of the year. Bessemer steel was also found to be suited to other railway materials - thanks to trials on the London & North Western Railway - and rails, tyres, axles and even boiler plates in Bessemer steel soon became part of the new order.

The next few licences Bessemer granted were to concerns outside Sheffield, and these effectively heralded the spread of steelmaking technology away from the town. The development was more significant than was realised at the time, for it was nothing short of the beginning of the end of Sheffield's centuries-long monopoly in UK steel production.

True, two of the new licensees were only just outside Sheffield - Samuel Fox at Stocksbridge and Daniel Adamson at Penistone - but the process accelerated with a vengeance in 1865 when Bessemer converters were installed at the Barrow Iron Works in the Furness district of Lancashire on a site ideally located near an abundance of Cumberland haematite ores. Barrow Works, complete with blast furnaces and Bessemer converters, was also on the coast and thereby unwittingly provided the model for all the world's future 'state-of-the-art' integrated steel plants located alongside deep water ports.

Contemporary references to early Bessemer steelmaking exploits in South Yorkshire are not common. *The Engineer* for 2 May 1862, however, included an article covering The International Exhibition, in which it was stated that the exhibits provided by Henry Bessemer and Company included 'samples of steel wire, by Fox, of Deepcar'.

In the early days of the mild steel trade, Henry Bessemer had to be very much a salesman to promote his new product. Consequently, he often approached those who were engaged in metal processing, inviting them to try Bessemer metal for themselves so they could see how it compared with their regular feedstock. Having approached Samuel Fox in this fashion, Bessemer got back something of a bonus - mild steel wire which served to illustrate on his exhibition stand yet another use to which his new product could be put. Processing Bessemer steel to wire must have also made Samuel Fox more aware of the potential of this new material, so his decision to acquire a licence for Bessemer steelmaking was not altogether a surprise.

As events turned out, the Penistone and Stocksbridge Bessemer plants were contemporary, and shared a number of similarities. An old diary records that Stocksbridge blew its first charge of Bessemer steel in April 1863 and, using ingots from the initial casts, rolled its very first rails on 8 October 1863, to despatch them almost one month later (6 November) to the Great Northern Railway. The first Bessemer 'blow' at Penistone was made on 1 May 1863.[8] Apart from Bessemer's own works in Sheffield, Penistone proved to be the UK's first true greenfield site development for a Bessemer steelworks.

The Process Described

The existing steelworks in South Yorkshire which in the 1860s adopted the Bessemer process - Brown's, Cammell's (Cyclops) and Fox's - had all previously relied on traditional crucible melting techniques. Consequently, none operated blast furnaces, which would otherwise have been a valuable source of molten iron feedstock for their newly-installed Bessemer converters. Instead they, and indeed the other Bessemer plants subsequently established in South Yorkshire, were styled along the lines of what later became known as the 'classic' Bessemer layout, based on what Bessemer himself employed at Sheffield. At these plants, bought-in haematite pig iron was melted in coke-fired cupolas and fed alternately to one or other of a pair of converters for blowing down (Figure 4).

The melted pig iron (about six tons) was poured into a pear-shaped pre-heated vessel (the converter) lying on its side. The interior of the vessel was lined with heat-resisting ganister and at the base the lining incorporated fireclay plugs containing cylindrical holes (tuyeres).[9] On receiving the charge of molten pig iron, the vessel was turned upright on trunnions at the same time that pressurised air from a steam-driven blowing engine was forced

Figure 4. Engraving of works interior at Henry Bessemer & Company which appeared in the 1879 edition of Pawson and Brailsford's *Guide to Sheffield.* The upright converter (left, centre) is blowing down a charge; on the right a finished charge is being tapped from the tilted converter into a ladle carried on a carousel, or turntable. Note also the spout in centre, for filling converters from the cupola (visible through archway) in which pig iron was melted. The open pulpit, left, controls various converter mechanisms, including tilting, positioning upright, and supplying a pressurised air blast.

through the tuyeres into the melt. As a result, the non-metallic elements in the pig iron - principally silicon and carbon - were burnt away or oxidised in preference to the iron, a change accompanied by a noisy, spectacular display of fireworks. Heat generated by the oxidation was more than enough to keep the mass molten.

Judging the 'end-point' of a Bessemer blow was a crucial feature of the operation. The blowing period could not be fixed but had to be varied depending on the metalloid (carbon, silicon, etc.) content of the haematite iron feedstock. A skilled furnace hand knew when oxidation had reached the desired point by the length, type and colour of the flame issuing from the mouth of the converter. The importance of judging the end-point can be gauged from the fact that in the 1880s (at least) the blower at Stocksbridge was actually paid more than the Bessemer shop foreman, even though technically subordinate to him!

On reaching the end point, the vessel was tilted on its side once more, and the air blow shut off. Molten spiegeleisen from another cupola furnace was added and the charge briefly re-blown, leaving mild steel in the converter. The whole conversion process took something like 30 minutes.

The steel was then poured from the converter into a receiving vessel called a ladle, and after filling this was swung round on a fixed radius crane arm to allow the steel to be poured, or teemed, into a group of cast iron moulds set in a pit in the melting shop floor. The steel was left to cool and solidify into ingots, which were then removed by means of cranes and conveyed, while still red hot, to the forge or rolling mills for further processing.

The Products

The biggest industry which adopted Bessemer steel in its early proving period was that of railway engineering. This was an extremely important development since the country's rapidly expanding railway network, according to several economic historians, was the largest customer for wrought iron in the period 1840 - 1860. From then on steel would increasingly usurp wrought iron from this dominant role. The manufacture of steel rails, in particular, became a principal focus of the UK's early Bessemer steelplants. [10]

Bessemer received a particular fillip when Britain's largest railway, the London & North Western Railway (LNWR), accepted his steel as suitable for all manner of equipment including locomotives, rolling stock and track. This we can attribute largely to the open-minded attitude of John Ramsbottom, the railway's chief mechanical engineer. Yet when the matter was first mooted, both Bessemer and Ramsbottom viewed it with some trepidation. Initially, Bessemer was not keen for his steel to be used for making rails simply because they had such a poor market image - the last thing with which he wished Bessemer steel to be associated. Ramsbottom, on the other hand, had heard of the 'unreliable' nature of Bessemer steel, and when approached by Bessemer with a view to giving it a trial for rails had retorted, 'Mr Bessemer, do you wish to see me tried for manslaughter?'

Ramsbottom, to his credit, did give the steel a trial, and was so impressed with the results that he sought sanction from the LNWR's Board of Directors to have a Bessemer steelworks erected at the company's Crewe Locomotive Works in Cheshire. The vastly superior wearing qualities of the steel rails laid down as a trial by the LNWR at Chalk Farm (London) in 1862 finally dispelled any qualms others might have about steel rails, whereupon the whole business mushroomed.

Such was the growth in the steel rail trade that by 1875 there were eight Bessemer steelplants in the Sheffield district alone, at seven of which rails were a major product. Indeed, for a brief but glorious decade (1865 - 74) Sheffield was actually the world's largest producer of steel rails. The quality of steel rails shipped from Sheffield to the USA quickly established a pedigree for Bessemer steel, and acted as a powerful incentive for the creation of Bessemer steelplants there. This spread of the technology, an important secondary phase in the history of Bessemer steel, has been considered by others.[11]

Of all the products fashioned from Bessemer steel, the steel rail was undoubtedly that which had the greatest effect on the civilised world. Bessemer himself finally acknowledged this in *Engineering Review* on 20 July 1894, where he wrote:

> *This new material has covered with a network of steel rails the surface of every country in Europe, and in America alone there are no less than 175,000 miles of Bessemer steel rails binding together its widely scattered cities.*

At their works on Carlisle Street in Sheffield, Bessemer and his partners did not produce rails but rather concentrated on supplying to niche markets. This was a sensible decision because it meant that Bessemer was able to monitor the various new applications for which the steel was tried, and make modifications to the manufacturing process if this improved matters.

With the manufacture of tool steel - a Sheffield celebrity - Bessemer went to great lengths to beat the crucible steelmakers at their own game. It has to be admitted, however, that for technical

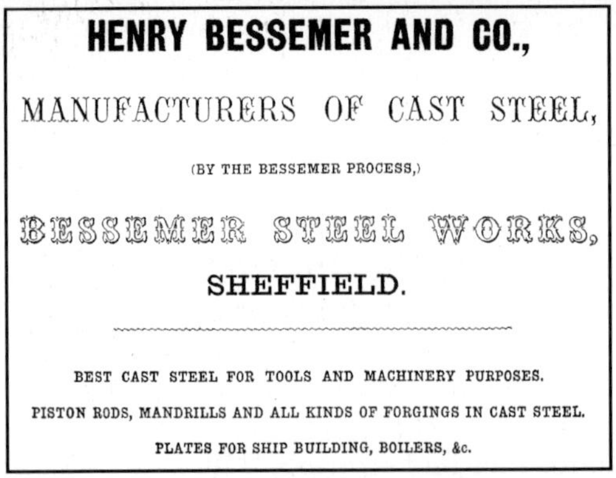

Figure 5. An early advert from White's *Sheffield Directory*, 1861. The mention of tool steel was discontinued in later advertisements, whilst the use of Bessemer steel plates for shipbuilding never really caught on.

reasons (largely control of composition) he was never able to achieve this by conventional use of the converter. He developed instead a complex two-stage process (not dissimilar to that used by orthodox crucible steelmakers!) and tool steel manufacture seems to have been quietly dropped from the company's product range as other, more appropriate outlets for Bessemer steel were developed. Tool steel, in fact, only appears to have been advertised in the earliest years of the company (Figure 5).

One ideal field in which Bessemer steel could compete with crucible steel was in the manufacture of rolled tyres, particularly for steam locomotives. Such tyres would remain a major product for the Carlisle Street works for the whole of its existence (Figure 6). Axles, too, especially the more highly stressed axles of steam locomotives (rather than those in carriages and wagons) were ideally suited to be manufactured from a one piece forging which could now be produced economically from a large Bessemer steel ingot. Much early work was done on this subject at Crewe, using its own Bessemer steelplant and forge to produce such axles for its own locomotives. Attention soon turned to crank axles, which had to withstand the highest levels of stress, being responsible for transmitting all the power of the locomotive from the steam cylinders to the driving wheels. Breakage rates for conventional wrought iron crank axles were alarmingly high - it was not unusual for 10 per cent of the locomotives within a fleet to be affected each year - and often these resulted in spectacular fatal accidents, with all the attendant bad press.[12] In 1867 Henry Bessemer & Company supplied the Lancashire & Yorkshire Railway with a batch of one piece forged steel crankshafts for locomotive construction and twenty-five years later was able to record that six of the axles concerned had each completed over 500,000 miles in service without failure - a vastly superior performance to wrought iron.

Other products were not so successful, though acceptance by the customer could play a crucial part in the matter. This particularly applied in the case of guns which were forged solid from a single Bessemer steel ingot, then bored out. Such guns were produced by Henry Bessemer & Company and John Brown & Company but the authorities at the Government's Woolwich Arsenal could not be persuaded out of their entrenched views on ordnance manufacture, and Bessemer

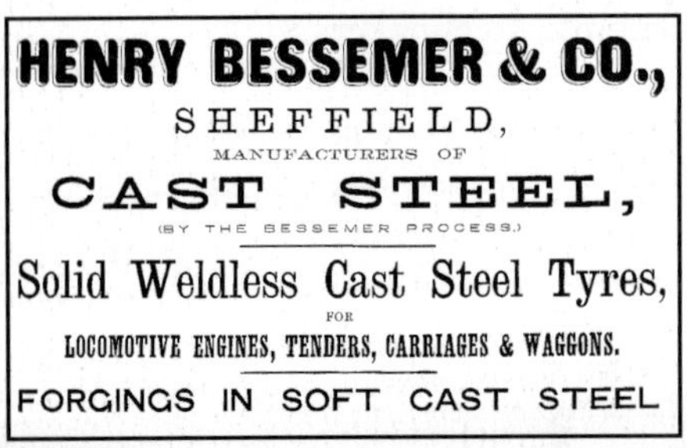

Figure 6. Henry Bessemer & Company advertised quite widely during the period that the original Bessemer patents on steelmaking were still valid. Note the prominence given to railway materials in this typical advertisement, which appeared in Kelly's 1869 *Post Office Directory of London.*

had to be content with selling his guns to overseas customers.

Similarly, Bessemer steel was destined never to make a major impact in metal shipbuilding, despite Bessemer's best promotional efforts in this direction. There was, however, sound technical reasons for the shipbuilders' reluctance, and not until the advent of the Siemens-Martin openhearth steel melting process could dead soft (i. e., low carbon) steels be produced with sufficient consistency to suit the needs of shipbuilders.

The End of an Era

Bessemer steelmaking and rail rolling had been relegated to secondary status within the South Yorkshire metallurgical scene well before the end of the nineteenth century. Quite simply, Bessemer steelmaking could be carried out far more economically at coastal sites near haematite ore fields. Many of Sheffield's former Bessemer converter operators survived by introducing more flexible, cost-effective Siemens-Martin openhearth furnaces and diversifying into new products. Brown's and Cammell's, for example, had each built up a large order book based on the lucrative production of ordnance, armour and general engineering by the 1870s. The former was, however, still advertising Bessemer steel in its range of products in 1893 whereas Charles Cammell & Company progressively concentrated its South Yorkshire Bessemer steelmaking activities at its Penistone Works, and the Cyclops Works converters closed down about 1900 (Figure 7).

Figure 7. 1890s view of the Bessemer shop at the Penistone Works of Charles Cammell & Co. Ltd., which was laid out in the classical Bessemer style. It makes for an interesting comparison with Figure 4. *Author's collection*

The firm of Henry Bessemer & Co. Ltd. remained very much a 'one-off ' of the South Yorkshire Bessemer plants (Figure 8). It never operated a rail rolling mill, concentrating its output on medium and heavy forgings - shafts, axles, crank axles, tyres and other related railway materials (Figure 9). About 1890 it installed acid Siemens-Martin openhearth furnaces and a few years later abandoned altogether the Bessemer process - once its very *raison d'être.* It survived until the mid-1920s Depression, and after closure the goodwill of the business was acquired by John Baker & Co. (Rotherham) 1920 Ltd., a firm also specialising in the manufacture of railway materials. The Baker family members on the board of directors were delighted to gain control of such a prestigious name in steel, and changed the name of the business to John Baker & Bessemer Ltd. to reflect its new status. [13] This successor company remained an important supplier in the UK's railway materials sector until it ceased trading in the mid 1960s, when it in turn was bought out for its order book by its two large rivals, the English Steel Corporation Ltd. and the United Steel Companies Ltd.

There is a particularly poignant aside to Bessemer's Sheffield business. The firm was initially managed by Bessemer's brother-in-law William D. Allen, and he was succeeded by his son Harry Allen when the original partners retired in the early 1870s and the business was floated on the Stock Exchange.[14] Harry became an active member of Sheffield's steel manufacturing establishment - the very clan which once so soundly re-buffed Henry Bessemer - and by 1899 he was serving as Senior Warden in the Cutlers' Company of Hallamshire, the Livery Guild organisation which had safeguarded the status of the region's metal manufacturers since the seventeenth century. Literally only months before he was due to be elected Master Cutler - the figurehead of all Sheffield's steel industries - Harry succumbed to influenza which turned to pneumonia and he died on 23 February 1899, aged 45.[15] Metallurgist and industrialist Robert Hadfield, as next in line, had the sad duty of taking up office as Master Cutler somewhat earlier than he had anticipated. One cannot help but think that had Harry Allen become Master Cutler, and had Henry Bessemer lived a little longer to see it, the latter might well have regarded the occasion as the ultimate recognition of his process and his faith in it.

At the turn of the century the only Bessemer plants in South Yorkshire with a reasonably assured future were those at Penistone, Rotherham and Stocksbridge. By this time all three were members of an Inland Rail Makers' Association, which ensured their mills continued to

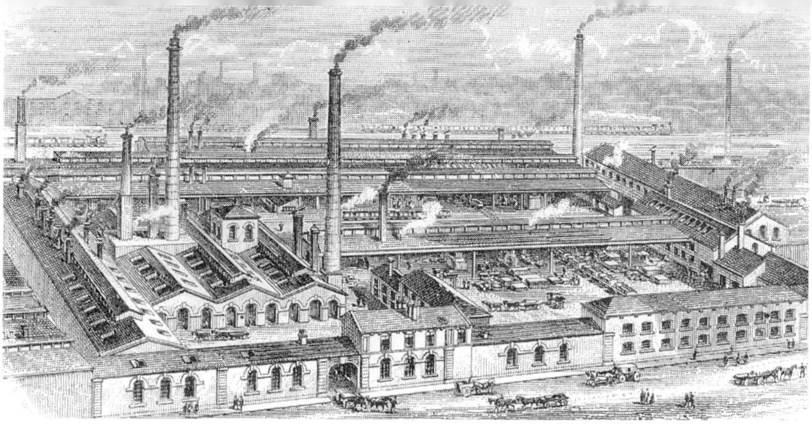

Figure 8. Artist's impression of the works of Henry Bessemer & Co. Ltd. as it appeared about 1890, with Carlisle Street in the foreground and the Midland Railway's goods only line to the Wicker Station beyond the buildings. *Courtesy K. P. Plant*

receive rail orders from British railway companies on an unofficial rota basis.

Stocksbridge closed its Bessemer plant during the First World War so that the adjacent rolling mill could be enlarged to increase the output of shell steel billets. The works continued to roll acid Bessemer rails, however, using ingots supplied by Rotherham steelmakers Steel, Peech & Tozer Ltd. under a special agreement. The Bessemer plants at Penistone and Rotherham survived somewhat longer, into the 1920s, though each by then was complemented with open hearth melting units. It was inevitable, once the post-war Depression began to bite, that the days of Bessemer steelmaking in South Yorkshire were numbered. An era ended when the region's last converters were finally silenced in the late 1920s (Figure 10). We can best appreciate the enormity of this event by considering it in context. During the four decades that the Bessemer process was a major part of the Sheffield steelmaking scene, the town rose from a cutlery and edge tool producer through the nation's largest roller of steel railway rails to become one of the

Figure 9. Advertisement from the early 1890s illustrating a selection of products offered by the Henry Bessemer & Company Limited. Single piece crank axles (top right; bottom left) were a speciality.

world's largest centres of armament and ordnance manufacture. The Bessemer process played the significant mid-field role in this important transition from light to heavy trades, and in consequence Sheffield owes it a great deal. The distrust of Bessemer by the town's orthodox steelmakers and their antagonism towards him was, to say the least, undeserved.

The Last Link

The last acid Bessemer converters in use in the UK - the two 30 ton capacity vessels at British Steel's Workington Works in Cumbria - were effectively direct descendants of those in the Sheffield plants of the nineteenth century. It was indeed fitting that one of the Workington converters was saved when its working life ended in 1974, and now graces in a most impressive manner the entrance to Sheffield's Kelham Island Industrial Museum complex, less than a mile distant from the site of the UK's first commercial Bessemer steelplant.

The Legacy

Bessemer's steelmaking invention provided an ideal vehicle to take forward the burgeoning Industrial Revolution of the 1860s and 1870s. Indeed, its commercial introduction marked the end of the first phase of that vast social, commercial and technological upheaval in which iron had played such a pivotal role. From now on the process would be more adequately supported by the Age of Steel.

The rate at which the new steelmaking technology spread through the western world was quite remarkable, but with good reason. Bessemer was practising efficient 'networking' of information before the word had ever been invented to describe this modern phenomenon we now associate with Information Technology. He actively encouraged the dissemination of 'best practice' techniques between Bessemer works as an extension of the pioneer school philosophy of his Carlisle Street Works. He was also prepared to provide managers experienced in Bessemer steelmaking techniques to licensees who had little or no previous steelmaking experience. Such frank and open interchanges within the industry created a whole new culture, and provided a major boost for the formation of a professional club in which the members would freely exchange (through lectures and publications) all manner of details relating to iron and steel

Figure 10. Acid Bessemer converter at the Ickles Works, Rotherham, of Steel, Peech & Tozer Ltd. in the late 1920s. It is thought the photograph records the very last Bessemer blow in South Yorkshire. *Author's collection*

processing. The whole business was formalised in 1869 with the creation of the Iron and Steel Institute, in which Bessemer was a founder member.[16]

Now, as we approach the new Millennium, thanks to new technology we have a myriad of materials at our disposal. And yet, despite the various advantages of plastics, or of aluminium and 'super-alloys' such as titanium, we remain firmly in the Age of Steel. It is a sobering thought to realise that virtually everything we employ in the modern world either contains steel, or has been manufactured on machinery which itself is largely made of steel.

Bessemer's prediction of 1861 has proved every bit as durable as the metal his invention brought into common use. We do well to honour his memory.

Notes and References

1. Much of the present account is based on Henry Bessemer's autobiography, completed posthumously by his eldest son. Entitled *Sir Henry Bessemer FRS: An Autobiography,* this was originally published in 1905 by Engineering (London) and reprinted in 1989 by The Institute of Metals. Understandably, the work is somewhat partisan, and I have attempted to produce a more balanced treatment by reference to other contemporary 'independent' sources.
2. *Sir Henry Bessemer, Father of the Steel Industry,* edited by C. Bodsworth and published in 1998 by the Institute of Materials.
3. Abram Hewitt addressing the American Meeting of the Iron and Steel Institute in 1890.
4. *Manchester Faces and Places,* Volume 5, 1894, John Galloway's obituary notice.
5. *Minutes of the Proceedings of the Institute of Civil Engineers,* Volume 18, Session 1858-9. Bessemer's paper was entitled 'Manufacture of Malleable Iron and Steel'.
6. Sir Allan Grant, *Steel and Ships,* 1950, Michael Joseph Ltd., London.
7. *Journal of the Iron and Steel Institute,* 1878, p. 615. Charles Cammell's obituary notice.
8. *Remarkable Occurrences and Interesting Dates* [of Penistone & District], published at Penistone in 1890 by the author, John Wood. The Penistone Bessemer Works quickly passed into the ownership of Charles Cammell & Company.
9. The use of ganister (a form of silica) as the lining, because it was chemically acidic, resulted in the process being called the acid Bessemer process. A later, important development was the substitution of burnt dolomite (a calcium-magnesium oxide) in place of ganister, and this was referred to as the basic Bessemer process.
10. For a more detailed account of the steel rail trade, see T.J. Lodge, 'South Yorkshire's Steel Rail Trade' in *Sir Henry Bessemer: Father of the Steel Industry.* See also Trevor Lodge, 'Rotherham's Railway Trades' in M. Jones (ed.), *Aspects of Rotherham 1,* Wharncliffe Publishing, 1995. The latter examines the manufacture of Bessemer steel rails as an important aspect of a wider manufacturing framework very reliant on the Victorian railway industry.
11. See, for example, 'Impact of Bessemer Steelmaking Technology in the United States' by E. T. Turkdogan in *Sir Henry Bessemer: Father of the Steel Industry.*
12. G. Dow, *Great Central,* Volume 2, Locomotive Publishing Company, 1962, London pp.84 & 200.
13. H. Baker, private correspondence.
14. Bessemer records that on expiration of the fourteen years' term of partnership the works was sold for exactly 24 times the amount of the original subscribed capital. Each of the partners in the meantime had received a sum equal to 57 times the gross capital as profit. In other words each partner made 81 times the amount of his subscribed capital.
15. *Journal of the Iron and Steel Institute,* Volume I, 1899, p. 261. Harry Allen's obituary notice.
16. Another legacy is the Bessemer Gold Medal, presented by the Institute of Materials (as successor to the Iron and Steel Institute) in recognition of outstanding metallurgical work on iron or steel. This highly-coveted prize has been awarded annually since 1873 and is funded from an investment sum which Bessemer bequeathed specially for the purpose during his tenure of President of the Iron and Steel Institute.

Acknowledgements

I wish to thank John Capes and Ray Heard for their continuing diligence on my behalf. John has actively supported my passion for Sheffield industry over many years, and Ray has enlightened me about several rich sources of relevant information of which I would otherwise have remained ignorant.

12. A CENTURY OF CINEMA

by Clifford Shaw and Christopher Stacey

THE STORY OF THE CINEMA in Sheffield begins with the flickering pictures of the new sensation of the music hall – the *Lumière Cinématographe* – seen for the first time in the city on 22 June 1896, at the newly-opened Empire Theatre in Charles Street (Figure 1).

A century later to the day – many of these 'snapshot' scenes, which have survived those first showings, were included in a commemorative programme at the Showroom, then Sheffield's latest cinema.

In the years between, the city has seen the rise and fall of 67 cinemas; the struggling attempts in the early years of the century to synchronise sound with picture; the advent of colour in 1912-13 with the pioneer system of Kinema-color; the masterpieces of D. W. Griffith; the slapstick of the Keystone Cops, Charlie Chaplin and Buster Keaton; the talkies; 3-D, wide screen and Cinemascope and now 'perfect' sound and pictures seen in the comfort of state-of-the-art multi-screen cinemas.

The rapidity with which this new phenomenon captured the entertainment world and audiences in Sheffield in particular was astonishing. By the end of 1896 films were being shown at Saturday night concerts at the Albert Hall in Barker's Pool and at the Grand Theatre of Varieties in West Bar. Fairground bioscope shows were also becoming popular and Randall Williams, a well-known travelling showman, brought his booth to Sheffield's Christmas fair in 1897.

Two men were to dominate the early cinema scene in Sheffield. Jasper Redfern had been quick off the mark to exploit an interest in new discoveries by combining a film show with a demonstration of Röntgen X-rays. This enterprise was to be closely matched with Frank Mottershaw (Figure 2),

Figure 1. Where it all started in Sheffield – the newly-opened Empire Theatre in Charles Street where, on the evening of 22 June, 1896, the first flickering pictures of the *Lumière Cinématographe* were shown to an astonished audience of music hall-goers.

Sheffield City Libraries, Local Studies Library

2

Wharncliffe Books
FREEPOST SF5
47 Church Street
BARNSLEY
South Yorkshire
S70 2BR

who was to place Sheffield firmly on the entertainment map.

At one time, Sheffield was hailed as an up-and-coming Hollywood of the North, thanks to the quite remarkable volume of films made by Mottershaw's Sheffield Photo Company. Many were shot on location but film studios established in Upper Hanover Street were fully equipped with facilities for developing and printing film stock. An open-air stage was built in the back garden for filming 'indoor' scenes, but plots were devised so that outdoor locations could be used. His most famous film was 'The Life of Charles Peace', the story of a notorious murderer who shot and killed a man in Banner Cross, Ecclesall, and which was shown far and wide in Britain and abroad. The scenes shot on location included Peace's attempt to escape arrest by leaping from a train between Kiveton Park and Shireoaks. Mottershaw's total output of fictional films was 63 of

Figure 2. Pioneer film-maker, Frank Mottershaw (left, nearer camera), whose studio was hailed as an up-and-coming Hollywood of the North, with his family (left to right, back row) Frank Storm Mottershaw, Arthur Mottershaw and Edith Mottershaw; (next row, right), Mrs Mary Mottershaw with Richard on her knee; Jessie is on her father's knee with Walter between his parents and Harry standing in front. The photograph is dated 1902. *Fiona Lloyd*

which 41 were made between 1904 and 1906. Sadly for Sheffield, film production at the Mottershaw studios effectively ceased by 1909, although Mottershaw's son, Frank Storm Mottershaw, an outstanding film maker, continued in the topical and documentary field.

Film producer and entrepreneur who stayed the course for many years was undoubtedly Jasper Redfern, optician and photographer, who established the city's first permanent cinema in 1905 by adapting the Central Hall in Norfolk Street, where he combined films and variety turns in programme planning that was a forerunner of the cine-variety that was a feature of the large 'super cinemas' of the late twenties and early thirties. Refurbished and renamed the Tivoli, Redfern's pioneer cinema became known as the 'ranch house' because of the number of westerns shown there in later years. Unlike Mottershaw, Jasper Redfern concentrated his film production on topical scenes. His newsreels of local events were swiftly supplied to his own as well as rival cinemas. His theatre empire extended to places as far apart as Manchester, Liverpool and Windsor.

Sheffield's first purpose-built cinema was the Union Street Picture Palace, which opened in August 1910 (Figure 3), followed the next year by the Electra Palace in Fitzalan Square (Figure 4), commissioned by Sheffield and District Cinematograph Theatres, one of three companies that would establish small local circuits. The façade of the Electra in glazed terracotta was in the style of fifteenth-century Arabian architecture with graceful minarets which were illuminated at night.

The Phoenix, opposite Hillsborough Barracks was the third purpose-built cinema combining films and variety turns. It was a family business. The first manager was Harold Phoenix, the owner's elder son who 'learned his trade' at Jasper Redfern's Central Hall.

Figure 3. Sheffield's first purpose-built cinema, The Palace, Union Street, was opened in August, 1910, and became one of the most popular picture houses in the city centre. The photograph shows the exterior, taken in 1959, when 'The Best of Everything', a Cinemascope picture, was being shown. *Leslie Johnson*

Figure 4. The Electra Palace, Fitzalan Square, the city's second purpose-built picture house, opened in 1911, was an imposing sight in Fitzalan Square with its glazed terracotta façade designed in fifteenth century Moorish architectural style with graceful minarets illuminated at night. In later years it became the News Theatre and later still it was renamed the Classic. *Sheffield City Libraries, Local Studies Library*

So the race was on. The big circuits with their flotations for capital in the money market, were yet to make their appearance; capital was raised locally and the men who jumped on the cinema band wagon were akin to 'butchers, bakers and candlestick makers'; one cinema, for instance, was built with the proceeds of pawnbroking.

Why so many years elapsed before purpose-built cinemas appeared is partly explained by the dominant position of the music hall in popular entertainment and the fact that, with a few exceptions, films were made and regarded only as extras to augment variety programmes. Large scale production in the United States and elsewhere did not begin until about 1907 and only then was the cinema able to come into its own.

Redfern made his debut as an exhibitor at the Albert Hall in February 1898, relying on topical interest in the Corbett v Fitzsimmons fight. In July he put on a show at the Attercliffe Alhambra, a music hall that from 1904 became known as the Palace. He continued to provide bioscope interludes at the Empire but from 1901 favoured the Montgomery Hall, opposite the Town Hall, where he would show complete film programmes but sometimes included variety turns. From 1905 he exhibited in Sheffield only at the Central Hall.

A major figure in the American film industry was James Stuart Blackton, who was born in Sheffield in 1875. His real name was Blacktin and he emigrated with his mother to the States about the age of eleven. By 1896, the young man had found his feet sufficiently to set up the Vitagraph company in partnership with Albert E. Smith, another 'Brit' who was struggling to make his way. Within a few years Vitagraph had become a leading film company. Blackton was at various times actor, cameraman, animator, script writer, director and publicist but his greatest contribution at Vitagraph was probably as producer. In October 1920, he paid a flying visit to Sheffield and the following year came to Britain to make 'The Glorious Adventure' in

Prizmacolor. In 1922 he directed two other films before returning to Vitagraph, where he worked until the company was taken over by Warner Bros. in 1926.

The early history of film exhibition, as we have seen, was closely tied in with the music hall. Frank MacNaghten was still feeling his way when he came to Sheffield in 1896 to try to revive the fortunes of the Grand Theatre, a rather seedy West Bar music hall. His efforts enjoyed some success and the backers of the Attercliffe Alhambra recruited him as managing director, but attendances were disappointing and his services were not retained beyond the contracted period of five years. In the meantime, he had acquired the Theatre Royal, Attercliffe, a drama house where plays were presented by touring companies. MacNaghten's main aim as a theatrical entrepreneur was to establish a chain of music halls and on the crest of the wave in 1910 he controlled three theatres, seventeen music halls and two cinemas. Except for the London halls, the circuit was managed from MacNaghten's office in Sheffield. Gradually the vaudeville circuit lost ground and in the 1930s several halls were turned into cinemas. MacNaghten died in 1938 but the business continued to be run from Sheffield until it was wound up in 1959.

The Theatre Royal, Attercliffe, introduced pictures for a summer season in June 1906 and, from February 1907, the hall mainly operated as a cinema, although often including a vocalist or variety turn in the programme. The Grand Theatre – no longer controlled by MacNaghten – also went over to films from December 1908, and from June 1909 the Attercliffe Palace followed suit. In the meantime the Hippodrome had opened in 1907 as a serious rival of the Empire and included a bioscope interlude in many of its programmes.

From 1909, films began to be shown in a number of makeshift halls and also on a Saturday evening at the recently-opened Wesley Hall, Crookes, and the Victoria Hall in Norfolk Street.

The Heeley Electric Palace opened in August 1911 and had a seating capacity of 1450 including 350 in the balcony. Although it had no stage, it had some of the trappings of a theatre with a number of private boxes. The Woodseats Palace opened in September 1911 with a seating capacity of 500, which was later increased to 800 when a balcony was constructed. The Picturedrome in Grimesthorpe opened in March 1912.

The pace of cinema building was gaining momentum and four halls were completed in November 1912. The Don, in particular, caught the attention of passers-by as an illuminated clown on one side of the entrance appeared to throw a ball of electric lights to a clown on the other side, who in turn threw it on a sign which spelt out Picture Palace.

Building continued, details of the various cinemas being summarised in an Appendix (pp. 197-200). Nine cinemas were completed in 1913, the Globe in Attercliffe opening in February. With a seating capacity of 1700, it was the largest yet built in Sheffield. Just below the roof was a globe, which at night revolved with constantly changing coloured lights. April saw the completion of the Coliseum, Spital Hill. Particularly impressive was the opulent Cinema House in the city centre (Figure 5), with its tower and the extensive use of white faience. This was the second cinema commissioned by Sheffield and District Cinematograph Theatres and opened in May 1913, the amenities including a café and billiards hall. July saw the opening of the Darnall Picture Palace, which became better known in later years as the Balfour. Somewhat unusually it was built in the style of a mock castle. The Park in South Street came on stream in August, the Darnall Cinema in September, the Heeley Coliseum in October, the Unity in November and nearby the Oxford opened in December in a converted Unitarian chapel with the altar remaining intact behind the screen.

The Weston, Woodhouse, and Wincobank picture palaces opened in 1914, followed by the Greystones, which was the first Sheffield cinema to be built with an associated ballroom.

The outbreak of war in August brought a halt to the building of new cinemas but those in the course of construction were mainly completed. The Walkley Palladium, the Lansdowne and the Norfolk were finished by December and the Rutland shortly afterwards but the Pavilion in Attercliffe and the Star on Ecclesall Road were

Figure 5. The sumptuous interior of Cinema House, Barker's Pool, which opened in May, 1913, was Sheffield's first 'super cinema' with tapestries on the side walls and concealed lighting. It was the first city cinema to show colour pictures in the Chronochrome process and also Edison's sound on disc films. *C. S. Stacey collection*

completed just in time for a Christmas opening in 1915. War conditions created many difficulties but the conflict brought a measure of prosperity to those in the cinema trade and, with the cessation of hostilities, there was no shortage of investors wishing to share in the bonanza.

Those companies in a position to move quickly had no difficulty in forging ahead. Heeley Green Picture House with its quaint Tudor frontage opened in April 1920, to be followed in May by two larger cinemas, the Chantrey Picture House and the Page Hall Cinema. The Chantrey had a ballroom, later used for billiards, and at the Page Hall there was a billiards saloon, a ballroom being added in 1929.

The Wicker Picture House fell into a rather different category. In 1916, the Ministry of Munitions commandeered the partially-completed building for use as a warehouse. It finally opened as a cinema in June 1920, with a high profile run of D. W. Griffith's 'Broken Blossoms'. October saw the completion of the Adelphi in Attercliffe (Figure 6) and in the following month the Lyric opened as Darnall's third cinema.

The crowning glory of the year came with the opening of the Abbeydale Picture House, although the ballroom and billiards hall were yet to be constructed. It was the first suburban 'super cinema' incorporating the latest techniques in design with a large stage for variety presentations and an organ. The Hillsborough Park Cinema was the last to escape the close scrutiny and delays arising from a decision of the City Council to use its emergency powers to ban non-essential building so that labour and materials would not be diverted from providing houses 'fit for heroes'.

Most of the cinemas in the pipeline eventually went ahead,

Figure 6. The Adelphi in Vicarage Road, Attercliffe, built in 1920, was a typical example of a type of 'back to front' cinema peculiar to Sheffield but not unique which resulted in access to stalls and circle from either side of the screen which was behind the entrance hall. *late Elsie Cable*

sometimes with a revision of the plans to avoid the use of materials needed for housing, but it was a period of quite serious inflation. Any postponement resulted in escalating costs, which crucially affected the viability of some projects, particularly as there had been a slump in cinema attendances.

The Victory, in Grimesthorpe, was eventually built but at a much higher cost and, within four years, the company was wound up, although fortunately the cinema survived. The Scala in the vicinity of Sheffield University fared rather better. It had a wider appeal with a ballroom on the second floor, a café on the first floor and an assembly room in the basement used for whist drives.

The Central Picture House on the Moor became one of Sheffield's leading cinemas. Despite the restricted frontage, the auditorium was large with a seating capacity of 1600. It also had a café–restaurant and a billiards saloon. The New Roscoe was a much humbler affair constructed as a replacement for an original hall. The Sunbeam, Barnsley Road, which opened in December 1922, was the last of the thirteen cinemas erected in the aftermath of the war.

In 1920, E. C. Clayton promoted Heeley and Amalgamated Cinemas, a small local circuit including the Heeley Palace, the Woodseats, the Oxford and the Pavilion, Attercliffe. Clayton also had an interest in the Lyric, Darnall, and other cinemas in South Yorkshire and the Isle of Man.

In 1921, Hallamshire Cinemas established a third local circuit by taking over the Crookes, Darnall and Weston picture palaces and had close association with the Lansdowne. The directors of the Sunbeam were also on the board of Hallamshire Cinemas. Sheffield and District Cinematograph Theatres had acquired the Globe in 1919 and in 1927 the Don also came under its control.

Later, the outsiders moved in. J. F. Emery, a Salford based circuit, took over the running of the Star, the Wicker and the Regal in the mid-thirties. Star Cinemas acquired the Lyric in 1943 and by 1955 had become a major force in the district after taking over the Emery halls and those of Heeley and Amalgamated Cinemas. To these would be later added the Manor, Hillsborough Park, the Ritz and Cinecenta.

The Albert Hall opened in 1873 as a concert hall with its Cavaille-Col organ that was reputed to be the largest in the world. From 1896 to 1912 films were shown frequently interspersed between music or other forms of entertainment. In 1913, the hall operated principally as a cinema and during the war years a few spectacular films were shown, but the hall was not used solely as a cinema until

June 1918. By the 1930s the Albert Hall was playing in tandem with the Regent as both were now part of the Gaumont British circuit. The end came when, suddenly, a rapidly spreading fire broke out on 14 July 1937, a few minutes after the audience had left, completely destroying the interior and the Cavaille-Col organ (Figure 7). Plans were drawn up to rebuild it but Gaumont British finally abandoned all thoughts of restoring it.

Spectacular fires seriously damaged the Tivoli in 1927, the Roxy (formerly the Page Hall) in 1958 and Studio 7 (formerly the Wicker) in 1967. Damage was also caused by fire at the Greystones Palace in 1956.

In December 1927, after a gap of some five years, Sheffield gained two new cinemas within a fortnight – the Manor at the top of City Road and the Regent in Barker's Pool.

The Manor was intended to cater for those living on the Manor

Figure 7. The morning after the night before – crowds gather outside the shell of the Albert Hall, Barker's Pool, devastated by fire which swept through the historic building destroying the renowned organ after the evening's cinema performance on 14 July 1937. The building on the left is the Regent. *Sheffield Newspapers*

estate. The cinema was on a sloping site with the circle at the level of the entrance hall; the stalls were at parterre level and there was a billiards saloon in the basement.

The Regent was something special and could be truly termed a 'super cinema'. The crush hall and lounge were elaborately decorated and a feature of the auditorium was a huge double dome and a beautifully-proportioned proscenium arch (Figure 8). Seating capacity was 2300 of which 850 were in the circle. As films were still silent, an orchestra of 25 musicians supplied the 'mood' music. Programmes included a quality stage show and an organ recital on the 'mighty Wurlitzer'. The coming of talkies eighteen months later resulted in the disappearance of cine-variety.

The race between the Regent and the Central to install sound equipment resulted in a dead heat as both went over to talkies from 17 June 1929. Curiously the Electra had jumped the gun as it had been showing shorts since March. These accompanied silent features and relied on disc recording.

Of the other city centre cinemas, the Albert Hall converted to sound in September and the Palace, Union Street in December 1929. Several of the district cinemas also went over to sound in 1929 - the Hillsborough Kinema, the Walkley Palladium, the Norfolk, the Star, the Scala and the Theatre Royal, Attercliffe. The last of the Sheffield cinemas to take the plunge were the Heeley Coliseum in August 1931 and the Page Hall Cinema in November 1931.

In the dying months of the silent era the Abbeydale, the Scala, the Coliseum, Spital Hill, and even the Palace, Union Street, had sought

Figure 8. The magnificent double dome of The Regent (renamed The Gaumont in 1946) and the graceful proscenium arch – both of which disappeared in 1968 when the cinema was reconstructed to provide twin cinemas. At its opening in 1927, it had a seating capacity of 2,300 with an orchestra of 25 and a 'mighty' Wurlitzer organ. *C. S. Stacey collection*

to turn back the tide through the introduction of cine-variety but the public knew what it wanted. Sound was a success and going to the pictures became a habit that revived the fortunes of the cinema industry. The response of those halls that had gone over to stage shows in the 1920s was not always predictable. The Attercliffe Palace mainly operated as a cinema from 1930 to 1937, as did the Regent, Grimesthorpe (formerly the Picturedrome) from 1930 to early in 1935. On the other hand the Phoenix remained a revue and variety theatre from 1925 to 1933, and the Heeley Green Picture House presented live entertainment – not films – between 1929 and 1938.

The Paragon, Firth Park, opened in 1934 and was the first in a series of cinemas built in the 1930s that were mainly intended to serve the developing housing estates. Two more were added in December 1937, the Ritz serving Parson Cross and the Plaza, Handsworth. The Carlton on the Arbourthorne estate was built by Sheffield and District Cinematograph Theatres and opened in 1938. An unusual feature was that it was constructed throughout in concrete and, despite its austere appearance, the interior was quite attractive.

The largest and perhaps finest of these cinemas was the Forum on Herries Road with a seating capacity of 1814. It was the work of George Coles, a leading cinema architect, the owner being M. J. Gleeson, whose main business was as a building contractor.

The Rex, Intake, was a beautifully designed cinema in the style of the period. It opened in July 1939 and survived until 1982, long after Sheffield's other suburban cinemas had closed.

The last of these pre-war cinemas was the Capitol, Sheffield Lane Top, which opened in September 1939 (Figure 9). It was the second of the cinemas designed by George Coles for Gleeson. One other new cinema, the Regal, constructed on the site of the Theatre Royal, Attercliffe, opened in 1935.

Figure 9. Interior of the Capitol, Sheffield Lane Top, (later to become the Essoldo and then The Vogue) which was designed by the noted cinema architect, George Coles, for M. J. Gleeson, building contractor-cum-cinema owner, and was the last pre-Second World War theatre to be built in Sheffield to serve the expanding Parson Cross area. *C. S. Stacey collection*

The Second World War broke out on 3 September 1939, and all theatres and cinemas were required to close. Cinemas in Sheffield were allowed to re-open from 15 September on condition that performances should not end later than 10 p.m., a requirement that was soon relaxed. The main aerial attacks on Sheffield were concentrated on the nights of 12 and 14 December 1940 and as a result the Central Picture House, the Tivoli, the Lansdowne and the Rutland were damaged and never re-opened. In the aftermath of the blitz the cinemas still in business opened in the mornings from 11 a.m. onwards but were required to close not later than half-an-hour after dusk. The Regal did not re-open until March 1941, followed by the Wicker in April, the Scala in July and the Star and the Hillsborough Kinema in October 1941. From November 1941 cinemas were allowed to remain open until 11 p.m. but Sheffield's central cinemas closed by 10 p.m. at the latest and usually much earlier. The Palace, Union Street normally closed by 9 p.m.

Sunday opening was the subject of recurring controversy and was not allowed in Sheffield until August 1944. The conditions imposed by the licensing authority were extremely restrictive, particularly the stipulation that performances could not begin until 6 p.m.; nor could children under school leaving age (then 14) be admitted to any programme. The only cinemas that initially opened on Sundays were the Regent, the Hippodrome, the Star, the Regal and the Wicker but the Lyric, Darnall, soon followed their lead and the News Theatre, formerly the Electra, also opened on Sundays from September 1945. The Page Hall (soon to become the Roxy) and the Victory went over to Sunday opening in 1946, and the Capitol and Forum introduced Sunday opening in 1948 after becoming part of the Essoldo circuit; but it was not until 1953 that the move toward Sunday opening really gained momentum, although sixteen Sheffield cinemas never opened on Sundays.

Construction of an Odeon began in 1939 on a site at the top of Pond Street originally intended for a second evening newspaper office. Work was suspended on the outbreak of war but a redesigned building was eventually completed in July 1956. It was a deceptively large cinema with a seating capacity of 2340. The Odeon took many of the large screen epics of the period before the Gaumont (formerly Regent) was 'twinned' in 1969. The Odeon had a short life as it closed in June 1971 and is now Mecca bingo.

Associated British Cinemas had been tenants at the Hippodrome since 1931 but failed to renew the lease in 1948. In May 1961 the company opened the ABC, Angel Street. The auditorium seated

1327 and was of the stadium type without a balcony. Instead of a traditional proscenium a vast curved curtain covered the screen and continued along the side walls.

The Regent was renamed the Gaumont in 1946. In 1968, it closed for nine months while the roof was raised fifteen feet and the interior was reconstructed to provide twin cinemas. Gaumont 1 was custom-built for showing Cinerama. It seated 737 and was on the upper floor. Gaumont 2 was the larger auditorium and had a seating capacity of 1150. Gaumont 3 seated 144 and was added in 1979 by converting the restaurant.

Cinecenta, which opened in 1969, was part of the Pond Street multi-storey car park development. The original intention was to show minority interest films but the cinema never prospered despite changes in ownership and the introduction of films with an X certificate.

Cineplex formed part of the Grosvenor House Hotel complex on Charter Square and opened in 1972. Shop units were combined to form three cinemas – the dream of Derek Williams, one-time regional manager for Rank Odeon. Initially the projectors were capable of showing only 16 mm prints but this limitation restricted the choice of recent releases and later a 35 mm projector was installed in the largest auditorium. After eleven years Williams decided to call it a day. Sheffield City Council agreed to take over the lease and to operate it as a municipal cinema in place of the 'art house' programmes that had been offered in the Library Theatre on a one-week-a-month basis. The Anvil, as Cineplex was renamed, managed to survive but rather precariously and, faced with mounting financial pressure, it caused regret but little surprise when the cinema closed in November 1990.

With cinema attendances at their peak in 1946 it would have been difficult to foresee the slow but steady drifting away of audiences, as ownership of television sets increased. The Scala closed in 1952 but this was due to the University making a compulsory purchase order with a view to expanding teaching facilities. The cinema industry tried hard to arouse the interest of audiences with a greater number of films in colour and the introduction of wide-screen processes. Cinemascope could make quite an impact if both the subject and the theatre were suited to the new format. The Palace, Union Street exploited Cinemascope with considerable success but other halls were less committed. Todd-AO, Supertechnirama 70, Cinerama and Vistavision attracted considerable attention at the time but failed to stay the course, and 3-D was a gimmick that never really caught on.

The first casualties resulting from a downturn in business were the Weston, the Victory, the Darnall Cinema and the Palace, Woodhouse, all of which closed in 1957, followed in 1958 by the Don and the Tinsley Palace. Soon the trickle became a flood, eight cinemas closing in 1959; two in 1960; five in 1961; six in 1962; three in 1963; two in 1964; one in 1965; three in 1966; two in 1967; one in 1968 and two in 1969. The Pavilion, Attercliffe, survived until 1970, although it had re-opened after earlier closures; later the hall was used for showing Asian films. The Essoldo, Lane Top (formerly the Capitol) and the Abbeydale remained open until 1975. The Rex (Figure 10) and Classic (formerly the Electra and News Theatre) succumbed in 1982 and Studios 5, 6 and 7 (originally the Wicker) in 1987.

Television had caused the closure of many cinemas in the late fifties and throughout the sixties. Those remaining were 'twinned' and eventually converted to three or more screens. In 1984 the outlook was bleak and audiences were still falling. The Gaumont was considered an expensive cinema to run and the lure of offering a prime site to property developers, resulted in the Rank Organisation deciding to close the cinema in 1984. A deal was negotiated to provide two auditoria within a shopping complex on the site. They were to be known as Odeon 1 and 2 and opened in 1987, access being from Burgess Street.

Their life was short – the concept of the multiplex resulted in the disused Fiesta night club building in Arundel Gate being converted to form a seven-screen complex (later increased to ten) that opened

Figure 10. Queues were all part of cinema-going in its pre TV heyday. Here is a panoramic picture of a crowd waiting in August, 1944, to see 'Lassie Come Home' at the Rex, Intake, one of the most perfectly-designed cinemas in the city, which opened in 1939 and survived unto 1982, long after other suburban cinemas had closed. *Dorothy Ward*

in 1992. With great ingenuity the twin screens of the former Cinecenta had been incorporated within the scheme. The Odeon, Arundel Gate, is constructed on three levels and now has a seating capacity of 1734. Understandably Odeon Cinemas decided to concentrate on one site and closed the Odeon, Burgess Street in 1994.

As a successor to the Anvil, the Showroom opened in March 1995 with two screens with seating capacities of 83 and 110. As a result of a substantial lottery grant it has been possible to provide two additional screens with capacities of 178 and 280. The complex re-opened in March 1998 with a seating capacity of 651. The proprietors are Sheffield Media and Exhibition Centre, a non-profit making trust.

The multiplex age really hit Sheffield with the opening of the AMC at Crystal Peaks in May 1988. It was an event that was more important than was probably realised at the time, as it provided ten screens and 2328 seats. The original proprietors (American Multi-Cinema) quickly withdrew from the British market, having reached an agreement with UCI (United Cinemas International) but the idea of the multiplex had already taken root.

Warner Cinemas opened a multiplex with eleven screens at Meadowhall in March 1993. Total seating is currently 2198, the capacity of the smallest auditorium being 72 and the largest 362.

The Virgin twenty-screen 'Megaplex' opened in November 1998 (Figure 11). It has a seating capacity of 4915 and is the latest and boldest attempt to entice folk back to the cinema, offering a choice of up to 30 films each week. The seating capacity of the auditoria range from 82 to 691 and all are designed to give an unrestricted

Figure 11. The latest state-of-the-art multi-screen cinema to open in the Sheffield area is the Virgin Complex in Broughton Road. Here is the imposing entrance to the 20-screen Megaplex opened in November, 1998, with a seating capacity of 4,915. *Clifford Shaw*

view of the screen which in the largest auditorium is a massive 20 metres wide.

In Sheffield none of the dream palaces have survived and even an élite cinema like the ABC/Cannon has closed and the modern cinemas forming the Odeon, Burgess Street, remain unused.

The city now has 55 screens and some 11,826 seats to accommodate cinema attendances that have been gradually edging up since they were at their lowest level in 1984. Multiplexes are proving popular. The danger is that the next may prove one too many.

Bibliography

1. Robert Benfield, *Bijou Kinema and Electric Theatres*, Sheffield City Polytechnic, 1976 (includes information on the Sheffield Photo Company).
2. Allen Eyles, *ABC: The First Name in Entertainment*, Cinema Theatre Association, 1993 (includes a description and photographs of the Sheffield ABC).
3. Allen Eyles, *Gaumont British Cinemas*, Cinema Theatre Association, 1996 (includes a description, photographs and programme information relating to the Regent/Gaumont in Barker's Pool).
4. Leslie Frost, *Seats in all parts. Memories of the Lyceum, Sheffield Empire and Attercliffe Palace*, published by the author 1986 (Revised 1989).
5. Geoff J. Mellor, *The Northern Music Hall*, Frank Graham, 1970 (in particular, Chapter nine on the MacNaghten Vaudeville Circuit).
6. Geoff J. Mellor, *Picture Pioneers. The story of the Northern Cinema*, Frank Graham, 1971.
7. Geoff J. Mellor, *Movie Makers and Picture Palaces. A Century of Cinema in Yorkshire 1896-1996*, Bradford Libraries, 1996.
8. Clifford H. Shaw and Stuart R. Smith, *The Early Years of Cinema in Sheffield 1896-1910*, Sheffield Cinema Society, 1995.
9. Fred Turley, *Mighty Music at the Movies. The Cinema Organ in Sheffield and the Surrounding Area*, Sheaf Publishing, 1990.
10. Richard P. Ward, *In Memory of Sheffield's Cinemas*, Sheffield City Libraries, 1988.
11. *Picture House*, Magazine of the Cinema Theatre Association No. 21, 1996 (includes an account of the Albert Hall and details of the publicity stunts devised by Reginald Rea, who was manager throughout the 1920s).
12. Newsletters of the Sheffield Cinema Society 1987 – to date (copies deposited in the Sheffield Local Studies Library).
13. *The A.B.C. of the Cinemas of Sheffield*, Sheffield Cinema Society, 1993 (Revised 1999).

Appendix

A SUMMARY RECORD OF SHEFFIELD'S CINEMA HERITAGE

Theatres that became cinemas	Date when films first shown on a regular basis	Date when use ceased
Theatre Royal, Staniforth Road, Attercliffe	9.2.1907	17.6.1933
Grand Theatre, West Bar	7.12.1908	Late 1920
Attercliffe Palace, Attercliffe Road	7.6.1909	17.7.37 but the hall remained open as a theatre until July 1955; it had also been used as a theatre from 1920 to June 1930.
Hippodrome, Cambridge Street	20.7.1931	2.3.1963

Miscellaneous halls mainly used as cinemas	Date when films first shown on a regular basis	Date when use ceased
Central Hall, Norfolk Street (from 1914 renamed the Tivoli)	10.7.1905	12.12.1940
Hillsborough Palace of Varieties, Broadfield Road	21.2.1909	May 1911

Imperial Hall, Cross Addy Street (from 1910 it was renamed Upperthorpe Picture Palace)	5.4.1909	1915
Roscoe Picture Palace, Infirmary Road	23.12.1910	Early 1922 (replaced by a new cinema)
Walkley Electric Theatre, Fulton Road	27.3.1911	1916
Olympic Electric Palace, Bramall Lane	21.9.1911	21.10.1911 (reverting to its former use as a roller skating rink)
Albert Hall, Barker's Pool	17.6.1918 (used as a cinema throughout 1913 and later sporadically)	14.7.1937 (due to a disastrous fire)

Purpose designed cinemas	**Date of opening**	**Date when use ceased**
Sheffield Picture Palace, Union Street	1.8.1910	31.10.1964
Electra Palace, Fitzalan Square (renamed the Sheffield News Theatre from 8.9.1945 and the Classic from 15.1.1962)	10.2.1911	24.11.1982
Phoenix, Langsett Road, Hillsborough	25.3.1911	10.9.1960 but from June 1925 to July 1933 the hall was mainly used as a theatre.
Heeley Palace, London Road/Oak Street	7.8.1911 (reopened 28.2.1965 after closure in March 1963)	22.6.1965, although children's matinées were still held until 1966.
Woodseats Picture Palace, Chesterfield Road	4.9.1911	24.9.1961
Picturedrome, Upwell Street, Grimesthorpe (from April 1925 it was renamed the Regent)	18.3.1912	Early 1935 but the hall remained open as a theatre until June 1940; it had also been used as a theatre from April 1925 to late 1930).
Crookes Picture Palace	2.11.1912	2.4.1960
Tinsley Picture Palace, Sheffield Road	16.11.1912	15.2.1958
Don Picture Palace, West Bar	18.11.1912	1.3.1958
Hillsborough Kinema, Proctor Place	On or about 18.11.1912	23.7.1966
Globe, Attercliffe Common/Kirkbridge Road	10.2.1913	29.6.1959
Coliseum, Spital Hill	24.4.1913	2.11.1963
Cinema House, Barker's Pool	6.5.1913	12.8.1961
Darnall Picture Palace, Staniforth Road/ Balfour Road	19.7.1913	28.2.1959
Park Picture Palace, South Street	1.8.1913 (reopened 12.9.1960 and again on 14.11.1963 after closures)	31.12.1966, although the hall had closed previously on 30.7.1960 and 2.6.1962.
Darnall Cinema, Catcliffe Road	15.9.1913	2.11.1957
Heeley Coliseum, London Road/ Guernsey Road	27.10.1913	14.1.1961
Unity, Langsett Road/Gertrude Street	7.11.1913	28.3.1959
Oxford, Addy Street/Shipton Lane	15.12.1913	15.8.1964
Weston, Upper St Philip's Road/Mitchell Street	Mid or late February 1914	2.2.1957
Woodhouse Picture Palace, Market Square	2.3.1914	28.12.1957
Wincobank Picture Palace, Merton lane	11.6.1914	21.2.1959
Greystones Picture Palace, Ecclesall Road	27.7.1914	17.8.1968

Walkley Palladium, South Road/Highton Street	17.12.1914	6.10.1962
Lansdowne, London Road/Boston Road	On or about 18.12.1914	12.12.1940
Norfolk, Duke Street/Talbot Street	24.12.1914	24.12.1959
Rutland, Rutland Road/Burton Road	On or about 1.2.1915	12.12.1940
Star, Ecclesall Road/William Street	23.12.1915	17.1.1962
Pavilion, Attercliffe Common	23.12.1915 (reopened 9.9.1963 and again on 2.3.1970 after closures)	24.10.1970, although the hall had previously closed as a cinema on 30.7.1960 and 2.6.1962.
Heeley Green Picture House, Gleadless Road	5.4.1920 (reopened 3.4.1961 as the Tudor)	14.7.1962, although closing previously on 7.3.1959. From April 1929 to 18.4.1938 the hall was in use as a theatre.
Chantrey Picture House, Chesterfield Road	22.5.1920	28.2.1959
Page Hall, Idsworth Road (from November 1946 renamed the Roxy)	24.5.1920	Probably 14.6.1959
Wicker Picture House, The Wicker (from October 1962, renamed Studio 7 and from April 1974 Studios 5, 6 and 7)	14.6.1920 (reopened 18.4. 1986 after closure)	20.8.1987, although the hall had previously closed on 4.12.1982.
Adelphi, Vicarage Road, Attercliffe	18.10.1920	28.10.1967
Lyric, Main Road, Darnall	22.11.1920	29.8.1962
Abbeydale Picture House, Abbeydale Road	20.12.1920	5.7.1975
Hillsborough Park, Middlewood Road	10.2.1921	29.10.1967
Victory, Upwell Street, Grimesthorpe	27.10.1921	6.7.1957
Scala, Brookhill/Winter Street	23.12.1921	5.7.1952
Central Picture House, The Moor	30.1.1922	12.12.1940
New Roscoe, Infirmary Road	17.4.1922 (reopened 8.10. 1961 after closure)	28.4.1962, although the hall had previously closed as a cinema on 23.9.1961.
Sunbeam, Barnsley Road/Skinnerthorpe Road	23.12.1922	2.9.1961
Manor Cinema, Manor Top	12.12.1927 (reopened 17.11.1963 after closure)	14.6.1969, although the hall had previously closed as a cinema on 17.11.1963.
Regent, Barker's Pool (from July 1946 renamed the Gaumont)	26.12.1927 (reopened 23.7.1969 after 'twinning')	7.11.1985
Paragon, Sicey Avenue, Firth Park	1.10.1934	28.2.1962
Ritz, Southey Green/Wordsworth Avenue	6.12.1937 (reopened 17.5.1965 after closure)	9.11.1966, although the hall had previously closed as a cinema on 7.11.1962.
Plaza, Richmond Road/Bramley Lane, Handsworth	27.12.1937	29.9.1963
Carlton, Eastern Avenue/Errington Road	15.8.1938	7.2.1959
Forum, Herries Road, Southey (from June 1956 renamed Essoldo)	17.9.1938	31.5.1969
Rex, Mansfield Road/Hollybank Road, Intake	24.7.1939	23.12.1982
Capitol, Barnsley Road, Sheffield Lane Top (from April 1950 renamed Essoldo and from April 1972 Vogue)	18.9.1939	4.10.1975
Odeon, Flat Street	16.7.1956	5.6.1971
ABC, Angel Street (from January 1987 renamed Cannon)	18.5.1961	28.7.1988

Cinecenta, Upper Concourse, Flat Street (from May 1986 renamed Cannon and from August 1989 Fiesta)	31.1.1969	29.9.1991 (but the auditoria were incorporated within the Odeon 7 multiplex)
Cineplex, Charter Square (from October 1983 renamed Anvil)	31.1.1972	3.11.1990
Odeon, Burgess Street	20.8.1987	20.2.1994
AMC, Crystal Peaks (from August 1989 renamed UCI)	26.5.1988	Currently exhibiting (10 screens)
Odeon 7, Arundel Gate (from December 1994 the '7' was dropped following the provision of additional auditoria)	5.3.1992	Currently exhibiting (10 screens)
Warner Cinemas, the Oasis, Meadowhall (from February 1997 renamed Warner Village Cinemas)	23.3.1993	Currently exhibiting (11 screens)
Showroom, Paternoster Row	2.3.1995 (reopened 27.3. 1998 with two additional auditoria)	Currently exhibiting (4 screens)
Virgin Megaplex, Valley Centertainment, Broughton Lane	5.11.1998	Currently exhibiting (20 screens)

Cinemas in fringe areas of Derbyshire and the West Riding that are now part of Sheffield	**Date of opening**	**Date when use ceased**
Chapeltown Picture Palace, Station Road	23.12.1912	16.3.1963
Central Hall, High Street, Beighton	7.8.1913	23.3.1963
High Green Picture Palace, Thompson Hill	29.1.1914	5.10.1957
Ecclesfield Cinema House, The Common/Coit Lane (from September 1950 renamed Essoldo)	1.1.1921	7.2.1959
Stocksbridge Palace, Manchester Road	12.5.1921 (reopened 13.6.1963 after closure)	23.7.1966, although previously closing as a cinema on 11.5.1963.

Other venues where films were shown from time to time	**Films first shown**	**Exhibition ceased**
Sheffield Empire, Charles Street	June 1896	1915
Montgomery Hall, Surrey Street	December 1897	1911
Victoria Hall, Norfolk Street	October 1908	1964
Surrey Music Hall, West Bar	February 1909	1912
Wesley Hall, Crookes/Carson Road	March 1909	1929
Central Hall, Market Square, Woodhouse	November 1909	1916
Fulwood Guild Hall, Fulwood Head	November 1909	1936
St Vincent's Hall, Solly Street	September 1911	1917
Wesleyan Hall, Attercliffe Road	January 1927	Uncertain (1936-38)
Library Theatre, Tudor Place (from October 1967 to April 1983 the venue was promoted as the Sheffield Film Theatre, exhibiting during monthly 'film weeks')	November 1947 but occasional films from 1936	1994, although projection facilities still available

Contributors

1. John Spencer's Baltic Trade in Sheffield Wares

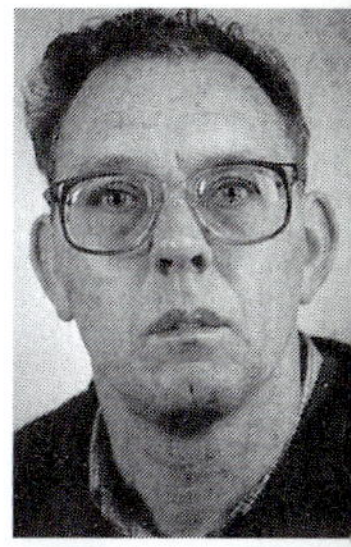

Dennis Smith was born in Sheffield in 1947, and has spent much of his life in the Walkley area. Educated at Morley Street County School and Myers Grove Comprehensive School, he worked variously as cutlery worker, food mixer and cemetery worker. A childhood spent exploring the ruined watermills of the Rivelin valley was partially responsible for his interest in industrial history. Other influences were his father's reminiscences of Sheffield trades and working conditions. He is possibly remembered by local librarians as the school boy who left grubby fingermarks on *The Oxford History of Technology*! Dennis has published booklets on aspects of life in the Bradfield and Cawthorne areas of South Yorkshire. His articles have appeared in the *Transactions of the Hunter Archaeological Society* and Sheffield University's *Lore and Language* journal. He contributed an article on the buttonmaking industry of Sheffield to *Aspects of Sheffield 1.*

2. Rev. James Wilkinson and The Church in Sheffield, 1754-1805

Born and bred in Sheffield, **Malcolm Mercer** left school at fourteen in 1939. After seven years in the retail trade disrupted by three years in the Royal Navy (1943-46), he trained as a teacher at Sheffield Training College and taught in several Sheffield schools before being appointed Head of Parson Cross School (1968-83). He gained a Diploma in Education Management at Sheffield Polytechnic in 1971 and an MA in Education at Sheffield University in 1979. He has contributed to the *Transactions of the Hunter Archaeological Society* and *The History of the City of Sheffield 1843-1993* (1993). He is the author of *The School at Parson Crosse* (1980) and a history of elementary education in Sheffield between 1560 and 1902 - *Schooling the Poorer Child* (1996). He contributed an article on Nonconformity in Sheffield, 1550-1660, to *Aspects of Sheffield 1.*

3. Early Sheffield Assay Masters and Assay Offices

Jackie Richardson was born in Sheffield and went to High Storrs Grammar School. After gaining an MA(Hons) in English at Edinburgh University she took a postgraduate librarianship course in Leeds. Her first job was in York Central Library. After a couple of years she and her husband missed the hills too much and they returned to live in Sheffield. A period as a school librarian in Dronfield followed by spells at Highfield Library in Sheffield and Sheffield Polytechnic convinced her that motherhood would be much more rewarding and she retired and had two children.

In 1981, out of the blue, she was offered the chance to work part-time at Sheffield Assay Office, building up the library. She has been there ever since and is now responsible for the library, archives and silver collection.

4. VISUAL REMINDERS OF SHEFFIELD'S TURNPIKE ROADS

Howard Smith was born and bred in Sheffield, and spent all his professional career as a schoolmaster and further education lecturer in the city. Immediately following early retirement he studied for an MA in Local History under the tutelage of David Hey. His thesis was converted into his first book *A History of Rotherham's Roads and Transport* (1992). He has also produced six 'Turnpike Trails' designed to make local history accessible to the layman. His specific research area of roads was triggered by his being invited to write a script on the history of local roads for BBC Radio Sheffield in its early days. Guide stoops caught his eye whilst researching old packhorse ways and he produced *The Guide Stoops of Derbyshire* in 1996. He contributed articles on roads to *Aspects of Sheffield 1* and *Aspects of Rotherham 3*.

5. JOHN CURR, 1756-1823, MINING ENGINEER AND VIEWER

Ian Medlicott was born in Doncaster where he spent his early years before moving to Sheffield. He was educated at High Green Secondary Modern School, Barnsley College of Technology and Ecclesfield Grammar School. After qualifying as a school teacher, he taught in primary and secondary schools in Sheffield and Barnsley. He gained a BA (Hons) and an MPhil with the Open University. He has been interested in local history for many years, especially early coal mining in South Yorkshire, about which he has published articles in archaeological journals. He contributed articles on the history of coal mining to *Aspects of Barnsley 5* and *Aspects of Rotherham 3*.

6. JOHN WATTS, LAMBERT STREET: A SURVIVING SHEFFIELD COMPANY WITH OVER 200 YEARS' HISTORY

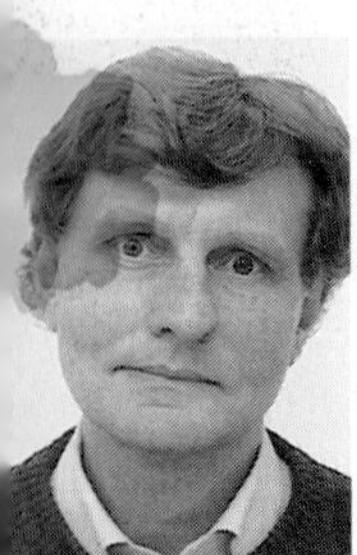

Peter Machan's father was an engineer who went into producing razor blades on Mary Street after the war, so Peter grew up to the smell and sound of metal grinding and polishing. After leaving Brincliffe Grammar and Myers Grove schools he trained as a teacher and he is presently headteacher at Bankwood Primary School in the Gleadless Valley. In the 1970s he became fascinated with the fast disappearing survivals of the Sheffield trades and toured their Dickensian workshops, taking hundreds of photographs before they were swept away in the 1980s. He has also organised the Little Mesters festivals at the Leadmill and given talks to hundreds of Saga Holiday visitors to the city. He also served for a spell on the council of the Sheffield Trades Historical Society. In 1994 he gained an MA in Local History, and the research on John Watts was conducted as part of that course. His publications include *Made in Sheffield* (1986), a survey of surviving cutlers' premises, and a *Pictorial Map of Historical Sheffield. The Dramatic Story of the Sheffield Flood* is due for publication later this year.

7. Ecclesfield's Literary Connection

Chris Morley was born in Manchester but served his apprenticeship as a design draughtsman with the Light Castings Division of Newton Chambers & Co. Ltd. (Redfyre). Until his early retirement he worked as a designer for several domestic appliance manufacturers. He qualified as a mechanical engineer, and went on to study industrial design, and the utilisation of gas. He is a chartered engineer. He has studied social and economic history as an extra-mural student, specialising in the history of the stove grate and domestic appliance industries. He and his long-suffering wife have travelled widely in the UK and abroad, following leads into early ironmaking and casting. When they have not been spending 'Casting' holidays, they have been 'Gattying', researching the biography of the family of the Rev. Alfred Gatty, erstwhile vicar of Ecclesfield. Chris is also an expert on the Walkers of Grenoside and Masbrough and his *The Walkers of Masbrough: a re-examination* was published in 1996. He contributed articles on the stove grate industry to *Aspects of Sheffield 1* and *Aspects of Rotherham 3*.

8. Juliana Ewing, Children's Writer, and Ecclesfield's Countryside

Melvyn Jones was born in Barnsley and educated at the Holgate Grammar School and the universities of Nottingham and Leeds. He taught for seven years at Myers Grove, Sheffield's first comprehensive school, and then for nine years at Sheffield City College of Education before its amalgamation into Sheffield City Polytechnic in 1976. He retired from the post of Head of Academic Resources in the School of Leisure and Food Management at Sheffield Hallam University in 1997. He is now Visiting Professor at the Countryside Research Centre at Sheffield Hallam University. He has written extensively on the economic and social history of South Yorkshire. Recent publications include *Chapeltown and High Green* (1996), in Chalford Publishing's Archive Photographs series and *Ecclesfield, Grenoside, High Green and Chapeltown* (1998) in Tempus Publishing's Images of England series (both with Joan Jones). Besides editing *Aspects of Sheffield*, volumes 1 and 2, he is the editor of *Aspects of Rotherham* , volumes 1-3. He is currently working on a book on *The Making of the South Yorkshire Landscape.* Wearing another hat he is BBC Radio Sheffield's 'History Man' with a live weekly local history spot.

9. REGULATING AN INDUSTRIAL TOWNSHIP: RELIGION, POLITICS AND LEISURE IN ATTERCLIFFE, *C*.1851-1881

Andrew Walker teaches history at the University of Lincolnshire and Humberside. He gained an MA in Local History, Literature and Cultural Tradition from the University of Sheffield in 1989 and went on to obtain a doctorate there in 1994. His PhD examined the social and cultural development of the South Yorkshire coalfield in the second half of the nineteenth century. His publications include 'Migration into the South Yorkshire Coalfield, 1861- 1881' in *Northern History,* Vol. XXIX, 1993, and ' "Pleasurable Homes ?" Victorian Model Miners' Wives and the Family Wage in a South Yorkshire Colliery District', *Women's History Review,* Vol. 6, No. 3, 1997.

10. AN ILLUSTRATED HISTORY OF IZAL

Joan Jones (née Gregory) was brought up in Charlton Brook near Chapeltown and was educated at Ecclesfield Grammar School, Matlock College of Education and what is now Sheffield Hallam University. She has taught in primary schools in the West Riding, Nottingham and Sheffield, and was Deputy Head at Bankwood School. She was a Senior Lecturer in the School of Education at Sheffield Hallam University from 1995 to 1998 teaching history to intending primary school teachers. She is Honorary Secretary of the Chapeltown and High Green Archive which was founded in 1987 and which is noted for its wide range of publications. Between 1983-86 Joan acted as adviser to the award-winning BBC TV's schools history series *Now and Then*. She is co-author of *Chapeltown and High Green* (1996), in Chalford Publishing's Archive Photographs series and *Ecclesfield, Grenoside, High Green and Chapeltown* (1998) in Tempus Publishing's Images of England series. She has contributed to the *Aspects of Barnsley* and *Aspects of Rotherham* series. She is currently co-editing a book on oral history.

11. HENRY BESSEMER: SHEFFIELD'S RADICAL STEELMAKER

Sheffield born and bred, **Trevor Lodge** was educated at Abbeydale Grammar School, and Manchester and Sheffield universities. An industrial chemist by training, he had an early career which comprised spells of teaching interspersed by a period as a research chemist with Newton Chambers & Co. Ltd., once famous for its range of Izal products derived from coal tar distillation. He retrained as a metallurgist in the early 1970s, largely through development work carried out at British Steel's Templeborough Steelworks. Possessing considerable working knowledge of many of South Yorkshire's other steel-works, both past and present, he currently works as an information officer in South Yorkshire's special steels industry. He has been actively researching the UK's heavy industries (coal, steel and engineering, and the railways that served them) for over thirty years. In a related capacity, he is Vice-Chairman of the Industrial Railway

Society, whose quarterly journal he edited between 1971 and 1979. His histories of the Park Gate Iron & Steel Co. Ltd.; Steel, Peech & Tozer Ltd.; and Samuel Fox & Co. Ltd. appeared in serialised form in British Steel's *Steel News* and United Engineering Steels' Journal, *Stocksbridge Gazette* between 1981 and 1993. He was a major contributor to *Sir Henry Bessemer: Father of the Steel Industry,* published in 1998 by the Institute of Materials, and is currently working on a full length appraisal of Bessemer's life, times and influence.

12. A Century of Cinema

Clifford Shaw was born in Bolton, Lancashire. He studied medicine at St Bartholamew's Hospital and qualified in 1942. After serving in the RAMC he chose a career in public health. His first job involved working in the child health services in Rotherham from 1947-49. After an appointment as lecturer at the London School of Hygiene he moved to Ipswich and Nottinghamshire, before coming to Sheffield in 1956. In 1965 he was promoted to Medical Officer of Health on the retirement of Dr Llewelyn Roberts, with whom he had collaborated in preparing a new edition of *A Synopsis of Hygiene.* The position of Medical Officer of Health lapsed when the NHS was reorganised in 1974 but he remained in medical administration. From an early age he has been an inveterate filmgoer and is interested in the theatre and foreign travel. Since his retirement he has been compiling a history of Sheffield cinemas and has also contributed a chapter on 'Aspects of Public Health' in the *The History of the City of Sheffield 1843-1993.*

Christopher Stacey has had a lifelong interest in the cinema since the time as a schoolboy when he was given a toy projector and 'cadged' odd lengths of film from a friendly local cinema manager. As a result, his interest has always been in the technical side of the cinema industry and, in recent years, following his retirement as associate chief sub-editor of *The Star*, Sheffield - earlier he had held senior sub-editorial positions with the old *Sheffield Telegraph* - he has acted as consultant for South East Arts advising on several projects and supervising installations of cinema equipment at the Platform Theatre, Haywards Heath, and more recently at Cinematheque, at Brighton Media Centre. He is a member of the British Film Institute, the Projected Picture Trust, which rescues and preserves old cinema equipment, and is a trustee of Mercia Cinema Society which specialises in promoting and aiding research of the history of cinemas in the United Kingdom. He is an authority on early cinema projectors but no longer has that toy projector that first enlivened his interest!

Index of People and Places

PLACES